Undergraduate Topics in Computer Science

Undergraduate Topics in Computer Science (UTiCS) delivers high-quality instructional content for undergraduates studying in all areas of computing and information science. From core foundational and theoretical material to final-year topics and applications, UTiCS books take a fresh, concise, and modern approach and are ideal for self-study or for a one- or two-semester course. The texts are all authored by established experts in their fields, reviewed by an international advisory board, and contain numerous examples and problems. Many include fully worked solutions.

For further volumes:
http://www.springer.com/series/7592

John Cowley

Communications and Networking

An Introduction

Second Edition

 Springer

John Cowley
Kingswinford, West Midlands, UK

Series editor
Ian Mackie

Advisory board
Samson Abramsky, University of Oxford, Oxford, UK
Karin Breitman, Pontifical Catholic University of Rio de Janeiro, Rio de Janeiro, Brazil
Chris Hankin, Imperial College London, London, UK
Dexter Kozen, Cornell University, Ithaca, USA
Andrew Pitts, University of Cambridge, Cambridge, UK
Hanne Riis Nielson, Technical University of Denmark, Kongens Lyngby, Denmark
Steven Skiena, Stony Brook University, Stony Brook, USA
Iain Stewart, University of Durham, Durham, UK

ISSN 1863-7310   Undergraduate Topics in Computer Science
ISBN 978-1-4471-4356-7   ISBN 978-1-4471-4357-4 (eBook)
DOI 10.1007/978-1-4471-4357-4
Springer London Heidelberg New York Dordrecht

Library of Congress Control Number: 2012948286

Springer is part of Springer Science+Business Media (www.springer.com)

Preface

Overview

Communications and Networking: An Introduction, Second Edition provides a clear and easy to follow treatment of the subject, written specifically for undergraduates who have no previous experience in the field.

Organisation and Features

- Topics retained from the previous edition include:
    - Networking models and standards, local area and wide area networks, network protocols, TCP/IP-based networks and network management
    - Plenty of material on wireless communications, both fixed and mobile
    - Authoritative coverage of network security
    - Many explanatory diagrams
    - Comprehensive glossary
- All these topics continue to be important and relevant today.
The new edition contains several changes and additions.
- Several sections have been added to illustrate the most recent developments in networking and communications. The most significant additions are the following:
    - There is a much greater emphasis on mobile computing, particularly modern mobile phones.
    - The section on Internet protocol version 6 (IPv6) has been considerably expanded.
    - New threats to data and new ways of countering these have been included in the chapter on network security.
    - There is a greater emphasis on security in other chapters too.
    - Grid computing, cloud computing, microblogging, mobile ad hoc networks, near field communication, Power over Ethernet and the Ground Positioning System (GPS) are covered in the new edition.

- Mistakes and typos have been corrected, and some concepts have been further clarified, based on observations received from readers.
- Coverage of some older technologies has been reduced.
- The glossary has been revised.
- The language used has been simplified to some extent, for the benefit of non-English speakers.
- A number of new diagrams have been added, some modified and a few removed.

Target Audiences

Primary

First- and second-level undergraduates studying modules on communications and/or networks.

Secondary

First- and second-level undergraduates studying modules that contain some material on communications and/or networks.

Suggestions to the Instructor

- Base your lectures on the PowerPoint slides.
- Use the end-of-chapter questions and supplementary exercises for tutorials and/or self study and class tests.
- Use this book itself for self study (under your guidance if necessary).

Supplementary Resources

The following supplementary resources are hosted on a website:
- PowerPoint teaching slides (updated so as to complement the new edition)
- Revised solutions to the end-of-chapter questions
- Updated supplementary exercises with solutions

Why Should I Buy/Recommend This Book?

The author takes a step-by-step approach, with examples and exercises designed to give the reader increased confidence in using and understanding communications systems. The text takes the reader through the essentials of networking and communications technologies and provides a comprehensive, reliable and thorough treatment of the subject. It is organised in such a way that readers without a strong knowledge of the subject matter can grasp the material quickly.

Contents

Abbreviations

2G	Second-generation mobile phone network
2.5G	General packet radio services mobile phone network
3G	Third-generation mobile phone network
3D	Three-dimensional
4G	Fourth-generation mobile phone network
10-Gb E	10-gigabit Ethernet
10GBASE-ER	A 10-Gb E Ethernet variant
40-Gb E	40-gigabit Ethernet
100-Gb E	100-gigabit Ethernet
100BASE-T	A twisted-pair variant of 100-Mbps Ethernet
1000BASE-T	A twisted-pair variant of gigabit Ethernet
802.1p	A prioritisation standard for IP telephony
802.1q	A standard that supports virtual LANs
802.1X	An authentication standard for LANs
802.3	The basic IEEE standard for Ethernet
802.3af-2003	The original power over Ethernet standard
802.3at-2009	The improved power over Ethernet standard
802.5	The Token Ring standard
802.11a	A 54-Mbps wireless LAN standard
802.11ac	A newer and faster wireless LAN standard than 802.11n
802.11ad	A faster wireless LAN standard than 802.11ac, but with a shorter range
802.11b	An 11-Mbps wireless LAN standard
802.11g	A 54-Mbps wireless LAN standard
802.11i	An official WLAN security standard which was agreed after WPA2
802.11n	A high-speed wireless LAN standard that uses MIMO technology
802.11x	A generic term used to refer to the 802.11 family of WLAN standards
802.15.1	The Bluetooth standard
802.15.4	The standard that ZigBee is based on
802.16-2004	A fixed wireless WiMAX standard

802.16-2005	A standard for mobile WiMAX
802.16e	A standard for mobile WiMAX
802.16m	The WiMAX 2 standard
802.20	A high-speed mobile wireless standard
1901.2010	Standard for HomePlug networks
ABR	Available bit rate
AC	Alternating current
ACK	Positive acknowledgement
ADSL	Asymmetric DSL
AES	Advanced encryption standard
AH	Authentication header
AM	Amplitude modulation
ANSI	American National Standards Institute
AP	Access point
API	Application programming interface
APT	Advanced persistent threat
ARP	Address resolution protocol
ARQ	Automatic repeat request
ASCII	American standard code for information interchange
ASN.1	Abstract syntax notation.1
ATM	Asynchronous transfer mode
AV	Anti-virus
B channel	Bearer channel
BAP	Battery-assisted passive
BOOTP	Bootstrap protocol
BRI	Basic rate interface
BSI	British Standards Institution
CA	Certificate authority
CAT 5e	Category 5e
CBR	Constant bit rate
CCITT	Consultative Committee on International Telegraph and Telephone
CDMA	Code division multiple access
CIDR	Classless interdomain routing
CIR	Committed information rate
CRC	Cyclic redundancy check
CSMA/CA	Carrier sense multiple access/collision avoidance
CSMA/CD	Carrier sense multiple access/collision detection
CSS	Cascading style sheets
CSU/DSU	Channel service unit/data service unit
D-channel	Delta channel
DAD	Duplicate address detection
DC	Direct current
DCE	Data circuit terminating equipment
DDOS	Distributed denial of service

DECnet	Network architecture of the Digital Equipment Corporation (now defunct)
DF	Don't fragment
DHCP	Dynamic host configuration protocol
DHCPv6	Dynamic host configuration protocol version 6
DIX	The original Ethernet standard, developed by the Digital, Intel and Xerox companies
DLCI	Data-link connection identifier
DMZ	Demilitarised zone
DNS	Domain name system
DOCSIS	Data over cable service interface specification
DOD	The US Department of Defense
DOS	Denial of service
DSL	Digital subscriber line
DSLAM	DSL access multiplexer
DSSS	Direct sequence spread spectrum
DTE	Data terminal equipment
DWDM	Dense wavelength division multiplexing
E3	A digital leased line standard that offers a data rate of 34.368 Mbps
EAP	Extensible authentication protocol
EAP-TLS	An authentication protocol
EIA	Electronic Industries Alliance
EIA/TIA-232	A physical-layer protocol
ESMTP	Extended SMTP
ESP	Encapsulating security payload
ETSI	European Telecommunications Standards Institute
EUI-64	Extended unique identifier-64
EV SSL	Extended validation SSL
FCoE	Fibre channel over Ethernet
FCS	Frame check sequence
FDD	Frequency division duplex
FDDI	Fibre distributed data interface
FDM	Frequency division multiplexing
FDMA	Frequency division multiple access
FEC	Forward error correction
FHSS	Frequency hopping spread spectrum
FIN	Finished (TCP packet)
FM	Frequency modulation
FRAD	Frame relay access device
FSO	Free space optics
FTP	File transfer protocol
GLONASS	GLObal NAvigation Satellite System
GPRS	General packet radio services
GPS	Global positioning system
GSM	Global system for mobiles

GUI	Graphical user interface
HAN	Home area network
HDLC	High-level data link control
HSDPA	High-speed downlink packet access
HSUPA	High-speed uplink packet access
HTML	HyperText markup language
HTTP	HyperText transport protocol
IaaS	Infrastructure as a service
ICMP	Internet control message protocol
IDS	Intrusion detection system
IEEE	Institute of Electrical and Electronics Engineers, a standards body
IETF	Internet Engineering Task Force
IKE	Internet key exchange
IM	Instant messaging
IMAP	Internet message access protocol
IMT	International mobile telecommunications
INMS	Integrated network management system
IOS	Internetwork operating system (Cisco proprietary operating system)
IP	Internet protocol
IPS	Intrusion prevention system
IPSec	IP security protocol
IPv4	IP Version 4
IPv6	IP Version 6
iSCSI	Internet small computer system interface
ISDN	Integrated services digital network
IS-IS	Intermediate system-to-intermediate system
ISO	International Organisation for Standardisation
ISP	Internet service provider
IT	Information technology
ITU-R	International Telecommunication Union Radio-communication Sector
ITU-T	International Telecommunication Union Telecommunication Standardisation Sector
LAN	Local area network
LAPB	Link access procedure balanced
LAPD	Link access procedure D-channel
LAPF	Link access procedure for frame mode services
LED	Light-emitting diode
LEO	Low earth orbit
LLC	Logical link control
LSA	Link-state advertisement
LTE	Long-term evolution
MAC	Media access control
MAN	Metropolitan area network
MANET	Mobile ad hoc network
MEO	Medium earth orbit

MIB	Management information base
MIME	Multipurpose Internet mail extensions
MIMO	Multiple input, multiple output
MP3	MPEG-1 audio layer 3
MPEG	Moving Picture Experts Group
MPLS	Multiprotocol label switching
MSC	Mobile switching centre
MTA	Message transfer agent
MTBF	Mean time between failures
MTTR	Mean time to repair
MTU	Maximum transmission unit
NAK	Negative acknowledgement
NAT	Network address translation
NFC	Near field communication
NIC	Network interface card
NOS	Network operating system
NRZ	Non-return-to-zero
OC-192	Optical carrier level 192: a SONET standard for transmission over optical fibre
OFDM	Orthogonal frequency division multiplexing
OS	Operating system
OSI	Open systems interconnect
OSPF	Open shortest path first
P2P	Peer-to-peer
PaaS	Platform as a service
PAN	Personal area network
PC	Personal computer
PCI	Peripheral component interconnect
PCMCIA	Personal Computer Memory Card International Association
PIN	Personal identification number
PKI	Public key infrastructure
PM	Phase modulation
PN	Pseudo-noise
PNG	Portable network graphics
POe	Power over Ethernet
POP	Post office protocol
POP3	POP version 3
PRI	Primary rate interface
PSTN	Public switched telephone network
PVC	Permanent virtual circuit
QoS	Quality of service
RAID	Redundant array of independent disks
RAM	Random access memory
RARP	Reverse address resolution protocol
RFC	Request for comments

RFID	Radio frequency identification
RIP	Routing information protocol
RJ-45	Registered jack-45
RMON	Remote monitor
RQ	Request
RS232-C	The former name of EIA/TIA-232
RTCP	RTP control protocol
RTP	Real-time transport protocol
RTSP	Real-time streaming protocol
SaaS	Software as a service
SAN	Storage area network
Sat Nav	Satellite navigation
SATA	Serial advanced technology attachment
SCSI	Small computer system interface
ScTP	Screened twisted-pair cable
SDH	Synchronous digital hierarchy
SDSL	Symmetric DSL
SETI	Search for Extraterrestrial Intelligence
SFTP	Secure file transfer protocol
SIP	Session initiation protocol
SLAAC	StateLess address auto-configuration
SMON	Switch monitoring
SMS	Short message service
SMTP	Simple mail transfer protocol
SNMP	Simple network management protocol
SNMPv1	Version 1 of SNMP
SNMPv2	Version 2 of SNMP
SNMPv3	Version 3 of SNMP
SONET	Synchronous optical NETwork
SPF	Shortest path first
SPSL	Security policy specification language
SQL	Structured query language
SQLi	SQL injection
SRTP	Secure real-time transport protocol
SSH	Secure shell
SSID	Service set identifier
SSL/TLS	Secure sockets layer/transport layer security
STP	Shielded twisted pair
SVC	Switched virtual circuit
SYN	A packet used in TCP to synchronise the initial sequence numbers on two computers that are initiating a new connection
T3	A T-carrier digital leased line that offers a data rate of 44.736 Mbps.
TCP	Transmission control protocol
TDD	Time division duplex
TD-LTE	Time division LTE
TDM	Time division multiplexing

TDMA	Time division multiple access
TDR	Time domain reflectometry
TFTP	Trivial file transfer protocol
TIA	Telecommunications Industry Association
TIA/EIA-232	A physical-layer standard for serial data communications
TLS	Transport layer security
TOS	Type of service field
TTL	Time to live
UA	User agent
UBR	Unspecified bit rate
UC	Unified communications
UDP	User datagram protocol
UMTS	Universal mobile telecommunications system
UPS	Uninterruptible power supply
URL	Uniform resource locator
USB	Universal serial bus
UTM	Unified threat management system
UTP	Unshielded twisted pair
UWB	Ultra-wideband
V.92	A modem standard
VANET	Vehicular ad hoc network
VBR	Variable bit rate
VBR-NRT	Variable bit rate—non-real time
VBR-RT	Variable bit rate—real time
VDSL2	Very high-speed digital subscriber line 2
VLAN	Virtual LAN
VLSM	Variable-length subnet mask
VoIP	Voice over IP
VPLS	Virtual private LAN service
VPN	Virtual private network
W3C	World Wide Web Consortium
WAN	Wide area network
WCDMA	Wideband CDMA
WDM	Wavelength division multiplexing
WEP	Wired equivalent privacy
Wi-Fi	Wireless Fidelity
WiMAX	Worldwide interoperability for microwave access
WLAN	Wireless LAN
WPA	Wi-Fi protected access
WPA2	The second version of WPA
WUSB	Wireless USB
X.25	A standard protocol suite for packet-switching WANs
xDSL	A generic term for all forms of DSL
XHTML	Extensible HyperText markup language
XML	Extensible markup language
XOR	Exclusive or

Introduction

Abstract

This short chapter starts by considering how we can define what a network is. Next, there is a short discussion of different types of networks. This is followed by an account of the reasons why networks are used. Then, there is a discussion of communication between computers. Several basic terms used when discussing computer communication are introduced.

1.1 What Is a Network?

A network consists of a number of interconnected, autonomous computers. Being 'interconnected' means that the computers can send information to each other. We need to include the word 'autonomous' in our definition so as to exclude *distributed systems*. These consist of many processors linked together but acting as one computer under the control of one copy of the operating system. In a network, however, all the computers have their own operating system and can act independently. The hardware and software of which a network is composed are considered in later chapters of this book.

1.2 Types of Networks

Local area networks (LANs) are limited to a small geographical area. LAN data transfer rates tend to be very high. The whole LAN—computers, cables and all other components—is usually owned by one organisation, for example, a business. Further details of LAN technologies are given in Chap. 4. Figure 1.1 shows a LAN.

Wide area networks (WANs) connect computers over long distances, even right round the globe. WAN data rates are typically lower than those of LANs. WANs are normally used to interconnect LANs. It is uncommon for an entire WAN to be owned by one organisation. Almost always, third-party telecommunications carrier

J. Cowley, *Communications and Networking: An Introduction*, Undergraduate Topics in Computer Science, DOI 10.1007/978-1-4471-4357-4_1,
© Springer-Verlag London 2012

Fig. 1.1 LAN

Fig. 1.2 WAN

companies will provide the long-haul links. Further details of WAN technologies and services are given in Chap. 5. Figure 1.2 illustrates a WAN.

You may also encounter the term *metropolitan area network* (MAN). MANs are a halfway house between LANs and WANs. They can span an entire city and its suburbs, but their reach is not as great as that of WANs.

Fig. 1.3 Source, destination and transmission medium

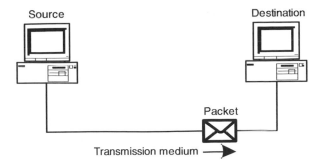

Personal area networks (PANs) and *home area networks* (HANs) are very short-range networks. These are described in Chap. 10.

1.3   Reasons for Networks

LANs make it possible to share computer hardware, software applications and data files. They also make communications such as e-mail or instant messaging possible. WANs enable the same possibilities as LANs, with the added advantage of a world-wide reach.

1.4   Communication Between Computers

1.4.1   Source, Destination and Transmission Medium

Whenever information is sent through a network, there is always a *source* (the sending computer), a *medium* along which the data travels (often, but not always, a cable) and a *destination* (the receiving computer). This is shown in Fig. 1.3. Further information about transmission media is given in Chap. 2.

1.4.2   Packet

The data is usually sent in a *packet*, a unit of information suitable for travelling between one computer and another (see Fig. 1.3). In addition to the data itself, the packet will contain *addressing* information. The source address in a packet identifies the sending computer. The destination address identifies the receiving computer. Besides address information, the packet will also contain other items that are needed to facilitate communication. Details of the structure of various kinds of packets will be given later in this book.

1.4.3   Protocol

When we want to send a packet of data from one computer to another, it is vital that the source, the destination and any other devices on the network all use the same *protocol*. A protocol is a set of rules. These rules make communication via a network work satisfactorily. Outside the field of computer science, one meaning of the word 'protocol' is a code of conduct. We find the word used this way in the phrase 'the protocols of the Geneva convention'. An explanation of how various protocols work together to facilitate communication can be found in Chap. 3 (Sect. 3.1).

1.5   Summary

This introductory chapter started by considering the definition of a network. Next, different types of networks were briefly discussed and then some reasons why networks are used were given. Finally, computer communication and some of the basic terms used were introduced.

1.6   Questions

1. What are the differences between *WANs* and *LANs*?
2. What benefits do networks offer?
3. Why do data packets need to include addresses along with the data?
4. What is a *network protocol*?

Communications Technologies

2

Abstract

In this chapter, we look at some of the technologies that are used for computer communications. The chapter starts with an explanation of the differences between serial and parallel data transfer, asynchronous and synchronous communications and duplex, half-duplex and full-duplex communications. There are explanations of the distinctions between data rate, bandwidth and throughput. Next come discussions of modulation and encoding, error control methods, switching and multiplexing. The topologies used in networking are described. Finally, we explore network transmission media.

2.1 Serial and Parallel Communications

Inside the case of a computer, data is often moved around on parallel pathways. Multiple wires are used to transfer whole units of data simultaneously. Parallel transfer is used inside the processor, for example. Outside the processor itself, a parallel bus (a bus is a common path for moving information about) is often used to transfer data. In a peripheral component interconnect (PCI) bus, for example, 64 parallel wires can be used to transfer data between components. If we want to transfer, say, 8 bytes of data, with a 64-bit parallel system, all 8 bytes can be transferred at once. An 8-bit parallel transfer is illustrated in Fig. 2.1. A whole byte of information is transferred at once, with each bit of the byte moving along its own wire.

Even inside the computer case, parallel data transfer is not always used. For example, a serial advanced technology attachment (serial ATA or SATA) cable may be used to attach a hard disk drive to its controller. It is possible to use parallel connections over short distances to external peripheral devices, for example, a parallel printer. Usually, however, serial connections are used for external connections. In serial transfer, only one wire carries the data, and only one bit is transmitted at a time. Figure 2.2 illustrates serial transfer.

J. Cowley, *Communications and Networking: An Introduction*, Undergraduate Topics in Computer Science, DOI 10.1007/978-1-4471-4357-4_2,
© Springer-Verlag London 2012

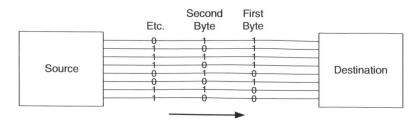

Fig. 2.1 Parallel data transfer

Fig. 2.2 Serial data transfer

Fig. 2.3 Serial and parallel data transfer to/from an NIC

One vital piece of hardware for communication over a network is the *network interface card* (NIC, usually pronounced 'nick'). Inside the computer, the NIC sends and receives data via a parallel connection; outside the computer, the NIC is connected in serial fashion to the network. These connections are shown in Fig. 2.3. NICs are covered in more detail in Chap. 4.

Fig. 2.4 Asynchronous transmission

2.2 Asynchronous and Synchronous Communications

In serial transmission, the receiving device has to know when a new character begins. This can be done using either asynchronous or synchronous transmission.

2.2.1 Asynchronous Transmission

Asynchronous transmission is used in low-speed applications where communication is only sporadic. An example of this kind of situation is the connection of a console (terminal) to a router. In an asynchronous transmission, a special bit called the 'start' bit is sent before the bits that make up the character, and one 'stop' bit (or possibly two stop bits) is sent at the end. For this reason, an alternative term for asynchronous transmission is start–stop transmission. The start bit alerts the receiving device to the fact that a character is about to be transmitted. The stop bit tells the receiver that no more bits will be sent for a while.

Figure 2.4 illustrates asynchronous transmission. In the diagram, the transmission of the capital letter 'J' is shown. A 7-bit ASCII code is being used (1001010). The diagram should be read from right to left. The communications line is initially in the idle condition—nothing is happening. Then, out of the blue, a start bit arrives. This warns the receiver that the next bit will be the least significant bit of a character. The remaining bits of the character follow. The 0s and 1s are represented by different voltages on the communications line, for example, +5 and 0 V.

After the most significant bit of the character, there is a parity bit—a check for errors. In Fig. 2.4, even parity is being used. This means that over the whole of the character and the parity bit, there is an even number of '1' bits. If the received bit pattern does not accord with this, then it is assumed that there has been a transmission error. Alternatively, odd parity could have been employed, in which case with no errors there would be an odd number of '1' bits over the whole of the character and the parity bit. An 8-bit code could have been used instead with no parity check. There is further coverage of error control methods later in this chapter (see Sect. 2.6). After the parity bit, there is a stop bit to tell the receiver that transmission has ceased for the time being. EIA/TIA-232 (RS232-C), mentioned in Sect. 3.2.1, is an example of an asynchronous protocol.

Fig. 2.5 Synchronous transmission

2.2.2 Synchronous Transmission

In asynchronous transmission, roughly 30% of the bits that have to be transmitted are not data bits. This is a rather large overhead, and, so, for high-speed transmission, synchronous transmission is used instead. In synchronous transmission, data is sent as a continuous stream at a constant rate, making maximum use of the available line capacity. To achieve this, the clocks on the transmitting and receiving devices are synchronised by sending synchronising bits. Once the sender and receiver clocks are synchronised, the receiver can distinguish the beginning of the data stream and can pick off each byte by counting the number of bits. Figure 2.5 illustrates synchronous transmission. High-level data-link control (HDLC) is a typical synchronous protocol. A description of HDLC can be found in Sect. 6.3.

2.3   Simplex, Half-Duplex and Full-Duplex Communications

Simplex transmission is transmission that can take place only ever in one direction. An example of simplex communications is a household radio set, which can receive data from radio stations but cannot transmit. In half-duplex transmission, data can be transmitted in either direction across a communications link but in only one direction at a time. A walkie-talkie radio is an example of a half-duplex device because only one person can talk at a time. In full-duplex transmission, data is transmitted in two directions at the same time. A telephone is an example of a full-duplex device because the people at both ends of the line can talk at the same time.

Many fibre-optic systems are simplex, with a different strand of fibre having to be used for each direction. Many satellite services are also simplex. In such systems, a satellite is used for downloads, and some other system is used for communication in the other direction. Satellite and optical fibre are covered in more detail later in this chapter. Simplex transmission is illustrated in Fig. 2.6. In computer communications, half-duplex and full-duplex working are more commonly found, however.

Half-duplex working is fine for transferring files between computers when most data is flowing in one direction at a time. However, when used for other applications, it may cause delays. When low-speed versions of the popular LAN protocol Ethernet are used with a hub instead of a layer-2 switch (see Chap. 4), they can use half-duplex transmission only. Two computers connected to a half-duplex Ethernet LAN must take turns to send information to each other. A computer has to wait for the transmission that

Fig. 2.6 Simplex
transmission

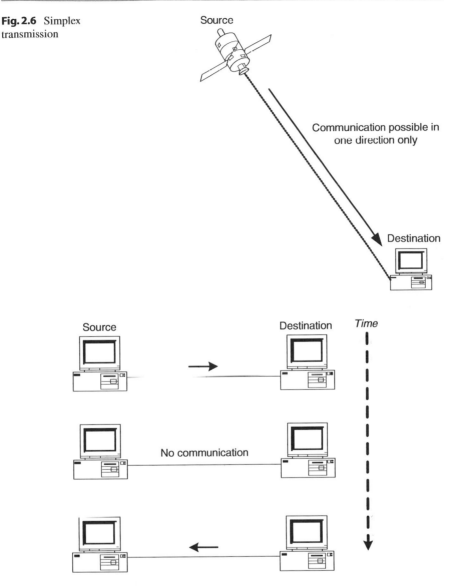

Fig. 2.7 Half-duplex transmission

it is sending to end before it can receive data. Full-duplex working removes this restriction. Half-duplex transmission is illustrated in Fig. 2.7.

Full-duplex transmission is illustrated in Fig. 2.8. Full-duplex working is ideal for interactive applications because it eliminates the waiting time referred to in the previous paragraph. Ethernet used with a layer-2 switch is an example of full-duplex transmission. The switch can automatically sense whether the device at the other end of the wire, for example, the NIC of a PC, has a full-duplex capability. If full-duplex transmission can be used, this has the effect of speeding up the operation of the LAN.

Fig. 2.8 Full-duplex transmission

2.4 Data Rate, Bandwidth and Throughput

The terms data rate, throughput and bandwidth are related, but their meanings are not exactly the same.

2.4.1 Data Rate

The data rate is the amount of data transferred per second. This term is used to describe the performance of many different kinds of computing device, for example, disk drives, as well as networks. Data rates are expressed in bits per second (bps). For example, 2 Mbps is 2,000,000 bps. The units used to express data rates are shown in Table 2.1. Note that the meaning of the prefixes kilo-, mega- and so on differs from the meaning when these are used for storage units. When indicating the capacity of storage units such as hard disk drives, these prefixes stand for powers of 1,024. For example, 1 Kb of storage is 1,024 bytes.

2.4.2 Data Transfer Calculations

A formula for calculating how long a data transfer takes is as follows: time taken = file size/data rate. How long will it take to transfer a 600-Kb file over a network running at 100 Mbps?

Time = total number of bits / data rate

File size $= 600 \text{kb} = 600 \times 1,024 \text{bytes} = 614,400 \text{bytes} = 614,400 \times 8$

$\qquad = 4,915,200 \text{bits}$

So, the total transfer time $= 4,915,200 / 100,000,000 \text{s} = 0.049152 \text{s}$.

This result is only an estimate. In practice, the file would not be transferred in its raw form but would have to be packaged up into the right format to travel over the network. This would involve extra, non-data, bits being added. Also, as we shall see in the following section, the data rate would not be at its ideal maximum.

Table 2.1 Units used to express data rates

Unit	Equivalent in bits per second
Bits per second (bps)	–
Kilobits per second (Kbps)	1,000 (10^3 bps)
Megabits per second (Mbps)	1,000,000 (10^6 bps)
Gigabits per second (Gbps)	1,000,000,000 (10^9 bps)
Terabits per second (Tbps)	1,000,000,000,000 (10^{12} bps)

Fig. 2.9 Analogue signal

2.4.3   Throughput

In a real network, various factors militate against the theoretical data rate of a channel being realised. The devices attached to the network (user workstations, server computers, switches, routers and so on) will all affect throughput to some extent. The layout of the network, the characteristics of the data being sent and how many people are using the network will also affect throughput. We can define throughput as the actual amount of data successfully transferred from one place to another in a given time. This figure is unlikely to be as high as the notional data rate.

2.4.4   Bandwidth

The term *bandwidth* is used in two different ways for analogue and digital communications. Let us first have a brief look at bandwidth as used to describe analogue signals.

Analogue data transmission is performed by manipulating electromagnetic waves. These waves vary continuously, and they can be sent over various kinds of media, for example, copper wire. Figure 2.9 shows an analogue signal. The variation in the waves directly mirrors (is an analogue of) the variations in the light or sound waves that a transmitter produces. For example, a dial-up modem (see Chap. 5) produces shrieking sounds, which are sent over the analogue sections of the telephone network as continuously varying electrical waves. The bandwidth of an analogue signal is the difference between the highest and lowest frequencies contained in the signal. The frequency is the number of times the wave goes up and down per second. Frequency and analogue bandwidth are measured in cycles per second or hertz (Hz).

Digital transmission, on the other hand, is done with a series of electrical (voltage) pulses. Figure 2.10 shows a digital signal. With digital signalling, the information

Fig. 2.10 Digital signal

that is being sent out over the medium is turned into a stream of bits. A digital signal is not affected by noise (interference) or attenuation (weakening of the signal) as easily as an analogue signal. In the digital context, the term bandwidth is commonly used to mean the same as data rate and is expressed in bits per second. It can be argued that this is an incorrect use of the term bandwidth, but in computer networking, it is very frequently encountered with this meaning. So the phrases 'a data rate of 100 Mbps' and '100 Mbps of bandwidth' can be taken to mean the same thing.

2.5 Modulation and Encoding

2.5.1 Amplitude Modulation, Frequency Modulation and Phase Modulation

The term *modulation* refers to ways of encoding information onto a carrier signal. The device that carries out modulation is called a modulator. For example, we may need to turn a digital signal from a computer into an analogue signal in order to send it out over a network. At the other end, conversion from analogue to digital will be carried out to give the original digital signal. The device that does these conversions is called a *modem* because it is both a modulator and demodulator (see Chap. 5 for details of how various kinds of modems are used).

There are three fundamental ways of altering the carrier signal: *amplitude modulation* (AM), *frequency modulation* (FM) and *phase modulation* (PM). In AM, the amplitude of the carrier signal is manipulated, changing the height of the wave. In FM, the frequency of the carrier signal is manipulated, altering how many peaks and troughs of the wave there are in a given time. In PM, the phase of the carrier signal is manipulated: The wave is made to start at a different point in its cycle. These three different modulation methods are illustrated in Fig. 2.11. A combination of AM and PM works well in modems and combined with other techniques such as echo cancellation can give remarkably high speeds considering that the analogue phone system is being used.

2.5.2 Codes for Transmitting Digital Data Using Digital Signals

If we want to send digital data using a digital signal, the most obvious way of encoding the bits would seem to be simply to use a high voltage level to represent a 1 bit and a low voltage level to represent a 0 bit. However, if this were done, the receiver could misunderstand the significance of a low voltage. Such a voltage

Fig. 2.11 AM, FM
and PM

Fig. 2.12 Encoding schemes

might signify a 0 bit, but it might alternatively mean that nothing was being transmitted. This form of encoding is called non-return-to-zero (NRZ) and is illustrated in Fig. 2.12.

There are many different coding schemes, but we shall look at just one other besides NRZ. As can be seen in Fig. 2.12, Manchester encoding uses a transition in voltage to represent 1 s and 0 s. A transition from low to high (representing a 1 bit) or high to low (representing a 0 bit) voltage occurs in the middle of a bit time. One advantage of such a scheme is that the receiver only has to look for a change in voltage (easier to detect than voltage value). Furthermore, always having a transition in the middle of a bit time provides a clock signal as well as data. Manchester encoding is used in 10 Mbps Ethernet (further details of Ethernet are given in Chap. 4). More complicated encoding schemes than Manchester are used in higher speed versions of Ethernet.

2.6   Error Control Methods

Signal impairment can lead to errors in bit transmission. Data error rates are usually defined in terms of a ratio. For example, 1/1,000 means that for every 1,000 bits, one bit will be transmitted in error. This can also be represented as an error rate of 10^{-3}.

Finding out whether errors have occurred (error detection) and correcting these errors (error correction) can be important because of the potential cost of data error. As a simple example of this, consider the following: A figure representing a bank balance is sent over a network. An error occurs in only one digit of this balance, but that is enough to make the received figure differ by thousands of Euros from what it should be.

All error control methods involve adding extra, redundant bits to the message that is to be transmitted. We can classify these methods as automatic repeat request (ARQ) or forward error correction (FEC).

2.6.1   Automatic Repeat Request

The idea behind ARQ is for the transmitter to add enough redundant bits to the block of data that it is sending out to make it possible for the receiver to tell if there has been an error during transmission. The receiver cannot correct the error itself, and so it asks for a retransmission of the data block that contains the error.

Parity (see Sect. 2.2.1) could provide a simple form of ARQ. A parity failure would provoke the receiver into asking the sender to resend the data block in question. However, if there were more than one error, such a simple system might fail to detect any error. For example, let us imagine that even parity is in use. The data that the sending computer transmits is 1010111. To give even parity, it adds a 1 bit, making the message 10101111. During transmission, two bit errors occur, and the bits get changed to 00100111. But when the receiver checks for parity, it finds an even number of 1 bit and is satisfied that there have been no errors. For this reason, simple parity is not used for ARQ in practice.

A more satisfactory alternative to simple parity is the *checksum* method. Here, the sending computer adds up all the data bytes of the message to be transmitted. The resulting figure, the checksum, is transmitted along with the data. At the other end, the receiver performs the same operation on the data and compares the checksum it has calculated with the one that the sending computer included in the message. If these two checksums are not the same, the receiving computer concludes that there has been an error during transmission and asks for a retransmission. The size of checksums is kept within reasonable bounds by, for example, the sending device throwing away any carries beyond 8 bits. One protocol that uses checksums is TCP (although the calculation involved is slightly more sophisticated than that described here). The TCP protocol is explained in Chap. 6.

2.6.1.1 Cyclic Redundancy Check
The *cyclic redundancy check* (CRC) is a more sophisticated error detection method than checksums. This technique lends itself to implementation in hardware, which is fast, since it requires merely a shift register and an exclusive-OR (XOR) function.

Fig. 2.13 CRC calculation

$$
\begin{array}{r}
\text{Divisor} = 1101 \\
\text{Data} = 101010 \\
\text{Bits transmitted} = 101010011
\end{array}
$$

```
                   110111
            1101 │ 101010000
                   1101
                   ────
                   1111
                   1101
                   ────
                    1000
                    1101
                    ────
                    1010
                    1101
                    ────
                     1110
                     1101
                     ────
         Remainder = 011
```

The transmitting device divides the outgoing block of data by a certain number (chosen because it gives good results). It is the remainder that results from this division that is sent out with the data. At the other end, the receiver does a similar calculation and compares the result it gets with the CRC that the sender has sent it. If there is a discrepancy, then the receiver assumes that there has been a transmission error and asks the sender to retransmit the data.

As can be seen in Fig. 2.13, the division is actually carried out modulo 2 in binary. In modulo-2 arithmetic, there are no carries and no borrows, and there is no difference between addition and subtraction. When done on paper, the calculation is a binary 'long division sum'. However, it is easier to do than a normal long division sum because instead of having to perform subtractions and use borrows, we can utilise XOR. See, for example, the first stage in the division process in Fig. 2.13, where we take the XOR of 1010 and 1101, giving a result of (0)111. In CRC division, one number is said to 'go into' another merely by virtue of having the same number of digits. Before starting the division, some zeros need to be added to the end of the data. We add the number of digits in the divisor (four in this example) −1 (i.e. three zeros). When we finish, the result (the remainder) must be one digit shorter than the divisor. That is the reason for the leading zero in the remainder in Fig. 2.13. We then append the remainder (011) onto the end of the data (101010) and transmit 101010011.

CRCs are very good at detecting burst errors (most data transmission errors occur in bursts). There are several international standards for CRCs. A prime example is the 32-bit CRC which is used for error control in the Ethernet frame (see Chap. 4).

2.6.1.2 Automatic Repeat Request Mechanisms

We shall now look at two different ways of organising ARQ: *idle RQ* and *continuous RQ*. In idle RQ (or *stop-and-wait RQ*), the transmitter sends a block of data and then waits for an acknowledgement from the receiver. The receiver checks what it has received. If there are no errors, it sends back a positive acknowledgement (ACK). If the receiver finds an error, it discards the block and sends back a negative acknowledgement (NAK). If the block is completely lost or destroyed, there is no

Fig. 2.14 Idle RQ

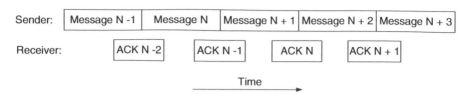

Fig. 2.15 Continuous RQ

ACK. If the transmitter receives an ACK, it sends the next block. If it receives NAK, it sends the previous block again. (It always keeps a copy of the block that it has just sent out, in case it is needed.) If the transmitter does not receive an ACK within a given time, there is a timeout and the block is resent. The idle RQ system is illustrated in Fig. 2.14.

It can be seen in Fig. 2.14 that time is wasted while the sender waits for the receiver to acknowledge receipt of a block. As the term idle RQ suggests, the transmitter is idle while awaiting an acknowledgement. Continuous RQ is a way of increasing efficiency over what idle RQ offers. The aim of continuous RQ is to transmit data blocks continuously so that there will be no idle time. The sender sends off several data blocks in succession, without waiting for an acknowledgement. The sender gives every block that is transmitted a *sequence number*. Every acknowledgement uses the correct sequence number such that the sender knows which block is being acknowledged. Continuous RQ is illustrated in Fig. 2.15.

2.6.1.3 Automatic Repeat Request Retransmission Mechanisms

If an error occurs when continuous RQ is in use, there is a choice of ARQ retransmission mechanisms. These mechanisms are *go-back-N* and *selective retransmission*. In go-back-N, after an error, the receiver sends a NAK. This means that the block having that sequence number should be sent again. The sender sends that block again and then sends the following blocks, even though these may already have been transmitted successfully. In Fig. 2.16, block N is positively acknowledged but block $N+1$ is negatively acknowledged. By the time the NAK for block $N+1$ arrives, the sender has already sent out blocks $N+2$ and $N+3$. Since blocks $N+2$ and $N+3$ are out of sequence, the receiver ignores these and waits for block $N+1$ to arrive again. Having retransmitted block $N+1$ (which this time is received with no errors), the sender retransmits blocks $N+2$ and $N+3$.

Selective retransmission is illustrated in Fig. 2.17. When selective retransmission is in use, the sender's response to a NAK for block $N+1$ is to retransmit block $N+1$ only but not blocks $N+2$ and $N+3$. Despite the fact that blocks $N+2$ and $N+3$

Fig. 2.16 Go-back-*N*

Fig. 2.17 Selective retransmission

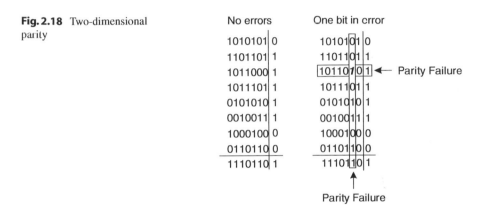

Fig. 2.18 Two-dimensional parity

are now out of sequence (because block *N*+1 has not arrived intact), the receiver accepts them. When the sender has retransmitted block *N*+1, it sends blocks *N*+4 and *N*+5 and so on.

The disadvantage of the go-back-*N* method is that some blocks will be retransmitted unnecessarily. This is a waste of bandwidth. The disadvantage of selective retransmission is that the receiver needs plenty of buffer (temporary storage) capacity in order to store temporarily data blocks that have been received out of sequence. Go-back-*N* is the more popular of the two methods, since buffer capacity is finite.

2.6.2   Forward Error Correction

The idea behind FEC is to add enough redundant bits to the data block to be transmitted so that the receiver can correct errors without having to ask for a retransmission. It is, of course, essential to use FEC instead of ARQ if only a simplex link is available because in such a situation, it is impossible to ask for a retransmission. When there is a duplex link, FEC is often used in combination with ARQ.

Two-dimensional parity offers a very simple form of FEC (see Fig. 2.18). In two dimensional parity, we not only add a parity bit to each character but also add a row of parity bits after a block of characters. The row of parity bits is actually a parity bit for each 'column' of characters. The row parity bits plus the column parity bits add a great amount of redundancy to a block of characters. Unfortunately, such a system can correct only single-bit errors. So, in practice, we need a more sophisticated system, as it is quite possible that there will be more than one error in a block.

Usually, special error-correcting codes known as Reed–Solomon codes are used for FEC. The applications in which these codes are used include wireless and mobile communications and digital subscriber line (DSL) modems. The sophisticated mathematical techniques used by Reed–Solomon codes are beyond the scope of this text.

2.7   Switched Connections

Switches are devices that can make a temporary connection between other devices. A switched network is shown in Fig. 2.19. As can be seen in Fig. 2.19, the computers have been given numbers and the switches letters. Each of the switches makes a connection between two of the links to which it is connected. There are three kinds of switching: circuit switching, packet switching and message switching.

2.7.1   Circuit Switching

Circuit switching is used in the traditional, analogue, public switched telephone network (PSTN). Circuit switching has three stages. Firstly, a circuit is set up from one end device to another. This circuit may involve several switches along the route. Next, the data is transferred. Finally, the circuit is disconnected. In circuit switching, there is a dedicated path between the end devices.

Setting up the circuit before any data can be sent takes some time. Let us assume that circuit switching is in use in the network shown in Fig. 2.19. If computer 8 needs to connect to computer 7, the complete circuit between them needs to be set up. Computer 8 will send a request to switch E to be connected to computer 7. Switch E will have knowledge of available routes and will be able to choose the best one. A dedicated path is set up between switches E and D. Switch D then asks for access to computer 7. If computer 7 permits access, then an ACK will be sent back to computer 8. Only now can the data be transferred. When the data is being sent, the only delay involved will be the time taken for it to propagate through the network. When data transfer is finished, more signalling takes place to 'tear down' the circuit (get rid of it) and make all the links that have been used available again for future use.

If there is only a little data to transfer, circuit switching is inefficient because of the time taken to set up the circuit. Also, a transfer will hog a transmission path that no other devices can use until the circuit is released. Despite these disadvantages, circuit switching has been very successfully used for voice transmission.

Fig. 2.19 Switched network

2.7.2   Message Switching

In message switching, the circuits are permanent, but it is the data that is switched. There is no need to set up a dedicated path before sending the data. If an end device needs to send a message, it adds the address of the destination to the message before sending it off. At every switch in the communication path, the message is briefly stored before being passed on to the next switch. For obvious reasons, this technique is known as *store and forward*.

Let us assume that message switching is in use in the network shown in Fig. 2.19. Computer 3 wants to send a message to computer 7. Computer 3 appends the address of computer 7 to the message. The message is stored briefly by switch B, which then forwards it to switch F. After having briefly stored the message, switch F forwards it to switch D. Switch D stores the message before forwarding it to computer 7.

For computer data transfer, message switching is more efficient than circuit switching. However, it is no longer used because of the large amounts of storage space required on the switches. Furthermore, the delays involved are unacceptable today.

2.7.3 Packet Switching

This technique is similar to message switching, in that addressing, storing and forwarding are all involved. What is different is that, instead of complete messages being forwarded between switching devices, the source divides the data into much smaller packets before it is sent off. It is these packets that are given addresses and then sent through the network.

There are several advantages to sending packets rather than messages. Firstly, there is much less delay, since the packets are short. The small size of the packets means that less storage is needed in the switches compared with message switching. We have already discussed the concept of sequence numbers (see Sect. 2.6.1). When combined with addressing, sequence numbers permit the interleaving (multiplexing) of packets from more than one source (multiplexing is explained in Sect. 2.8). When this is done, the communications channel can be used more efficiently. Packet switching is a very popular method of communication. There are two variants: *datagram* packet switching and *virtual circuit* packet switching.

2.7.3.1 Datagram Packet Switching

In datagram packet switching, each packet contains the destination address. The route that datagrams take between the same source and destination can vary. For example, let us assume that datagram packet switching is in use in the network shown in Fig. 2.19. Computer 3 sends two successive datagrams to computer 7. The first datagram travels, say, via switches B, A, F, E and D. The second travels via B, C and D. It is possible that the datagram that was sent out first will arrive after the second one because the route it took was shorter. This problem is taken care of by each datagram having a sequence number. The datagrams can be reordered at the destination using the sequence numbers.

2.7.3.2 Virtual Circuit Packet Switching

In virtual circuit packet switching, a route from sender to receiver is set up before any transfer takes place. This is not the same as the dedicated path that is set up in circuit switching. The physical path along which successive packets travel may vary. Addressing of the packets is carried out by means of virtual circuit numbers, which indicate the virtual circuit a packet belongs to. Virtual circuits come in two forms: switched virtual circuits (SVCs) and permanent virtual circuits (PVCs).

2.7.3.3 Switched Virtual Circuits

An SVC is set up temporarily whenever it is needed. The virtual circuit does not persist when the data transfer is finished. For example, let us assume that computer 8 in Fig. 2.19 is going to send some data to computer 3 using an SVC. Computer 8 sends out a set-up call to computer 3. The virtual circuit is established automatically with no human intervention. When all the data packets have been sent, the virtual circuit is automatically torn down.

2.7.3.4 Permanent Virtual Circuits

As the name suggests, a PVC is somewhat longer lasting than an SVC. It has to be set up by a network administrator. There is no need for a set-up call; the virtual circuit is always available whenever it is needed. We will mention PVCs again when X.25 and frame relay are discussed in Chap. 5.

2.8 Multiplexing

In multiplexing, signals from several sources are sent down one long-distance channel at the same time. At the destination, these signals are separated again. The advantage of this is that an expensive WAN link can be used very efficiently. There are two major varieties of multiplexing: *time division multiplexing* (TDM) and *frequency division multiplexing* (FDM). A third kind of multiplexing, *wavelength division multiplexing* (WDM), can be classified as a variant of FDM.

2.8.1 Time Division Multiplexing

The idea of time division multiplexing (TDM) is to interleave bits (or bytes) from several sources. Figure 2.20 shows how it works. In the diagram, there are eight low-speed channels feeding into the multiplexer. The multiplexer takes a bit or a byte (depending on the system in use) from each low-speed channel in turn and outputs it onto the high-speed communications link. The multiplexer cycles through all the eight channels on a round robin basis. What is not shown in Fig. 2.20 is that there is another multiplexer at the destination, which demultiplexes the multiplexed data into low-speed channels. Simple TDM is a fairly efficient way of using a high-speed, long-distance communications link. However, it is wasteful if low-speed channels have nothing to send when it is their turn. A more complicated technique called statistical multiplexing gets round this by filling the slots on a first-come-first-served basis, rather than using a round robin system.

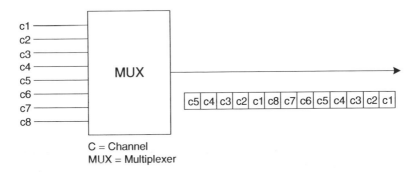

Fig. 2.20 Time division multiplexing

Fig. 2.21 Frequency division multiplexing

Fig. 2.22 Wavelength division multiplexing

2.8.2 Frequency Division Multiplexing

In FDM, a high-speed link is divided into several bands of frequencies. Each channel is carried within one of these frequency bands. This is an analogue technique, whereas TDM is digital. FDM is illustrated in Fig. 2.21.

2.8.3 Wavelength Division Multiplexing

WDM is similar to FDM in that multiple signals are sent simultaneously over one transmission path. However, instead of electrical signals being sent, light signals are transmitted. Data from different channels (different colours of light) is carried at very high rates over a single strand of optical fibre. (For a discussion of optical fibre, see Sect. 2.10.2.) The sender multiplexes the source channels before they are sent over the long-haul link; the receiver demultiplexes these. WDM is illustrated in Fig. 2.22. For the sake of simplicity, only four colours are shown in the diagram, though many more are possible. Dense wavelength division multiplexing (DWDM) allows even greater bit rates than does simple WDM.

2.9   Topologies Used In Networking

The term *topology* as applied to a computer network refers to the structure of the network. A distinction is drawn between the physical and logical topologies. The physical topology is the way in which the network is laid out. The logical topology is concerned with how the transmission medium, for example, a cable, can be accessed by the computers attached to the network. In this section, the discussion is confined to physical topologies. The concept of logical topology will be introduced later (see Sect. 4.2.2).

2.9.1   Bus

Outside the computing context, the term *bus* can be used to denote an electrical conductor that is used to connect several circuits together. Inside a computer (as we saw in Sect. 2.1), a bus is a common path for moving information about, for example, a data bus. In a computer network, a bus is a single piece of cable to which all the computers are attached. At the two ends of this cable, there are resistors that absorb unwanted signals so that they are not reflected back along the bus. If the bus fails, communication ceases. A physical bus was used in old types of Ethernet LAN (further details of Ethernet are given in Chap. 4). The bus topology is illustrated in Fig. 2.23.

2.9.2   Ring

As the name suggests, in the ring topology, the computers are laid out in a ring. An endless cable (ring) connects the computers together. If the ring fails, there can be no further communication, and so sometimes a double ring is used. The ring topology is illustrated in Fig. 2.24.

Fig. 2.23 Bus

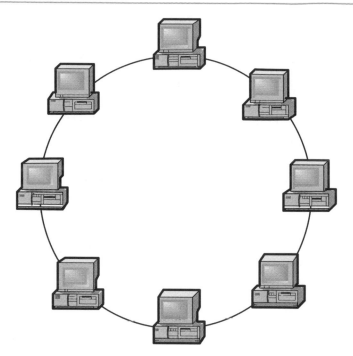

Fig. 2.24 Ring

2.9.3   Star

As shown in Fig. 2.25, the star topology looks rather like a wheel without a rim. The devices at the ends of the spokes of the wheel can communicate with each other only via a central hub. Originally, this central hub was a computer and the other devices were usually dumb terminals (devices with a keyboard and screen but no processing power). In modern star networks, the devices at the outer ends of the spokes are computers, but the hub is a device that will not necessarily have any intelligence. Irrespective of how much intelligence it possesses, if the hub fails, this has a catastrophic effect on the functioning of the network. Despite this, the star topology is a very popular one for LANs.

2.9.4   Tree (Hierarchical)

The tree or hierarchical topology is illustrated in Fig. 2.26. The computer at the root of the tree (shown at the top of Fig. 2.26) controls all the traffic in the network.

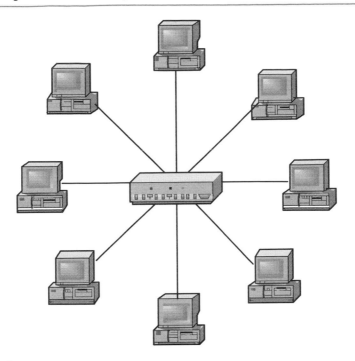

Fig. 2.25 Star

Fig. 2.26 Tree

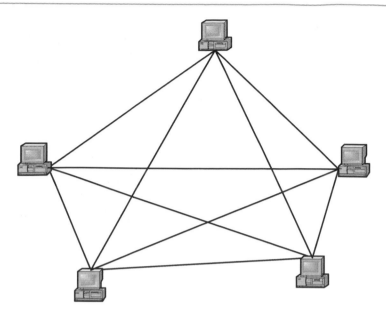

Fig. 2.27 Mesh

2.9.5 Mesh

In the mesh topology (Fig. 2.27), every computer is directly connected to every other one. If one link between any two computers stops working, an alternative route will be available. A topology such as this is expensive, but it may be necessary for applications where it is vital that computers do not lose contact with each other. An example of such an application is controlling a nuclear power station.

2.10   Network Transmission Media

The word *media* is the plural form of *medium*. As we saw in Sect. 1.4.1, in networking, these terms are used to refer to the pathways along which data travels. The pathway is often a cable of some kind but not always. There are three classes of media: copper cable, fibre-optic cable and wireless media.

2.10.1 Copper Cable

Copper cable is the most common kind of cabling in LANs. There are several different forms of copper cable, each with particular advantages and disadvantages. All these forms carry an electrical current that represents the data.

Fig. 2.28 Coaxial cable

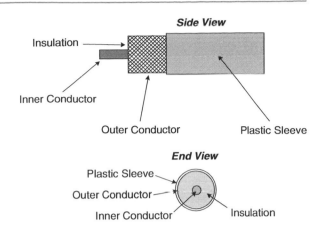

2.10.1.1 Coaxial Cable

This cable consists of two copper conductors, one inside the other, separated by plastic insulation. The inner conductor is a thick copper wire. The outer conductor is a cylindrical mesh of thin copper wire. This layer also acts as a shield for the inner conductor, helping to cut down on electromagnetic interference from outside the cable. A plastic sleeve protects the cable. A coaxial cable is illustrated in Fig. 2.28. As can be seen from the illustration, the kind of coaxial cable that is used for computer network installations is very similar to a television aerial cable.

A coaxial cable has some useful features. Fewer repeaters are needed to boost the signal than with twisted-pair cable. It is less expensive than fibre-optic cable. It was used for cabling Ethernet LANs. However, for some years, it has not been used for new Ethernet installations as it is expensive to put in compared to twisted-pair cable. It is also tricky to connect the outer conductor properly. A coaxial cable is commonly used for carrying cable television signals (and computer data as well if a cable modem is in use) into the home.

2.10.1.2 Unshielded Twisted-Pair Cable

As the name suggests, in a twisted-pair cable pairs of copper wires are twisted together in a helix. This is done to cut down on *crosstalk* (electromagnetic interference between the signals carried on adjacent wires). Most twisted-pair cables are unshielded twisted pair (UTP). In UTP cable, there are four pairs of wires. Each individual wire is covered with plastic insulation. The most common form of UTP cable is category 5e (CAT 5e). A UTP cable is shown in Fig. 2.29.

UTP cable is very popular in LANs for several reasons. It is cheap, easy to install and small enough to fit into wiring ducts easily. The main disadvantages are susceptibility to electrical interference and the short distance that is permissible between repeaters.

Fig. 2.29 UTP cable

Four Pairs of Wires

Plastic Sleeve

Fig. 2.30 ScTP cable

Four Pairs of Wires

Plastic Sleeve

Screen

2.10.1.3 Shielded/Screened Twisted-Pair Cable

In shielded (STP) or screened (ScTP) twisted-pair cable, shielding or screening is added to a four-pair cable to give more protection from interference, both from inside and outside the cable. In STP cable, each pair of wires is surrounded by a metallic foil and then the whole bundle of wires is shielded. In ScTP, the individual pairs of wires are not shielded. An ScTP cable is illustrated in Fig. 2.30. The shielding/screening makes ScTP and STP cable much more difficult to install than UTP, but interference is greatly reduced.

2.10.1.4 Straight-Through and Crossover Cables

Normally, computers on a LAN are connected together via a hub or switch. In this case, the type of cable that is needed is a *straight-through* cable, in which the transmit pin at the computer end is directly connected to the transmit pin at the hub or switch. The respective receive pins are also directly connected to each other. The use of a straight-through cable is illustrated in Fig. 2.31.

However, if we wish to connect two computers directly to each other without using a hub or switch, we have to connect the transmit pins at each end to the receive pins at the other end. The kind of cable that is necessary in such a situation is called a *crossover* cable. The way in which a crossover cable is used is shown in Fig. 2.32. Both these kinds of cables would normally be UTP, but STP or ScTP could be used instead.

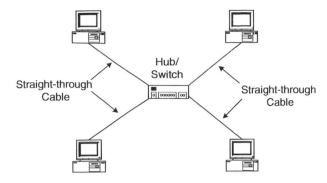

Fig. 2.31   Straight-through cable

Fig. 2.32   Crossover cable

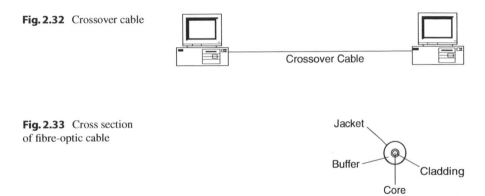

Fig. 2.33   Cross section
of fibre-optic cable

2.10.2 Fibre-Optic Cable

Instead of using electrical currents to represent data, optical fibre carries a beam of light. The fibre cores are made of glass (or plastic). Cladding, consisting of glass (or plastic) of a refractive index different from that of the core, surrounds each fibre. The cladding stops the light beam getting out of the fibre, relying on the principle of *total internal reflection*. There is a buffer layer (usually plastic) around the cladding to protect it from damage. Finally, a plastic jacket surrounds the other layers. A cross section of a fibre-optic cable is shown in Fig. 2.33. The cables are often used in pairs, with a fibre for each direction.

Fibre-optic cable has several advantages over copper. It offers higher data rates and needs fewer repeaters. It is light and occupies little space. It is completely immune to electrical interference. It is difficult to tap, which gives greater security. The disadvantages are that it is more difficult to splice (join together) than a copper

Fig. 2.34 Single-mode and
multimode fibres

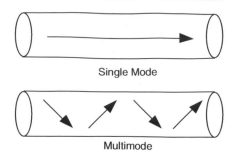

cable and, crucially, is more expensive. Fibre-optic cable is commonly used for
trunk telephone lines and for 'vertical' cabling for LANs. For connections to LAN
desktop computers, however, copper still predominates.

The diameter of the core of *single-mode* fibre is just sufficient for one wavelength of light. The light source is a laser diode, and the light travels in a straight line
along the fibre. Few repeaters are needed to transmit signals for long distances, and
data rates can be very high. *Multimode* fibre has a greater diameter, which allows
multiple wavelengths of light to take multiple paths through the fibre core.

Multimode fibre uses a cheap light-emitting diode (LED) as the light source.
Both single-mode and multimode fibres use a photodiode, which generates an
electrical pulse when light falls upon it, to detect the received light signal. Single-
mode and multimode fibres are illustrated in Fig. 2.34.

2.10.3 Wireless Media

Laying a cable can often be difficult, expensive or inappropriate. In such circumstances, wireless media can be used instead. For example, if a temporary link is
needed between sites, it may not be worth laying a cable, and a wireless network may
be the answer. If a deep ocean trench separates an island from the mainland, laying a
cable might be impossible, and so a wireless link can be installed instead.

Any kind of mobile computer system will need a wireless link. Compared to
wired links, wireless links tend to have relatively low capacity and high-error rates.
They tend to be affected by weather, and installation is often highly regulated.
Despite these disadvantages, wireless transmission is very popular (see Sect. 10.4.1
for some of the advantages of wireless LANs (WLANs)).

2.10.3.1 Microwave Radio
Microwave radio is the commonest form of transmission without wires. Two places
where it is used are 802.11x LANs and mobile telephone networks (see Chap. 10).
The information is carried through the air by ultra-high, super-high or extremely
high-frequency radio waves. Microwave signals (unlike ordinary radio signals)
can be aimed to travel in a particular direction, and so the signals can be targeted

Fig. 2.35 Line-of-sight microwave transmission

precisely at those who need to receive them. Microwave transmission offers high bandwidth. A line of sight is preferable between transmitter and receiver because buildings have an adverse effect on the signal. For this reason, high towers are commonly used to relay microwave transmissions (see Fig. 2.35). Rain can interfere with microwave signals. Various ways in which microwave transmission can be used are explored in Chap. 10.

2.10.3.2 Satellites

Microwave signals can be sent over very long distances using satellites. Although the cost of launching a satellite is high, it can carry a vast amount of traffic. It carries a number of *transponders* (transmitter/responder). These listen for incoming radio signals, boost them and then retransmit them at a different angle from the angle at which they arrived. Each transponder works on a different frequency.

Communications satellites are usually in a *geosynchronous* orbit, 35,785 km above the earth's surface. At this distance, a satellite is synchronised with the rotation of the earth. To an observer on the earth, it does not appear to move in the sky. A geosynchronous satellite is illustrated in Fig. 2.36.

Alternatives to the geosynchronous satellite are the *low earth orbit* (LEO) and *medium earth orbit* (MEO) satellite. The orbit of these satellites is much closer to the earth's surface than that of a geosynchronous satellite. This means that they appear to move relative to the surface of the earth. An array of 64 LEO satellites is sufficient to cover the whole of the earth's surface. MEO arrays are used in satellite navigation systems such as the Global Positioning System (GPS), Galileo and GLObal NAvigation Satellite System (GLONASS). GPS is explained further in Sect. 10.11.

Fig. 2.36 Geosynchronous satellite

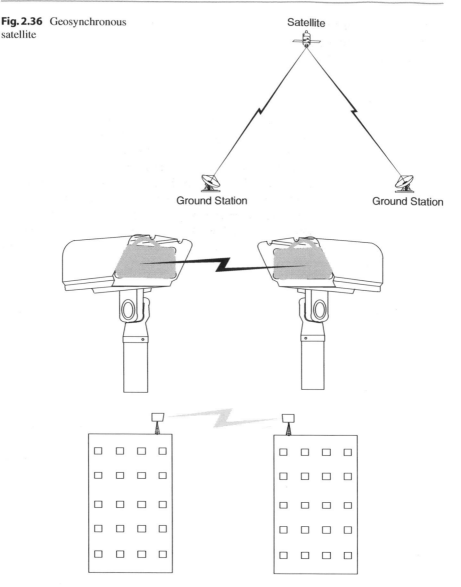

Fig. 2.37 Free space optics

2.10.3.3 Infrared

Infrared signals can be used for networking over short distances. While a line of sight is merely preferable for microwave communications, for infrared this is absolutely essential because the signal cannot pass through most solid objects. This is both an advantage (because of lack of interference with other systems and good security) and a disadvantage (because of shortness of range). With no need for aerials (antennae, antennas) on the devices, an infrared system can be very successful at linking together small, portable devices within a room. Unlike microwave, no spectrum licensing is needed. However, infrared networks are very much less popular than microwave-based networks.

2.10.3.4 Free Space Optics

We have already seen (Sect. 2.10.2) how light signals can be used to transmit data when constrained within fibre-optic cables. It is also possible to use lasers for computer communications without a cable. This is known as *free space optics* (FSO). In FSO, light beams are transmitted from one transceiver (transmitter/receiver) to another using low-power lasers. A line of sight is essential. Fog and snow can impede the light beam, which is a serious disadvantage in many parts of the world. Despite this, FSO is often used for connecting LANs together across a street, using equipment such as that shown in Fig. 2.37. FSO systems can work over distances of several kilometres. The transceivers will work through windows, and so it is not even necessary to mount them on the roof of a building. As with infrared systems, no licensing is necessary.

2.11 Summary

This chapter has looked at some of the technologies that are used for computer communications. The chapter started with an explanation of the differences between serial and parallel data transfer, asynchronous and synchronous communications and duplex, half-duplex and full-duplex communications. The distinctions between data rate, bandwidth and throughput were then explained. Modulation and encoding, error control methods, switching and multiplexing were then discussed. The topologies used in networking were described. Finally, network transmission media were explored.

2.12 Questions

1. The lowercase letter 'w' is being transmitted using asynchronous transmission. The 7-bit ASCII code for 'w' is 1110111 (77 hexadecimal). Even parity is being used, and there is one stop bit. Draw a timing diagram illustrating this. Base your diagram on Fig. 2.4.
2. Describe hub-based Ethernet LANs in terms of the following dichotomies: *serial/parallel* transmission, *synchronous/asynchronous* transmission and *full-duplex/half-duplex* transmission. In addition to reading this chapter, you may have to do a bit of further research to answer this question.
3. How long, in theory, will it take to transfer a 1-Mb file over a network running at 1 Gbps?

Table 2.2 Two-dimensional even parity

0	0	1	0	0	0	0
0	0	1	1	0	0	0
0	1	0	0	0	1	1
1	0	0	1	0	0	0
0	0	0	0	0	1	0
1	0	0	0	1	1	1
1	1	0	0	0	1	0

4. Explain the difference between *analogue* and *digital* transmission.
5. Investigate the *8B/10B* encoding scheme that is used in gigabit Ethernet. In addition to reading this chapter, you may have to do a bit of further research to answer this question.
6. (a) If even parity checking is in use, what are the parity bits assigned to the ASCII characters capital 'B', 'F', 'J' , 'P' and 'W'?
   (NB: The ASCII code for capital 'A' is 41 hexadecimal, i.e. 1000001 binary. The other codes can be worked out by counting on from 41 in hexadecimal and then converting to binary.)
   (b) What are the parity bits if odd parity is used?
7. A message is transmitted using cyclic redundancy coding to check for errors. The message is 101011. The divisor that is used for the CRC is 1101. Give the total bit pattern that is sent (see Fig. 2.13 for an example).
8. Two-dimensional even parity is being used. Fill in the column and row check bits for the block of data in Table 2.2.
9. Explain the differences between *TDM* and *FDM*.
10. Distinguish between *physical* and *logical* topology.
11. Distinguish between *UTP, single-mode optical fibre* and *multimode optical fibre*.
12. What kind of cable would be best for the following applications?
   (a) Horizontal wiring in an office
   (b) Vertical wiring in a building
   (c) A connection under the Atlantic Ocean
13. Describe the physical form of a *coaxial cable*.
14. In what circumstances would a *crossover cable* be needed?
15. What are the advantages and disadvantages of *infrared transmission*?

Networking Models and Standards

3

Abstract

In this chapter, we look at layered models, which are standard ways of organising networks. The chapter starts with an explanation of network layering and its advantages. Next, there is a description of one of the most important networking models, the open systems interconnection (OSI) 7-layer model. An explanation of the principles of data encapsulation follows. Another important networking model, TCP/IP, is then explained and compared with the 7-layer model. Finally, we look at several important networking standards bodies.

3.1 Layering of Networks

Most networks are organised as a series of layers or levels. At the lowest layer, physical communication takes place; at higher layers, virtual communication happens. At the higher layers, *peer processes*—the entities comprising the corresponding layers on different machines—appear to communicate directly with each other. For example, in Fig. 3.1, layer 3 at the source and layer 3 at the destination are peer layers.

In reality, these peer processes communicate via protocols. The protocol at a particular layer carries out a sequence of operations on the data. Next, this protocol passes the data to another layer, and there a different protocol carries out a different sequence of operations. Thus, the data gets passed down from layer to layer at the source until finally it is ready to be sent over the physical network medium, for example, a cable, to the destination. At the destination, the data gets passed upwards from layer to layer through the *protocol stack*. At each layer, a protocol performs operations on the data that reverse what was done at the corresponding layer at the source. Eventually, the data is in the form in which it was when it started out at the source. The data is now ready to be dealt with by the receiving application. The set of layers and protocols is the *network architecture*.

J. Cowley, *Communications and Networking: An Introduction*, Undergraduate Topics in Computer Science, DOI 10.1007/978-1-4471-4357-4_3,
© Springer-Verlag London 2012

Fig. 3.1 Communication
between layers

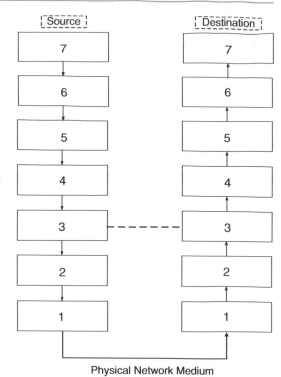

Physical Network Medium

3.1.1 Advantages of Layering

Organising a network architecture in layers as described above has a number of
advantages. It makes design less complex because any problem is broken down into
separate components. It is a more flexible way of working than having one big,
monolithic program that performs all functions needed by the network. If it is
necessary to enhance or modify the system, only one module needs to be changed,
and this should have no knock-on effects on the rest of the system. The application
programming interfaces (APIs) between the layers are tightly defined, and programmers write network software to these APIs.

3.2   OSI 7-Layer Reference Model

The OSI 7-layer reference model was devised by the International Organisation for
Standardisation (ISO). During the 1980s, different computer manufacturers had
their own network architectures and protocols. This situation often made it difficult
to network together computers made by different manufacturers. The aim of OSI
was to devise an architecture containing standard protocol layers that all vendors

Fig. 3.2 OSI 7-layer model

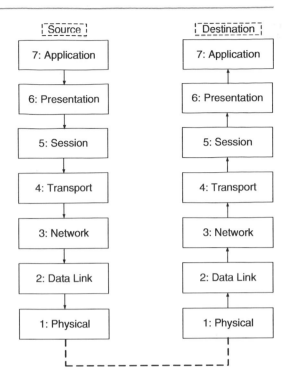

would use, resulting in complete *interoperability* between all network devices and network software. The OSI model had seven layers (see Fig. 3.2). Some new protocols were devised and some existing protocols were incorporated into the model. Although a few protocols that were designed for OSI are still in use, for example, the Intermediate System to Intermediate System (IS–IS) routing protocol, overall OSI was a failure as a practical network architecture. However, the OSI model is still important as a means of describing and teaching about network protocols. Each of the seven layers performs a particular network function. Summaries of these functions are given below.

3.2.1   Physical Layer

The physical layer is concerned with the transmission of bit patterns over a communications channel. It is responsible for how the binary 0s and 1s are represented, for example, what voltage levels are used. It is also concerned with the control signals to set up and tear down connections. Connectors and pin assignments are also specified by the physical layer. EIA/TIA-232 (or RS232-C) is an example of a physical-layer protocol.

3.2.2   Data-Link Layer

The data-link layer handles the errors that result from the physical transmission media. In this layer, the raw bit patterns from the physical layer are organised into *frames* (for examples, see Sects. 4.2.2.2 and 6.3). These frames are acknowledged by the destination if they are received correctly. The data-link layer also performs *flow control*. It can speed up or slow down the rate at which the source is sending data, according to how much buffer space is available at the receiver. HDLC (see Sect. 6.3) is a typical data-link protocol.

3.2.3   Network Layer

The network layer is concerned with the routing of packets across a network. The message from the source is split up into packets. The packets are then sent off to the destination. The network layer is concerned with addressing. The source address in a packet identifies the sending computer. The destination address identifies the computer that finally receives the packet. Internet Protocol (IP) is an example of a network layer protocol.

3.2.4   Transport Layer

The transport layer is responsible for end-to-end connections between *hosts* (a host is an end user's computer that is connected to a network). This layer masks the characteristics of the underlying network, which may change with advances in technology. Transport-layer protocols are implemented on the hosts, not on each machine in the chain that links these hosts.

The commonest type of transport-layer connection involves the establishment, maintenance and termination of a logical connection (virtual circuit) between two hosts, where the data that is sent from the source is delivered in the order in which it was sent. Any errors are detected and corrected and flow control is carried out. Transmission Control Protocol (TCP) is the most important example of a transport-layer protocol.

3.2.5   Session Layer

The session layer deals with the establishment, maintenance and termination of *sessions* between two users. This is similar to logging in and out of a time-sharing computer system but over a network rather than from a directly connected terminal. Security precautions, such as authentication of users by password, belong in this layer. The UNIX X Window system, a client–server system that offers a windowing environment over a network, is an example of a session layer protocol.

3.2.6 Presentation Layer

The presentation layer deals with data formatting, data compression and data encryption. Examples of data formatting are the need to convert between different character codes such as ASCII and EBCDIC and between different ways of representing integers such as big-endian and little-endian. The presentation of graphical images, sound and moving images is also dealt with in the presentation layer. For example, the portable network graphics (PNG) binary file format, used for displaying images on the Internet, is part of the presentation layer.

The presentation layer also looks after data compression. Compression is carried out using algorithms that make files smaller than they originally were. Any repeating bit patterns are replaced by shorter bit patterns (*tokens*). If the files are made smaller in this way, they can be transmitted in a shorter time.

Encryption is another function carried out in the presentation layer. Using a mathematical key, the outgoing file is scrambled to make it unintelligible to anyone who intercepts it. At the other end, the same key or a mathematically related key can be used to unscramble (decrypt) the data and turn it back into its original form.

3.2.7 Application Layer

The application layer contains a number of protocols that users need to be able to communicate over a network. HyperText Transfer Protocol (HTTP), which is used to transfer pages on the World Wide Web, is but one example out of many application layer protocols.

3.3 Encapsulation

Data is sent over a network from a source to a destination. The data cannot be sent until it has been encapsulated, that is, packaged up into a suitable form to be transmitted over the network. During the encapsulation process, the data has protocol information added to it as it is passed down through the OSI layers. This protocol information consists of headers (address information), trailers (for error control) and other items.

The data encapsulation process is illustrated in Fig. 3.3. Having been sent from the source, the data travels through the application layer and on down through the other layers. As the various layers carry out their services, the packaging of the data changes. A number of steps must be performed in order to encapsulate the data.

1. First of all, the data has to be built. If, for example, an e-mail is being sent, the alphanumeric characters of which it is composed will have to be converted into a form that can travel across the network. If compression and/or encryption is necessary, these functions will be performed.

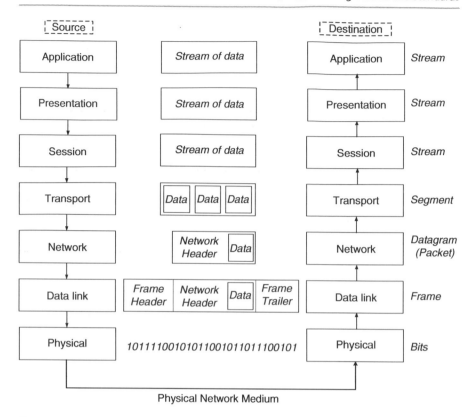

Fig. 3.3 Data encapsulation

2. Next, the data will have to be packaged up for transport from one end to the other. The data is divided up into *segments*. This will ensure that the sending and receiving hosts are able to communicate reliably.
3. The data must now be put into a *packet* or *datagram*. The datagram will include a header containing the addresses of the source and destination. Devices in the network will use these addresses to route the packet.
4. The packet must be put into a *frame* so that the data can be sent to the network device at the other end of the link. Every network device in the chain of links leading from source to destination needs framing so that it can connect to the next device.
5. Finally, the frame needs to be converted into a bit pattern (1s and 0s) so that it can actually be transmitted over the medium. The medium does not need to be the same along the complete path from source to destination. For example, an e-mail might start out from a portable machine connected wirelessly to a LAN, then pass onto a network wired with copper cable, then onto a WAN link wired with fibre-optic cable, then onto a satellite (microwave radio) link and so on.

Fig. 3.4 TCP/IP model

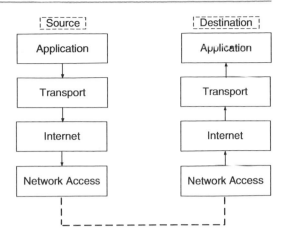

3.4   TCP/IP Model

The OSI 7-layer model was devised before the OSI protocols. As we saw, relatively few OSI protocols are in use, but the model is widely used as a means of classifying protocols. In the case of TCP/IP, on the other hand, the protocols came first, and the model was devised later. The instigator of TCP/IP was the US Department of Defense (DOD). The aim of TCP/IP was a robust communication system that would still function even if it were partially destroyed in a war.

The model has four layers: application, transport, Internet and network access. Beware! Although the TCP/IP application layer has the same name as the OSI application layer, the functions that it performs are not quite the same. The layers of the TCP/IP model are shown in Fig. 3.4.

Figure 3.5 shows how the protocols fit together into the TCP/IP suite. Many more TCP/IP protocols exist than are shown in the diagram, but those shown are some of the commonest. HyperText Transfer Protocol (HTTP), File Transfer Protocol (FTP), Simple Mail Transfer Protocol (SMTP) and Domain Name System (DNS) are all explained in Chap. 7. Dynamic Host Configuration Protocol (DHCP) is explained in Chap. 6 and Simple Network Management Protocol (SNMP) in Chap. 9. At the transport layer, the two main protocols are TCP and User Datagram Protocol (UDP). These are explained in Chap. 6. IP, also explained in Chap. 6, is the sole protocol at the Internet layer and allows universal communication between computers. The network technology that is being used by protocols in the top three layers resides in the network access layer.

3.5   The OSI and TCP/IP Models Compared

Figure 3.6 shows the OSI and TCP/IP models side by side. An obvious similarity between the two models is that the TCP/IP transport and Internet layers have very similar counterparts in the OSI transport and network layers. Both models have an

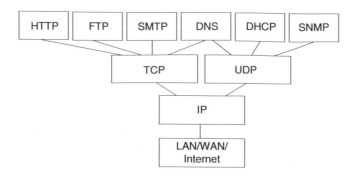

Fig. 3.5 TCP/IP

Fig. 3.6 The OSI and TCP/
IP models compared

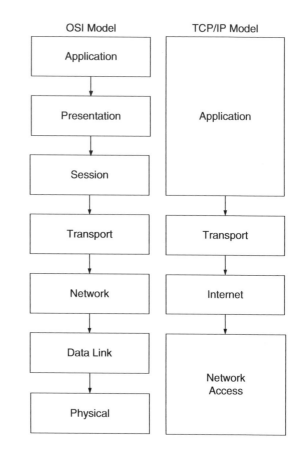

application layer, but the TCP/IP application layer performs the functions of the
OSI application, presentation and session layers combined. Another difference is
that the TCP/IP network access layer carries out the functions of the OSI data link
and physical layers. The OSI model is of more use for classifying protocols, but few

of its protocols are used to any great extent. TCP/IP protocols on the other hand, are very heavily used, but the model itself is less useful than the 7-layer model. The upshot is that networking students need to know about both models.

3.6 Networking Standards

It is important to have networking standards. The main reason for these standards is to make sure that hardware and software from different vendors can work together. We can classify standards into three categories: formal standards, proprietary standards and de facto standards. Formal standards are those developed by an official body, for example, the OSI 7-layer model and TCP/IP. Proprietary standards are those devised by one vendor for use with the company's products. An example of a proprietary standard is the now defunct Digital Equipment Corporation's DECnet, which worked only with DEC's products. De facto standards are those supported by more than one vendor but which have no official standing. An example of such a standard is the AT command set for modems. This was devised by the Hayes modem company (a proprietary standard initially) but was then taken up by every other modem manufacturer.

3.6.1 Networking Standards Bodies

There are many standards bodies that issue formal standards relevant to computer networking and telecommunications. Below are brief descriptions of just a few of these.

The Institute of Electrical and Electronics Engineers (IEEE) produces standards for electrical engineering, computers and control technology. It is responsible for the 802.3/Ethernet standards, among others (http://www.ieee.org). 802.3/Ethernet is discussed in Chap. 4.

The Internet Engineering Task Force (IETF) is concerned with the Internet architecture and the operation of the Internet (http://www.ietf.org). Among other standards, it is responsible for the TCP/IP protocols. It maintains a repository of Request for Comments (RFC) documents, a set of technical and organisational notes about the Internet. Some RFCs contain definitions of Internet standards, such as protocols.

The American National Standards Institute (ANSI) is an independent, non-profit organisation that administers and coordinates the US standardisation and conformity assessment system (http://www.ansi.org). The fibre-distributed data interface (FDDI) is an example of an ANSI networking standard. FDDI is briefly discussed in Chap. 4.

As we saw in Sect. 3.2, ISO is the International Organisation for Standardisation (http://www.iso.org), which devised the OSI 7-layer model. ISO is a network of many national standards institutes, including the British Standards Institution (BSI) and ANSI.

The International Telecommunication Union Telecommunication Standardisation Sector (ITU-T) produces telecommunications standards such as the V.92 modem standard (http://www.itu.int/ITU-T). The ITU-T was formerly called the Consultative Committee on International Telegraph and Telephone (CCITT).

The Electronic Industries Alliance (EIA) and the Telecommunications Industry Association (TIA) are US organisations that issue such standards as TIA/EIA-232 (formerly known as RS232-C). TIA/EIA-232 defines an interface between data terminal equipment (e.g. a computer) and data circuit terminating equipment (e.g. a modem). The EIA and TIA websites can be found at http://www.tiaonline.org and http://www.eia.org.

The European Telecommunications Standards Institute (ETSI) is an independent, non-profit organisation which produces telecommunications standards (http://www.etsi.org).

The World Wide Web Consortium (W3C) develops specifications and software for the World Wide Web (http://www.w3.org). HTML (see Sect. 7.3.1) and Extensible Markup Language (XML) are specified by W3C.

3.7 Summary

This chapter has looked at networking models and standards. The chapter started with an explanation of network layering. The OSI 7-layer model, an important way of describing networks, was examined. The principles of data encapsulation were then explained. Another important networking model, TCP/IP, was then described. The OSI and TCP/IP models were then briefly compared. The importance of networking standards was highlighted. Finally, several important networking standards bodies were mentioned.

3.8 Questions

1. What are the advantages of organising network architectures in *layers*?
2. Which of the following does a *physical-layer protocol* deal with?
   • Control signalling
   • Plugs and sockets
   • Checking for errors
3. Match the layer of the ISO/OSI 7-layer model to the facts about it:
   Layer
   (a) Physical layer
   (b) Data-link layer
   (c) Network layer
   (d) Transport layer
   (e) Session layer
   (f) Presentation layer
   (g) Application layer

Facts

(i)   Uses the raw transmission facility provided by the physical layer and makes the communication channel appear free of errors

(ii)   The environment in which users' programs operate and communicate

(iii) Concerned with establishing and maintaining a communication path between two users

(iv)   Concerned with the format of the data being exchanged by the communicating parties

(v)   Concerned with routing 'packets' across a network

(vi)   Concerned with the mechanism for transmitting bit patterns over a communication channel

(vii) Hides all the network-dependent characteristics from the layers above it

4. What are the layers in the *TCP/IP model*?

5. What is the *TCP/IP suite*?

6. What is an *RFC*?

7. Match the organisation to the facts about it:

Organisations

(a)   IEEE

(b)   ISO

(c)   ITU-T

(d)   W3C

(e)   IETF

Facts

(i)   Responsible for specifications and software for the World Wide Web

(ii)   Produces LAN standards, among others

(iii) Concerned with the operation and evolution of the Internet

(iv)   Responsible for the OSI 7-layer reference model

(v)   Responsible for world telecommunications standards

Local Area Networks

4

Abstract

In this chapter, we look at various aspects of LANs. The chapter starts with an account of some of the factors that we need to consider when planning a LAN. We look at the choices between a peer-to-peer and client–server LAN and between a wired and wireless network. There are descriptions of various components and devices for both wired LANs and wireless LANs (WLANs). Brief descriptions of several wired LAN technologies come next, but the chapter concentrates on Ethernet, which is the commonest of those technologies by far. Finally, we consider storage area networks and grid computing.

4.1 Building LANs

Several decisions need to be taken when planning a LAN. Should it be peer-to-peer or client–server? Should it be a wireless network? What kind of network technology should be used?

4.1.1 Peer-to-Peer and Client–Server LANs

Whether the network is organised on a peer-to-peer or a client–server basis, the same fundamental client–server technology and request–response protocol are used. (Client–server technology is explained in Chap. 7.)

4.1.1.1 Peer-to-Peer LANs

In a peer-to-peer network, the computers are equals (peers). None of the computers has control over the LAN, and the computers act as client or server computers as necessary. In a peer-to-peer LAN, a given computer can be acting as client or server at different times. Peer-to-peer LANs usually exist principally to

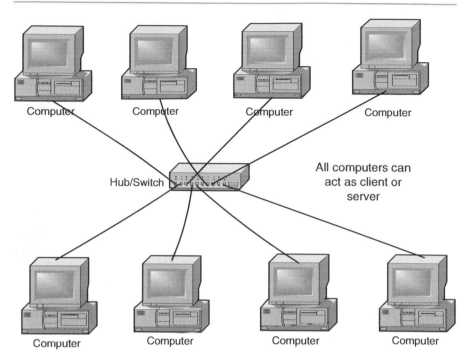

Fig. 4.1 Peer-to-peer LAN

share files and are normally based around a hub or switch. A peer-to-peer LAN is illustrated in Fig. 4.1.

Peer-to-peer LANs are easy to install and require little maintenance. There is no need for a network administrator. Users are in control of their own resources, and they can choose whether to share their files with other users. This can cause security problems. It is advisable to limit a peer-to-peer network to about ten *nodes* (a node is a computer that is attached to a network), or it may not work efficiently.

4.1.1.2 Client–Server LANs

Client–server technology is described in Sect. 7.1. In a client–server network, not all the computers are equal. There is a special server computer, which is dedicated to the server role. It responds to requests from all the other computers (the client computers). Typically, it provides file and print services and perhaps some other applications. The client computers are usually ordinary desktop computers, but the server computer is rather more powerful. The server computer may have extra memory and a more powerful processor or multiple processors. It will always have special software. Its operating system (OS), known as *a network operating system (NOS)*, is likely to be either a different version from that running on the client computers or else a completely different OS. The NOS controls the interaction of the

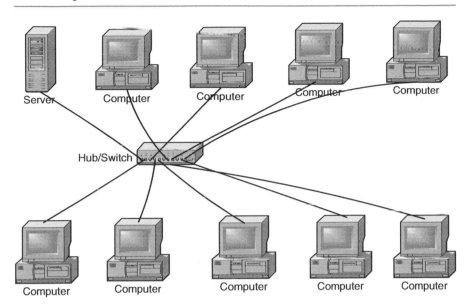

Fig. 4.2   Client–server LAN

client computers with the server computer and with each other. The most popular
NOS for PC LANs is Microsoft® Windows®. There may be more than one server
computer in the network. A client–server LAN is illustrated in Fig. 4.2.

User accounts and security are centralised on the server computer, which
makes administering a large network much easier than if it were organised on a
peer-to-peer basis. It is also easier to back up the files because they are all kept
in one place.

There are a few disadvantages to client–server LANs. The server computer is a
single point of failure: the network cannot function without it. The network needs a
trained, dedicated administrator, which increases the cost. The special software
needed also makes the client–server LAN more expensive than a peer-to-peer LAN.

4.1.2   Transmission Medium

When planning a LAN, one must decide whether to use cabling or wireless communications. The options for cabling were set out in Sect. 2.10. The default choice
for a wired LAN would be UTP cable laid out in a star topology. Wireless networks
are described in Chap. 10. The chief disadvantages of WLANs are poor security and
a relatively low data rate. However, WLANs are easy to set up compared with wired
LANs and make it very easy to move the computers about. A typical WLAN is
illustrated in Fig. 4.3. As shown in Fig. 4.3, a WLAN is usually connected to a
wired network, which facilitates long-distance communications.

Fig. 4.3   WLAN

4.1.3   Components and Devices

4.1.3.1 Components and Devices for Wired LANs

Each PC on the network will contain a network interface card (NIC). This is a circuit board that fits into a slot on the motherboard of the PC. Alternatively, the NIC circuitry might already be built into the PC's motherboard. The NIC lets the PC connect into a network. It encodes the data that is to be sent out, following the rules for the physical medium that is in use (a cable system or some other medium). Also, if the medium is shared, the NIC ensures that only one computer sends data at a time. In addition, it detects errors in transmission. Each network technology needs a particular kind of NIC. For example, an Ethernet NIC is necessary to connect to an Ethernet network. There are different kinds of NIC for the various types of PC bus (e.g. peripheral component interconnect (PCI)). The connector that the NIC has will vary according to the cabling used. With Ethernet, for example, there is a choice of twisted-pair cable or fibre-optic cable. Most NICs come with drivers for the most popular OSs. They are usually software configurable. A typical Ethernet NIC (for the PCI bus and fitted with an RJ-45 port) is illustrated in Fig. 4.4. NICs are usually built into PCs, whether server, desktop or portable, and do not normally need to be added.

Fig. 4.4NIC

48 ports

Fig. 4.5 Patch panel

Ethernet NICs usually support such standards as IEEE 802.1p and IEEE 802.1q. The first of these is an important prioritisation standard for voice over IP (VoIP, described in Sect. 7.7.2). 802.1p gives IP-based voice transmissions priority over data so as to reduce the latency (delay) and jitter (variation in delay) to which IP networks are prone and that voice cannot tolerate. IEEE 802.1q is a standard that supports *virtual LANs* (VLANs). (IEEE 802.1q and VLANs are discussed later in this section.) NICs can often process TCP/IP checksums too. If a NIC supports *wake on LAN*, its host PC can be switched on by sending it a special packet over the network.

Unless the LAN is very small, the network equipment apart from the workstations themselves is safely locked away inside one or more *wiring closets*. A wiring closet is simply a walk-in cupboard that contains racks of network hardware. The cable from each PC normally feeds into a *patch panel*. A patch panel is illustrated in Fig. 4.5. The patch panel acts like a small switchboard and is a convenient means of connecting various pieces of networking equipment together. Fixed into the patch panel from the back are many individual jacks (sockets). The plugs on the ends of the data cables plug into the jacks. If Category 5e UTP cable is in use, Registered Jack-45 (RJ-45) plugs and jacks are used. Other kinds of cable may need different plugs and jacks.

Fig. 4.6 Hub

10 ports

Fig. 4.7 Bridge

12 ports

Fig. 4.8 Ethernet switch

Other internetworking components which may be needed are hubs, switches and routers. To connect together more than two computers, either a hub or a switch is necessary. (A crossover cable, described in Sect. 2.10.1, can be used if we are just connecting one computer to one other.) A *hub* is an OSI layer-1 device which merely repeats (boosts) any signal sent from one of the computers on the network to which it is attached to all the other computers. An alternative name for a hub is a multiport repeater (a repeater with several ports). A hub is a very simple device, which does not understand network addresses of any kind. A typical hub is illustrated in Fig. 4.6.

Instead of a hub, it is more common to use a layer-2 switch. The switch is a computer in its own right, which understands layer-2 addresses such as Ethernet addresses. A switch can be used like its forerunner, the *bridge*, to connect LAN segments (a segment is a portion of a network). A bridge is shown in Fig. 4.7 and an Ethernet switch in Fig. 4.8.

The switch builds up tables of media access control (MAC) addresses (Ethernet addresses in the case of an Ethernet network) and can thus work out on which

Fig. 4.9 VLANs

segment a frame should be transmitted. (See Sects. 4.2.1 and 4.2.2 for a discussion of MAC addresses.) Bridges have only two or three ports but a switch has many. The high number of ports that a switch has means that it can be used in place of a hub. If a switch is used in an Ethernet network instead of a hub, it will effectively increase the available bandwidth in the network. This is because, unlike a hub, a switch permits several PCs on an Ethernet network to communicate at the same time and in full-duplex mode. In this case, there are no collisions, and Ethernet's CSMA/CD access protocol (see Sect. 4.2.2) is not used.

Layer-2 switches have so much intelligence that they are able to provide *VLANs*. A VLAN is a LAN that does not exist physically. It consists of a logical group of devices or users, selected from the devices or users on an actual, physical LAN. For example, users in a company's Accounts department can be grouped together into their own VLAN, while people in the Human Resources (HR) department might belong to another VLAN. The various members of these two departments might be dispersed over several floors of a building, as is the case in Fig. 4.9. The devices within a VLAN can communicate only with each other. Communication between VLANs needs a router. (Brief details of routers are given later on in this section and fuller details in Chap. 5.)

Preamble	Destination Address	Source Address	Tag	Length/ Type	Data	Frame Check Sequence

Fig. 4.10 VLAN tag

When the 802.1q VLAN standard is in use, every Ethernet frame contains a 4-byte *tag* that can be used to define the membership of the VLAN groups. The Ethernet switch inserts the tag into the Ethernet frame and recalculates the frame check sequence (CRC). The position of the tag is shown in Fig. 4.10. Please refer to Sect. 4.2.2 for an explanation of the other fields in the Ethernet frame.

VLANs are configured with software, and when establishing them, there is no need to move equipment about or reconnect cables. VLANs make it easy to add new stations or change the LAN in any way. VLANs also contribute to the security of the network. The traffic on the Accounts VLAN in Fig. 4.9 stays within that VLAN, and no one else can pry into the accounting files. Frames are switched only between switch ports that have been defined to belong to the same VLAN. VLANs also help networks to work more efficiently because those objects on the network (users and devices) that communicate with each other most often can be grouped together.

One disadvantage of network devices such as switches is that they add *latency* to the network. Latency is the delay between the time when a frame leaves the sending device and the time when the front of the frame reaches the receiving device. Layer-2 switches can operate in three different modes: cut through, store and forward, and fragment-free. In cut-through operation, the switch starts to transfer a frame that it has received as soon as it knows the MAC address of the destination. The advantage of doing switching in this manner is that the latency is very low. On the other hand, since the CRC is not checked, faulty frames as well as error-free ones are switched.

In contrast, in store-and-forward mode, the whole frame is read into the switch, stored briefly and then forwarded to the destination. This process takes longer than cut-through switching but has the advantage that invalid frames are thrown away by the switch rather than being passed on. Another advantage is that the frame can be sent out at a different data rate from that at which it was received.

Fragment-free mode is a compromise between cut through and store and forward. Here, the first 64 bytes of the frame are read. This is because any errors are likely to fall within the first 64 bytes. The fragment-free mode of operation is not as fast as cut-through switching, but it does give a greater chance that the frame being switched is worth sending on.

If we need to connect two or more networks or VLANs together, a router is necessary. Routers, as the name would suggest, can do routing. In other words, they can understand the addresses used by layer-3 protocols such as IP and make decisions about where an incoming network packet should be sent next. The kind of router that is usually used is a special computer, specifically designed to do routing and carry out a few other related network functions. Such a router is illustrated in

Fig. 4.11   Router

Fig. 4.12   Populated rack

Fig. 4.11. However, alternatively, it is possible to use an ordinary PC, running under an ordinary OS, such as Microsoft® Windows® or Linux. This PC will have special routing software running on it to allow it to act as a router. Routers are mainly used for connecting WANs together, so more details of routers are given in Chap. 5.

A rack containing networking equipment is shown in Fig. 4.12. Normally, such a rack would be safely locked up inside a wiring closet because security is very important. Racks are made in standard widths (e.g. 19″) and can accommodate equipment of standard thicknesses.

4.1.3.2   Components and Devices for WLANs

The *access point* (AP) shown in Fig. 4.3 is a hardware device, although alternatively the AP might consist of software running on a standard computer. It is the AP that lets the wireless devices connect to the wired LAN. The AP also helps to increase security.

Sometimes, the access point is built into a special router called a *wireless router*. Wireless routers are commonly used in the home. As well as providing routing and access point functions, they offer a network switch and often a firewall.

The wireless counterpart of the NIC (see Sect. 2.1, as well as above in the current section) that is used on a wired computer is the *radio*—a wireless transmitter/ receiver. For laptop computers, this is often a PC-card. PC-cards are built to Personal Computer Memory Card International Association (PCMCIA) standards. For desktop computers, universal serial bus (USB) and PCI radios are often used; compact flash radios are designed for small mobile computing devices. The radio is usually built into portable computers.

It is not essential to use an AP in a WLAN. Peer-to-peer (or ad hoc) WLANs can be constructed using only client radios. This is fine for a small or temporary network.

4.2   Types of Wired LAN

We will concentrate on Ethernet because it is the most popular kind of LAN by far. A few other types of LAN are briefly described in Sect. 4.2.3, however.

4.2.1   Logical Link Control and MAC Sub-layers

In Sect. 3.2.2, we encountered the OSI data-link layer (layer 2) and its functions. For LAN protocols, layer 2 is divided into two sub-layers: the logical link control (LLC) sub-layer and the MAC sub-layer. LLC is the upper sub-layer. It offers a common interface between the network layer (OSI layer 3) and the MAC sub-layer. It also offers reliability and flow control. LLC is a subset of high-level data-link control (HDLC), a wide-area data-link layer protocol, which is described in Sect. 6.3. When a computer wants to transmit, it is the MAC sub-layer that is responsible for putting the physical address of the destination computer into the data frame. The physical address is the address of the destination computer's NIC. Figure 4.13 shows the LLC and some of the more important MAC protocols.

4.2.2   Ethernet

Ethernet is far and away the most important standard for LANs. It has a fairly long history, during which it has evolved considerably. Its success is due to several factors. It is fairly simple, very reliable and above all cheap compared with rival technologies.

DIX was the first Ethernet standard. It got its name from the three companies that published it: Digital Equipment Corporation, Intel and Xerox. A few years later, the IEEE brought out the 802.3 standard. This is slightly different from the DIX Ethernet standard. It covers both OSI layer 1 and the lower part of layer 2, which can be seen in Fig. 4.13. At this stage in its history, Ethernet ran at 10 Mbps. Gradually, the

Fig. 4.13 LLC and MAC
sub-layers

maximum data rate of Ethernet has got faster and faster, moving from 10 to 100 Mbps
to 1 Gbps (1,000 million bps), then to 10, 40, 100 Gbps and so on. At all of these
data rates, the format of the Ethernet frame is almost identical, while the physical
layer can vary considerably.

The IEEE uses the following naming scheme for its family of Ethernet standards.
First of all, there is a number that indicates the data rate in megabits per second.
This number is followed by the word 'BASE', to indicate the use of baseband transmission (i.e. using just one unmultiplexed channel). After this, there are one or two
letters that show what type of medium is being used. For example, 100BASE-T
means that the data rate is 100 Mbps and that baseband transmission and twisted-
pair copper cabling are being used.

4.2.2.1 Carrier Sense Multiple Access/Collision Detection `

The MAC protocol that non-switched variants of Ethernet use is carrier sense multiple access/collision detection (CSMA/CD). In the original form of Ethernet, all the
computers were attached to a bus (a piece of coaxial cable which acted as a common
highway for data transmission). Only one conversation between two network stations at a time was possible, and a protocol such as CSMA/CD was needed to allow
a computer access to the bus. When CSMA/CD is in use, a station that wishes to
transmit listens to the bus. If there seems to be no activity, the station transmits
(carrier sense). Multiple access means that all stations have access to the network
medium (the cable). Once a station starts transmitting, all other stations will almost
immediately detect the transmission and will wait until it has finished before trying
to send anything themselves. However, it is still possible that two stations will both
detect that the bus is idle, and that both will start to transmit at about the same time.
Then, there will be a collision of data. The reason why this can happen is that any
signal takes some time to propagate along the bus. Collision detection is needed to
deal with this problem.

If a station detects a collision while it is transmitting, it sends a brief jamming
signal. This signal lets the other stations know that there has been a collision. After

8	6	6	2	46 -1500	4
Preamble	Destination Address	Source Address	Type	Data + Pad	Frame Check Sequence

Fig. 4.14 Ethernet II frame format

7	1	6	6	2	46 -1500	4
Preamble	Start Frame Delimiter	Destination Address	Source Address	Length/ Type	LLC Header + Data + Pad	Frame Check Sequence

Fig. 4.15 IEEE 802.3 frame format

sending the jamming signal, the station ceases transmission and then waits for a random time period. When this period is up, the station attempts to transmit again. If there are repeated collisions, this indicates a busy medium. To adjust for this, the time delay between repeated retransmission attempts is progressively increased. This is called the binary exponential backoff algorithm. If there are 16 unsuccessful attempts to transmit (a very rare occurrence), the frame transmission is abandoned, and the upper layer is informed of this.

4.2.2.2 Ethernet Frame Format

The Ethernet II (DIX) frame format is slightly different from the IEEE 802.3 version. The Ethernet II frame is shown in Fig. 4.14 and the IEEE 802.3 frame in Fig. 4.15. The first field of the Ethernet II frame is the 8-byte preamble. The purpose of this field is to warn the other stations on the network that a frame is coming. In IEEE 802.3, this field is split into two parts, but there is no difference in the bit patterns. The first 7 bytes carry timing information, while the eighth is the start frame delimiter, which indicates the end of the timing bits. The timing information was necessary for the operation of 10-Mbps Ethernet. Though it has not been needed for any higher speed versions, it has been kept for reasons of compatibility.

In both types of frame, the next two fields are for the destination (receiving station) and source (sending station) addresses. Both these addresses are 48 bits long and are usually shown as 12 hexadecimal digits. Every Ethernet card in the world has a unique MAC address. The first six hex digits indicate the manufacturer of the card; the second six are a unique identifier. For example, a certain Ethernet NIC has the following MAC address: 00-02-44-37-60-FA. The 00-02-44 part of the number identifies the manufacturer; 37-60-FA is the unique identifier.

The purpose of the next (two-byte) field differs in the two types of frame. In Ethernet II, the receiving station has to find out which higher layer protocol is being carried in an incoming frame. It needs to know this in order to tell to which upper-layer protocol it must give the data. It finds this out by looking inside the type field. In IEEE 802.3, this field can be used as a type field but alternatively can be used to carry the length of the data in bytes. There is no need to use this field to identify the

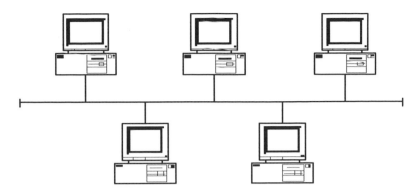

Fig. 4.16 Ethernet bus

protocol if the LLC field (missing from Ethernet II) is being used to do this. If the number is equal to or greater than 600 hexadecimal (1,536 decimal), then it is taken to indicate the length.

The whole point of sending an Ethernet frame is to carry some data. The data field is the place where the data is put. The greatest size of frame that is allowed in low-speed versions of Ethernet is 1,518 bytes; the minimum size is 46 bytes. If the frame would otherwise be below the minimum size, it is padded out with extra bytes to make it legal. The IEEE 802.3 frame also carries the LLC information within the data field. In high-speed Ethernet networks (1 Gbps or above) it is some-times possible to make a single frame carry much more data than the standard permits. This may be up to 9 Kb or even more. Such so-called *jumbo frames* can be used to make large file transfers more efficient, but not all switches, NICs or rout-ers support them.

Finally, in the frame check sequence (FCS) field, there is a 32-bit CRC code to check for errors. This checks the integrity of the whole frame except the preamble/start frame delimiter and, of course, the CRC field itself. (CRCs were explained in Sect. 2.6.1.) Any frame with an invalid CRC is simply thrown away without being processed any further because it is useless.

4.2.2.3 Ethernet Developments

Originally, Ethernet LANs always used coaxial cable. The cable formed a physical bus to which the stations were attached. To this day, the standard graphical repre-sentation of an Ethernet is normally a diagram such as that in Fig. 4.16, which shows the cabling as a bus. However, when the 10BASE-T standard was devised, the cabling became twisted pair, with the stations connected together via a hub. Modern Ethernet networks are 'physical star, logical bus': the network works on a bus principle but is wired as a star. Originally, Ethernet had both a physical and logical bus topology.

Gradually, Ethernet switches have supplanted hubs, and the fastest kinds of Ethernet are purely switch based. With high-speed forms of Ethernet, the pattern

Table 4.1 Some Ethernet physical-layer standards

Name	100 Mbps Ethernet	Gigabit Ethernet	10-Gb E	40-Gb E	100-Gb E
Data rate	100 Mbps	1,000 Mbps	10,000 Mbps	40,000 Mbps	100,000 Mbps

has been to bring out optical fibre-based standards first and then to introduce twisted-pair copper standards as soon as technology permitted. For example, the 1000BASE-T (twisted-pair) standard came out some time after the other gigabit Ethernet standards. In Table 4.1, details of some of the more important Ethernet physical-layer standards are given. There are several different variants of each of the standards shown in Table 4.1. There are different standards for twinax (twin coaxial) copper, twisted-pair copper, multimode fibre-optic and single-mode fibre-optic cable. Another recent trend has been to use Ethernet for WAN connectivity.

4.2.2.4 Power over Ethernet

Power over Ethernet (POe) was devised to carry an electricity supply along CAT 3 or CAT 5 cables at the same time as Ethernet signals. It is used to power such devices as IP phones, WLAN access points and LAN switches, which would otherwise need a separate power supply. There is a handshaking protocol (see Sect. 6.2.2 for an explanation of handshaking) which ensures that power is sent only to devices that request it. The original standard was IEEE 802.3af-2003. It was superseded by IEEE 802.3at-2009, which can supply up to 25 W DC.

4.2.3 Other Types of Wired LAN

Ethernet is not the only possible type of wired LAN, although it is by far the most important one.

4.2.3.1 Token-Passing LANs

In Token Ring (IEEE 802.5), access to the LAN is controlled by a token—a pattern of bits which constantly circulates around a ring of computers. Token Ring can guarantee that the maximum waiting time before gaining access to the network will not be above a certain figure. Such a network is termed *deterministic*. By contrast, Ethernet is regarded as *non-deterministic*. Token Ring was a good technology, but Ethernet was cheaper and has completely displaced it.

Fibre-Distributed Data Interface (FDDI) is a large-scale, ring-based, token-passing system, with built-in fault tolerance, that was designed to take advantage of fibre-optic cabling. Ethernet has supplanted it.

4.2.3.2 Asynchronous Transfer Mode LANs

A point-to-point network (see Sects. 5.5 and 5.10 for further information) that has been successfully used in LANs is asynchronous transfer mode (ATM). ATM is really a WAN technology, but it has also been used in LANs, where it is especially suitable for carrying multimedia information. ATM is more expensive than

Fig. 4.17 HomePlug system

Ethernet, and this is one reason why it has never been used in LANs to any great extent. It is a *cell*-based technology that uses switches (switches are described in Sect. 4.1.3.). Data is sent out in 53-byte cells, rather than in variable-length frames as in Ethernet or Token Ring. These fixed-length cells are what is switched through the ATM network.

4.2.3.3 HomePlug LANs

HomePlug is a power-line communication system. A modem that plugs into an electrical socket converts Ethernet signals into a special protocol. It then sends these over the mains electricity supply cables in a building. Such a system is very easy to set up because no wiring has to be installed. HomePlug can be as fast as standard Ethernet. IEEE 1901.2010 or HomePlug AV is a standard for networks like this. The more recent HomePlug AV2 offers better performance. Figure 4.17 shows a standard PC connecting to the Internet via a HomePlug system. Many kinds of device can make use of HomePlug, for example, specialised games computers and Ethernet-enabled TVs.

4.3 Storage Area Network

A *storage area network* (SAN) is a special network that is dedicated to storage. It links together one or more server computers with storage devices such as redundant array of independent disks (RAID) systems and tape libraries. A SAN is illustrated in Fig. 4.18. Note that it is a separate network from the LAN. The server(s) can access any device in the SAN's storage pool. A SAN usually offers a high data transfer rate.

The networking technology that is used is often Internet Small Computer System Interface (iSCSI). This carries Small Computer System Interface (SCSI) commands to control the storage devices over an IP-based Ethernet network. Figure 4.19 shows how SCSI commands are encapsulated within IP datagrams. Fibre channel, a high-speed fibre-optic network technology, is sometimes used instead of iSCSI. As well as hardware, a SAN usually includes special software to manage, monitor and configure it.

Fig. 4.18 SAN

Fig. 4.19 iSCSI

Another alternative to iSCSI is Fibre Channel over Ethernet (FCoE). Unlike iSCSI, FCoE does not run over IP. However, a SAN that uses FCoE can be easily integrated into an Ethernet LAN.

4.4   Grid Computing

Grid computing is a form of distributed computing (see Sect. 1.1). In a grid, multiple computers are networked together to give the equivalent of a very powerful supercomputer. The resources of all the computers are shared and brought to bear on a problem. One example is the Search for Extraterrestrial Intelligence (SETI), in which the unused processor cycles of thousands of computers are being used to search for signals from intelligent beings in outer space. Grid computing is illustrated in Fig. 4.20. The grid may consist of a wide variety of hardware running under various operating systems, as shown in the figure.

Often, the nodes in the grid are much more homogeneous, however. Also, there may not be one computer that directs operations, as in Fig. 4.20, but the computers may simply collaborate in solving a problem. With a complex system, there has to be

Labels within figure: Server Cluster · Back mounted Server Cluster · Server · Processor Cycles Stolen from Users' PCs · Server · Supercomputer · Resource Management Station

Fig. 4.20 Grid computing

a large degree of automation. Virtual servers (see Sect. 8.14.1 for further details) often form part of the grid, as do clusters. Clusters are sets of computers that are coupled together using some kind of fast LAN, working as if they were one computer. All the computers in the cluster have their own copy of the same operating system.

There are parallels with an electrical power grid. A power company uses its grid so as to be able to cope with peaks and troughs in electricity demand without letting its customers down. A business can use grid computing to offer computer resources to end users in a similarly flexible manner. Pieces of hardware and software can be pooled and brought into play when necessary. In real time, the system can adjust its supply of computing power to the demand. Grid computing allows expensive pieces of equipment to be used more efficiently. Elderly computers can be used if necessary, so as to get maximum benefit from them. Grid computing can help an organisation make the most of the space that is available to it. It is also more economical with electricity than using a disparate collection of separate server computers. Grid computing can deal with problems that need a vast amount of computer facilities.

4.5 Summary

This chapter has looked at various aspects of LANs. The chapter started with an account of some of the factors that need to be considered when planning a LAN. Factors affecting the choices between peer-to-peer and client–server LANs and between wired and wireless networks were then considered. Various components and devices for both wired LANs and WLANs were also described. Ethernet, being by far the most important LAN technology, was covered at some length. Then, some other wired LAN technologies were described. The chapter finished with brief sketches of SANs and grid computing.

4.6   Questions

1. What are the advantages and disadvantages of *client–server LANs*?
2. What is a *NIC* and what does it do?
3. What advantages do Ethernet switches possess over Ethernet hubs?
4. What are *virtual LANs (VLANs)* and why are they useful?
5. Explain the three different modes of operation of layer-2 switches.
6. Describe the two *sub-layers* at the data-link layer of LAN protocols.
7. Describe how shared Ethernet controls access to the medium.
8. Why is it necessary to have a maximum and a minimum frame length when using Ethernet?
9. (a) What is the purpose of *SANs* and what network technologies do they use?
   (b) How do *SANs* differ from network attached storage (*NAS*)? (Answering (b) will involve some research outside this text.)

Wide Area Networks

5

Abstract

Wide area networks (WANs) made a brief appearance in Sect. 1.2. We now look at WANs in a little more detail. The chapter starts with a consideration of the general characteristics of WANs. After a brief mention of the use of the public switched telephone network (PSTN) for computer networks, there is a description of the packet-switching technology frame relay. Integrated Services Digital Network (ISDN), an all-digital, circuit-switched service, comes next. Then, there is a description of digital leased lines. We follow this with coverage of digital subscriber line and cable modem, which offer alternative 'always-on' broadband services. Then, we look at some ways of accessing LANs remotely. Next is a section on routers, which are devices that are used to connect networks together. We cover the use in WANs of two technologies that were described in Chap. 4, ATM and Ethernet. Finally, we consider cloud computing, in which information technology services are offered over the Internet.

5.1 General Characteristics of WANs

WANs are used to carry data over long distances. This could be within a region of a country, across a whole country or even from one side of the world to another. The transmission facilities that are used nearly always belong to *carriers*—telecommunications companies that provide long-distance links for other companies or individuals to use. For example, if a company has more than one site, it can use a WAN to link up the LANs at those sites. This lets the sites share information. Such a situation can be seen in Fig. 1.2. WANs can carry several kinds of traffic, for example, voice, data and video. In terms of the OSI 7-layer model, WANs are located at the physical layer and data-link layer. WAN data rates are generally lower than those of LANs.

J. Cowley, *Communications and Networking: An Introduction*, Undergraduate Topics in Computer Science, DOI 10.1007/978-1-4471-4357-4_5,
© Springer-Verlag London 2012

Fig. 5.1 Use of modems

5.2   Public Switched Telephone Network

The PSTN is the ordinary, fixed-line (landline) network that has been in use for a century or so. When computer communications first started, the PSTN was a convenient network to use. Since the telephone network was designed to carry voice traffic rather than data, conversion of the digital signals from the computer into the kind of signals that can be carried over the PSTN is necessary. Most of the PSTN (the trunk lines) has been digital for several years, but the *local loop*, the line between the customer premises and the local exchange, is often analogue.

In Sect. 2.4.4, the differences between analogue and digital signalling were explained. Amplitude, frequency and phase modulation and how these can be made use of in the modem were also explained (see Sect. 2.5.1). Figure 5.1 shows modems being used to connect two PCs over a phone line.

5.3   Frame Relay

Frame relay is based on a much older technology called X.25, which was devised to connect devices with data terminal equipment (DTE) interfaces and devices with data circuit terminating equipment (DCE) interfaces to packet-switched data networks. A DTE is a device such as a computer or router. A DCE is the device that connects to the service provider's network. A modem is an example of a DCE. Figure 5.2 illustrates connection to an X.25 'cloud'. The term *network cloud* is often used to refer to a WAN when we are not interested in its internal details.

When X.25 is in use, the data is divided into packets and transmitted over virtual circuits. (Virtual circuits were explained in Sect. 2.7.3.) X.25 can be used with either switched or permanent virtual circuits. X.25 networks are reliable because error checking is carried out on a link-by-link basis. The reason for all this error checking is that X.25 was designed to run over analogue networks, where transmission errors were fairly common.

With the advent of digital networks, X.25 was found to be too slow, so a more modern approach to packet-switching networks, frame relay, had to be devised. Since digital networks were more reliable than analogue networks, there was no need for frame relay to include link-by-link error checking. Any error checks could be done by a higher layer protocol at the end stations. Frame relay functions only at OSI layers 1 and 2, while X.25 provides layer 3 services as well.

Fig. 5.2 X.25 connections

Fig. 5.3 Use of FRADs

As the name would suggest, data is broken up into frames before being sent out over the frame relay network. Just as in the case of X.25, the data is sent over virtual circuits (either SVCs or PVCs). PVCs can be used to construct *virtual private networks* (VPNs), which provide the equivalent of a private network but run over a public network. Before frame relay was devised, if an organisation needed a WAN, private lines or circuit switching over a leased line were necessary. Single, dedicated lines are not needed for WAN-to-WAN connections with frame relay. This reduces costs.

Frame relay is so much faster than X.25 that it can be used to connect LANs together. Frame relay is ideally suited to carrying a high volume of traffic which occurs unpredictably in bursts. Such traffic is typical of LANs. Even voice traffic can be sent using frame relay.

An important feature of frame relay is that frame relay service providers are able to offer their customers tightly defined service agreements. If the frame relay service fails to perform to the level that has been agreed, then the user can be compensated. There is a committed information rate (CIR) at which data is transmitted. But if the traffic and the service agreement allow this, data can burst above the committed rate for short periods.

The frame relay data frame, link access procedure for frame mode services (LAPF), is based on HDLC (HDLC is described in Sect. 6.3). The frame includes a field for the data-link connection identifier (DLCI). The DLCI, a number, represents the virtual circuit to which the frame belongs. In other words, it is the destination address of the frame.

To gain access to a frame relay network, a frame relay access device (FRAD) can be used. The sending FRAD breaks up the stream of data into frames for transmission over the network. The receiving FRAD carries out the complementary process, turning frames back into the original data stream. The use of FRADs is illustrated in Fig. 5.3. Inside the frame relay cloud are frame relay switches, wherein virtual circuits are set up. An alternative choice of device to a FRAD is a router equipped with an interface suitable for frame relay.

5.4   Integrated Services Digital Network

In Sect. 5.2, we saw that trunk telephone lines are usually digital, but the local loop is often analogue. ISDN is an all-digital telephone network, in which both the trunk lines and the local loop are digital. Such an arrangement means that all sorts of data can be sent using the same system, since everything travelling over the network is a stream of bits. In other words, the network can offer *integrated services* of several different kinds.

There are two different kinds of ISDN: basic rate interface (BRI) and primary rate interface (PRI). Both are circuit-switched services. BRI is for small businesses or home users. BRI has two 64-Kbps channels that can carry voice or data traffic. These are known as bearer channels (B channels). In addition, there is a 16-Kbps delta channel (D channel) that is primarily used for signalling. However, since this channel does not have to carry much signalling traffic, it can be used to provide a slow X.25-type packet-switching service.

For larger businesses ISDN PRI exists. This has 30 (23 in North America) 64-Kbps B channels and a 64-Kbps D channel. The total bit rate of ISDN primary rate (except in North America) is 2.048 Mbps. Many B channels can be simultaneously connected, making PRI ISDN suitable for such applications as videoconferencing. This can be rather expensive, however.

BRI has been very convenient for small businesses. Compared with the analogue PSTN (see Sect. 5.2 above), ISDN has a very short call set-up time of just a few milliseconds. Just one of its D channels offers a higher data rate than an analogue modem link. Using *bonding*, the two 64-Kbps channels can be combined to give an effective throughput of 128 Kbps. (Bonding has also been used with analogue modems.)

ISDN can be used to top up the capacity of a leased line connection (see Sect. 5.5 for information about leased lines). A router can be configured to open an ISDN link whenever the leased line is being used above a certain threshold. The leased line alone is normally in use. The ISDN line is used only when demand reaches a peak.

ISDN can also be used to back up a leased line. For example, a certain company might have a site in London and a site in Manchester connected by a leased line. If the leased line goes down, a backup ISDN line can replace it for as long as necessary. A router can be configured to bring the ISDN connection into play automatically.

Charges for ISDN lines are similar to those for ordinary fixed-line telephone lines. There is normally an installation charge and a quarterly line rental charge, but most of the money that the customer pays is for how long the line is used. Such a charging structure makes ISDN economical for fairly light usage.

Examples of ISDN BRI configurations are illustrated in Fig. 5.4. Connection to the network can be direct, as is the case for the ISDN telephones shown in Fig. 5.4, or indirect, using a router with an ISDN interface. An individual computer might be fitted with an ISDN card (very similar in appearance to the Ethernet card shown in Fig. 4.4). Alternatively, the computer might be connected via an ISDN *terminal adaptor* (essentially the same thing as the card but contained in a box that is separate from the computer).

Fig. 5.4 ISDN BRI configurations

5.5   Leased Lines

A leased line is used when an organisation needs a permanent, dedicated, *point-to-point* link. (A point-to-point link is a link from one place to another place.) The leased line provides a communications path that has been set up in advance from one site to another using the facilities of a telecommunications carrier company.

This system allows tight budget control because the cost does not depend on the amount of usage. For a monthly fee, the organisation is free to send as much data as it likes down the line, up to its maximum capacity. Usually, the cost of the rental depends on the data rate and the distance between the two sites that are being connected. Leased lines are usually more expensive than frame relay, particularly when many sites are connected. Two advantages of leased lines are that there is negligible latency and jitter and that the line is always available. Such features may be essential for certain kinds of application. The disadvantages include the cost compared with most of the alternative ways of setting up a WAN. Leased lines are not very flexible either. The data rate offered by a leased line seldom corresponds to the exact traffic requirements. (We have already seen in the previous section how it is often necessary to top up the carrying capacity of a leased line using ISDN.) If the capacity of the leased line needs to be changed, this usually entails an employee of the carrier visiting the site.

The equipment that organisations usually use with a digital leased line consists of a router and a device called a Channel Service Unit/Data Service Unit (CSU/DSU) at each end of the link. The CSU/DSU may take the form of a card that is fitted to a router or computer, or may be contained in a separate box, as is shown in Fig. 5.5. The CSU/DSU is the DCE device that connects to the digital line. It performs conversion between the kind of data frames used on the LAN and those used on the WAN link. The CSU/DSU also protects the carrier's network from damage that could be caused by the customer's network. The link between the router and the CSU/DSU in Fig. 5.5 is a serial cable using a protocol such as EIA/TIA-232 or a near equivalent at the physical layer.

Fig. 5.5 Typical leased line configuration

Fig. 5.6 Use of a multiplexer with a leased line

Leased lines can be shared using multiplexers (see Fig. 5.6). This helps to keep costs down because both voice traffic and data traffic can share the line. Some CSU/DSUs have multiple ports and have a built-in multiplexing capability.

The digital leased line services available in Europe and much of the rest of the world are the E-carrier series. The T-carrier series of digital leased line services is used in North America and a few other places. There are a few differences between the E-carriers and T-carriers, such as the data rates offered. For example, the E3 standard offers a data rate of 34.368 Mbps, whereas the equivalent T-carrier standard, T3, offers a data rate of 44.736 Mbps.

5.6   Digital Subscriber Line

Digital subscriber line (DSL) technology uses advanced modems to achieve high data rates over standard, twisted-pair, copper cable in the local loop. It is referred to as a *broadband* technology. Essentially, the term *broadband* means using a wide band of frequencies to transmit signals over more than one channel at the same time. This contrasts with the *baseband* technology typically used in LANs, where there is only one channel.

Fig. 5.7 ADSL equipment

The term *xDSL* can be used to refer to all kinds of DSL technology. The two main variants are symmetric DSL (SDSL) and asymmetric DSL (ADSL). SDSL uses all of the bandwidth of the line for data transmission. The data rate is the same in both directions. SDSL was intended for use by businesses as a cheap alternative to leased lines. ADSL was intended for home users. ADSL splits the bandwidth up, using most of it for digital data transmission but reserving a small amount for analogue voice transmission. The ADSL data rate is much faster in one direction than in the other, which is why it is termed *asymmetric*. ADSL was designed like this because home users were assumed to be downloading a relatively large amount of data from the Internet but sending out only a little data. It was also assumed that home users would want to keep their standard, fixed-line analogue telephone.

To be able to provide DSL, the service provider needs to place a *DSL access multiplexer* (DSLAM) inside the local telephone exchange. This device allows multiple subscriber lines to be multiplexed together for long-distance transmission over a high-speed leased line. If ADSL is in use, the subscriber needs, in addition to the ADSL modem itself, either a device called a *splitter* or individual *line filters*.

These separate the DSL signal from the analogue telephone service. Sometimes the splitter is built into the modem. ADSL devices are illustrated in Fig. 5.7.

Data rates offered by ADSL vary greatly, depending on the type of service. Very High Speed Digital Subscriber Line 2 (VDSL2) is claimed to deliver up to 100 Mbps in both directions. Other variants of DSL are much slower. Although DSL technology can potentially give very high data rates over the existing local loop, there are limiting factors. The greater the distance from the local telephone exchange, the slower the data rate. The quality of the copper cable in the local loop also affects the data rate. Although DSL services are much cheaper than leased lines, the service is unreliable in comparison.

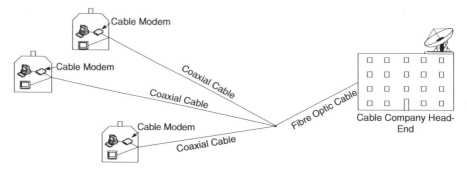

Fig. 5.8 Cable modem network

5.7   Cable Modems

Cable modems provide broadband connectivity to domestic users. The cable modem service depends on cable television being installed in the neighbourhood. Although the technology used is totally different from that used in ADSL, the experience that cable modems offer the consumer is rather similar. Like ADSL, a cable modem service is an 'always-on' service, which is always connected to the Internet. The data rates that can be obtained are similar to those offered by DSL. Many businesses do not use cable modems because they consider them too unreliable and insecure. Figure 5.8 shows a part of a typical cable modem network. The cable modem modulates and demodulates computer data for transmission and reception via the cable TV system. The *head-end* is the place where the cable company is connected to the Internet and where it receives television channels. Fibre-optic cable carries the signals most of the way from the head-end to the customer's house, but coaxial cable is generally used for the last part of the journey. Data over Cable Service Interface Specification (DOCSIS) defines the standards for transferring data using a cable modem system.

5.8   Remote Access to LANs

If a user needs to access a LAN remotely, for example, from a hotel or from home, he or she has the choice of a remote node connection, a remote control connection or connecting via a Web browser.

5.8.1   Remote Node

In remote node working, the remote computer acts as a node or workstation on the LAN. It can access all the resources of the LAN, for example, any attached printers. Remote node is useful if the remote user wants to look inside a file on the LAN's server computer or wants to copy a file from the server to the remote PC. All the data from the LAN travels to the remote computer as if it were a local PC. If the remote user has a high-speed connection, remote node is fine.

5.8.2   Remote Control

On the other hand, if either the connection or the remote PC is slow, then remote control is a better method. Here, all the data from the LAN is not transferred to the remote user's PC. Instead the user's PC on the LAN does the processing, but it is under the control of the remote PC. The remote user does not get the data files from the LAN PC but just sees the results of the processing on the screen of his or her computer. The remote user can capture and save these screens. For the remote user, it is just as if he or she were sitting at the keyboard of the PC on the LAN. The remote user's mouse clicks and keystrokes can control what is happening on the LAN PC. It is only the keystrokes and mouse movement that are sent from the remote user's PC and only screen changes that are sent back to that PC.

5.8.3   Remote Working via the Web

Alternatively, the remote user—perhaps working from home or perhaps on the road—may use the Internet to connect to the LAN. In this case, the LAN files are made available via the Web using Web server software. The remote PC acts as though it is part of the LAN. For security reasons, the remote user normally connects via a VPN. The VPN gives the remote user a secure tunnel through the Internet from the remote machine to the local machine. While in transit, the files are encrypted and cannot be interfered with by a third party. There are several techniques that can be used to provide a VPN over the Internet, but secure sockets layer/transport layer security (SSL/TLS) is very commonly used. These protocols are described in Chap. 8.

5.9   Routers

As we learnt in Sect. 4.1.3, when we need to connect two or more networks together, a *router* is usually necessary. With suitable software, any PC can act as a router. But usually the term *router* refers to a special machine that does not function as a general-purpose computer. The basic components of a specialised router are the same as those of a normal PC. There is a processor, some memory, a system bus and input/output interfaces. But in a dedicated router, unlike in an ordinary PC, there will also be a specialised operating system, which can run the router's configuration files. The configuration files contain rules and instructions to control the way in which data packets flow through the router. The router uses a *routing protocol* to decide on the optimal path for packets. Routing protocols are discussed in more

Fig. 5.9 Simplified rear
view of a router

Serial
Interface

Ethernet
Interface

detail in Chap. 6, but here let it suffice to say that the routing protocol is completely
different from the protocol that is being routed, such as IP.

Here is a very simple example of a router configuration file. Configuration files
can be much more complex than this.

interface Ethernet0/0
ip address 192.7.6.1/24
no shutdown
interface Serial0/0/0
ip address 201.26.12.1/24
no shutdown
router rip
network 192.7.6.0
network 201.26.12.0

This router has two interfaces—one Ethernet interface (Ethernet0/0) and one
serial interface (Serial0/0/0). Figure 5.9 shows a simplified rear view of such a
router. The Ethernet interface is used to connect to a LAN, and the serial interface
is used to connect to a WAN, perhaps via another device such as a CSU/DSU or a
modem. In each of the first two sections of the configuration file, the first line states
which interface is being configured. The second line gives the interface an IP address
and subnet mask (subnet masks are explained in Sect. 6.1.6). The third line ('no
shutdown') makes the interface active.

The last section of the file indicates that the router is to use the routing information protocol (RIP), which is a routing protocol. The command 'router rip' makes
the router exchange *routing tables* with neighbouring routers automatically every
few seconds. A router's routing table contains its knowledge about open paths
through networks. It is possible for a network administrator to configure static
routes, but it is usually more convenient to allow a routing protocol to maintain the
routing tables dynamically.

The networks to which the router is attached are listed in the last two lines of the
configuration file. These two lines tell the router that these are the networks about
which it must inform its neighbouring routers. This configuration file is for a Cisco®
router and uses commands from the Cisco Internetwork Operating System® (IOS),

Fig. 5.10 Routers in an internetwork

but configuration files for other makes of router are fairly similar. The interconnected networks are known as an *internetwork*. The internetwork that is referred to in the sample configuration file given above is illustrated in Fig. 5.10. The other router shown in Fig. 5.10 would also have its own configuration file.

Routers can be used to segment LANs, but their main use is in WANs. They work at OSI layer 3, the network layer. They examine layer-3 packets such as IP datagrams. Since they are able to understand layer-3 addressing, they can make decisions about where to send packets based on network addresses. The central capabilities of a router are an ability to select the best path for a packet and an ability to switch it to the correct interface. The router finds out the best path by consulting its routing table.

A router's routing table contains an entry for at least some of the routers in the system of which it is a part. The entry shows on which link a packet should be transmitted when the final destination is that node. Table 5.1 shows the routing table for router A in Fig. 5.11. This is a simplified example. The exact format of the routing table would depend on the type of router and the routing protocol in use. The symbol used in Fig. 5.11 that looks like a drum with arrows on top of it is the standard symbol for a router. This symbol is shown more clearly in Fig. 5.12.

In Table 5.1, there are multiple entries for all nodes (except A) in case of a failure. If either a router or a link goes down, it is important that there are alternative possibilities for routes. For example, imagine that a packet needs to be sent from a

Table 5.1 Routing table for router A in Fig. 5.11

Destination	Link	Alternative link	Alternative link
A	–	–	–
B	1	4	2
C	2	4	1
D	4	2	1
E	4	1	2

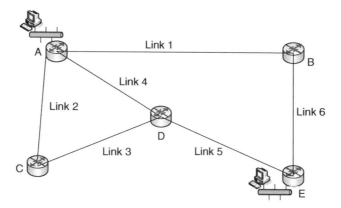

Fig. 5.11 Internetwork for Table 5.1

Fig. 5.12 Standard symbol for a router

PC on the LAN attached to router A to a PC on the LAN attached to router E. The routing table suggests that the packet should be sent out of the router on link 4. However, if this is not possible because either link 4 or router D is down, there is an alternative route via link 1 (or even link 2, though this would appear to be a more roundabout route to router E).

We cannot tell which routes are really the best ones merely by inspecting Table 5.1. Some routes use more links than others, but some of those links may be longer. It is quite possible that a route using four links may turn out to be shorter than one that uses only two links. Some links may have higher data rates than others, which might result in a route consisting of four links being better than one with only two links. As we shall see in Chap. 6, some routing protocols use more sophisticated *metrics* (ways of measuring how good routes are) than others.

5.10 ATM in the WAN

ATM was mentioned in Sect. 4.2.3 as a LAN technology. We learnt there that ATM is a point-to-point, switch-based and cell-based technology which was designed to be suitable for multimedia traffic. Though ATM never fulfilled its promise as a LAN technology, WAN carriers have used it heavily.

Figure 5.13 shows how ATM can be used for various kinds of traffic. It also shows the three layers of ATM (which roughly cover OSI layers 1 and 2) and the functions that they perform. We can see from the diagram that each ATM cell carries a payload of only 48 bytes. This is rather short for data, but for voice and video, the advantage is that an ATM switch causes minimal latency. The switching takes place over virtual circuits.

ATM offers several guaranteed classes of service. Constant bit rate (CBR) provides a virtual, fixed-bandwidth transmission circuit for applications that need a steady supply of bandwidth. Examples of such applications include voice and full-motion video, where it is important that latency and jitter are kept to a minimum. Variable bit rate (VBR) is for LAN-type traffic, which happens in bursts. VBR includes real-time and non-real-time service classes (VBR-RT & VBR-NRT). Unspecified bit rate (UBR) gives no guarantees as to when or if transmitted data will arrive at the destination. Available bit rate (ABR) gives minimal bandwidth guarantees.

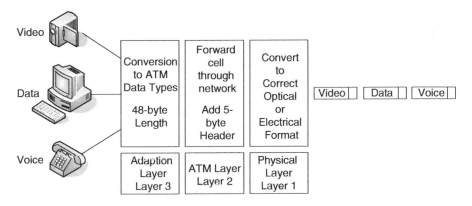

Fig. 5.13 ATM layers

5.11   Ethernet in the WAN

As we saw in Sect. 4.2.2, Ethernet has been the main type of network for LANs for many years. However, it is also used to provide WAN links. One variant of 10-Gb Ethernet, 10GBASE-ER, supports a link length of up to 40 km using single-mode fibre-optic cabling. It can do this because it has some compatibility with the WAN physical-layer standard Synchronous Optical NETwork/Synchronous Digital Hierarchy (SONET/SDH) OC-192, which has a data rate of 9.958464 Gbps. (SONET and SDH are very similar standards for synchronous data transmission over fibre-optic networks. SONET is the US (ANSI) version of the standard and SDH is the international (ITU) version. OC-192 is a standard data rate.)

Carrier Ethernet uses Ethernet technology to provide long-haul links that offer the same performance and availability as standard WAN services (such as the E- and T-series digital leased line services). It supports both data and voice. Carrier Ethernet can scale up and down flexibly through the range of Ethernet data rates according to need. Its principal attraction is its low cost compared with other communications carrier technologies. With carrier Ethernet, an organisation's various sites can be connected by Ethernet from end to end, as shown in Fig. 5.14.

5.12   Cloud Computing

The term *cloud computing* refers to the offering of information technology (IT) services over the Internet. It is generally agreed that there are three main kinds of cloud computing: infrastructure as a service (IaaS), platform as a service (PaaS) and software as a service (SaaS). We can also classify how these three are implemented: as public, private or hybrid clouds.

In SaaS, software (applications) is hosted by a vendor or service provider and made available to customers over a network, typically the Internet. Security as a service (see Sect. 8.14.1) is an example of SaaS. The differences between IaaS and PaaS are rather subtle. In both, computing facilities are provided to customers over a network, normally the Internet. IaaS provides computing infrastructure, such as server computers (usually virtualised) and networking equipment (e.g. routers and firewalls) on demand. Management software allows the customer to deploy this equipment at the click of a mouse. The customer is renting equipment which is being looked after by experts. PaaS too provides computing infrastructure on payment of a rental fee, but an operating system is also provided and kept up to date by the provider. PaaS users need to know less about the platform on which their software is being run than do IaaS users. IaaS gives users more control over the platform, but on the other hand obliges them to do more for themselves than PaaS does.

With a public cloud, services are made available to the general public over the Internet. The services may be free or paid for. A private (or internal or corporate) cloud offers services to a restricted population of users, hidden behind a firewall. A hybrid cloud is a mixture of private and public clouds.

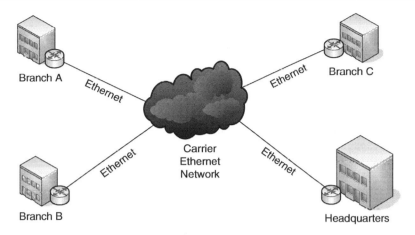

Fig. 5.14 Carrier Ethernet

5.12.1 Advantages and Disadvantages of Cloud Computing

The potential benefits of cloud computing include flexibility, speed of provisioning in response to changing workloads and speed of reaction to changes in the business environment. Cloud computing can save a business money because labour costs and end-user support costs are cut. The business only pays for what it consumes. Also, capital expenditure is less. The business can gain access to exactly the right amount of computing resources to suit its needs. It is quite common for much of a business's own computing capacity to be standing idle at any one time. On the other hand, the business still has to pay for the facilities that it is using, so the overall costs may be the same as they would be without cloud computing.

Cloud computing is not without potential disadvantages. Firstly, IT is so important to businesses that they may prefer to have complete control over it for themselves. They may be unwilling to risk the disruption that an unreliable cloud service could cause. Secondly, if cloud computing is to be beneficial to organisations, their connection to the Internet must be absolutely reliable. Sadly, that is not always the case. Thirdly, in the case of SaaS at least, it is possible that a cloud service could ultimately cost much more money than the software that it has replaced. Instead of a one-off payment for, say, a suite of office software, the rental for the cloud version of the suite could rise unpredictably.

5.13 Summary

This chapter has looked at various aspects of WANs. The analogue PSTN can be used for computer communications if nothing better is available. However, businesses usually use other WAN technologies. Frame relay is a popular packet-switching technology. ISDN is an all-digital, circuit-switched service, which can be used for voice and data of various kinds. Digital leased lines can be used for point-to-point connections. The various forms of DSL offer an 'always-on' broadband service, using the copper lines that were installed for the 'last mile' of the PSTN. Cable modem offers a similar service over a cable TV infrastructure. Three different ways of accessing LANs remotely were described. Routers are important devices that are used to connect networks. ATM, although it has been used in LANs to a limited extent, was expressly designed to carry multimedia information over long distances. Ethernet, though fundamentally a LAN technology, is also used for WANs. The chapter concludes with a brief treatment of cloud computing.

5.14   Questions

1. Explain the difference between *DTE* and *DCE*.
2. What does 'CIR' stand for and what is its purpose in frame relay service agreements?
3. What do 'BRI' and 'PRI' stand for? Explain the differences between these two kinds of ISDN.
4. How long would it take to transfer a 250-Mbyte file over an ISDN link of 64 Kbps? Is the answer realistic?
5. What does a *CSU/DSU* do?
6. What is the difference between *ADSL* and *SDSL*?
7. (a) Distinguish between the *remote control* and *remote node* methods for remote access to LANs.
   (b) Explain remote working via the Web.
8. Using Table 5.1 as a model, construct the routing table for router D in Fig. 5.11.
9. Explain the ATM *classes of service*.
10. Which WAN service would you recommend for the following applications?
    (a) Videoconferencing (i.e. transmitting video and audio back and forth between two or more different sites)
    (b) Low-speed connection to the Internet
    (c) High-speed connection to the Internet
11. Explain the differences between the three main kinds of *cloud computing*.

Network Protocols

6

Abstract

This chapter deals with network protocols of various kinds, especially transmission control protocol/Internet protocol (TCP/IP) and related protocols. It concentrates heavily on IP and TCP themselves. We give attention to both IP version 4 and IP version 6. A section on Internet control message protocol (ICMP), which is used in TCP/IP networks to send error messages and informational messages of various kinds, precedes the material on TCP. High-level data link control (HDLC), a layer-2 protocol that is used in WANs, features next. There is brief coverage of multiprotocol label switching, which permits highly efficient routing. Finally, there are descriptions of two different classes of routing protocols, which allow routers to inform each other about networks that they know about without human intervention.

6.1   Internet Protocol

IP was described very briefly in Chap. 3. In this chapter, more details of IP will be given. We shall be concentrating on version 4 of IP (IPv4) first. Later we switch focus to version 6 (IPv6) in Sect. 6.1.7. A diagram showing the format of the IPv4 datagram header can be found in Appendix A.

6.1.1   IPv4 Addresses

If two computers need to communicate with each other, then there must be some kind of addressing system that allows them to identify and find each other. In Sect. 4.2.2, we saw that Ethernet addresses are 48 bits long, equally split between bits indicating the manufacturer and a unique identifier. Whereas the MAC addresses used by a layer-2 protocol such as Ethernet are 'flat', IP addresses (layer 3) are hierarchical, consisting of a network part and a host part. The network part of the

J. Cowley, *Communications and Networking: An Introduction*, Undergraduate Topics
in Computer Science, DOI 10.1007/978-1-4471-4357-4_6,
© Springer-Verlag London 2012

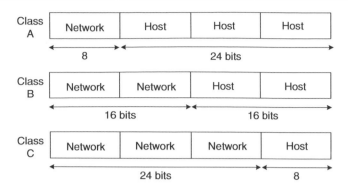

Fig. 6.1 IP address classes

address is used to identify and locate the network to which a host is connected; the host part identifies and locates the host on that network. Every computer on a TCP/IP network must have an IP address.

An IPv4 address is a 32-bit binary number. For the benefit of humans, it is usually written down as four decimal (denary) numbers separated by full stops (dots), for example, 192.168.1.33. This way of expressing IP addresses is called *dotted decimal*. Each of the four parts of the address is called an *octet* because it is 8 bits long. As an explanation of why we do not usually write down IP addresses in binary, consider the binary version of 192.168.1.33: 11000000101010000000001001000 01. A sequence of bits such as this is difficult for even highly numerate human beings to deal with, though it presents no problems at all to a computer.

When routers forward IP packets from the sending network to the destination network, the packets must include the addresses of both networks. The address of the destination network is needed so that the routers can deliver the packet to the right network. The router that is directly connected to the destination network can use the host part of the IP address to find the host. This hierarchical system somewhat resembles the postal system. For a letter to be delivered, first of all it has to reach the right post office using the name of the town. After that, the post office uses the house number and the name of the street to deliver the letter to its final destination.

6.1.1.1 Address Classes

Three classes of IP address cater for large, medium-sized and small networks. Class A addresses are for large networks, Class B for medium-sized networks and Class C for small networks. (In addition to these three classes, Class D exists for multicasting, sending the same message to a group of hosts, and Class E exists for research use.) Classes A, B, and C are illustrated in Fig. 6.1.

With three octets given over to host addresses, each Class A address makes available over 16 million host addresses. Only the leftmost octet is used for the network portion of the address, and the other three octets are for the host portion. The leftmost bit of a Class A address is always 0. The address 127.0.0.1 (*loopback* address or *localhost*) is used for testing IP software. Any address whose leftmost octet is a decimal value between 1 and 126 inclusive is a Class A address.

Table 6.1 IP address ranges

Class	Address range (decimal)	Address range (binary)
A	1–126	00000001–01111110
B	128–191	10000000–10111111
C	192–223	11000000–11011111

Fig. 6.2 Network address

Class B addresses were intended for medium-sized networks. The first two octets are used for the network part of the address and the last two are for the host part of the address. The leftmost 2 bits of the first octet are always 10 in a Class B address. An address whose leftmost octet is a decimal value between 128 and 191 inclusive is a Class B address.

Class C addresses were designed for small networks with no more than 254 hosts. All Class C addresses begin with the 3 bits 110. An address whose leftmost octet is a decimal value between 192 and 223 inclusive is a Class C address. The first three octets are used for the network part of the address and the last octet is the host part of the address. Table 6.1 shows the ranges of the leftmost octet in address classes A to C.

6.1.2   Reserved Addresses

There are some possible IP host addresses that we cannot use. First of all, we cannot use the network address, which identifies the network itself, as a host address. Please refer to Fig. 6.2. If a computer anywhere outside Network A sends data to a host on Network A, that host will be seen as 194.216.4.0. The individual addresses of the

Fig. 6.3 Broadcast address

hosts on Network A are used only when the data has reached Network A. Only the router that is directly attached to Network A will know about these; other routers will not. The situation in LAN B is just the same in this respect. As we can see in Fig. 6.2, LAN B's network address is 194.216.5.0.

Note that the router interface in Network A has an IP Address that belongs to Network A; the interface in Network B has an IP address from Network B. Not shown in Fig. 6.2 is the address of the router's WAN interface, which will be completely different from the addresses on its two Ethernet interfaces.

An example of a Class A network address is 117.0.0.0. 117.0.0.13, for example, is a host on that network. In a Class A address, the first octet is the network portion and the last three octets are the host portion. A Class B example is 183.22.0.0. 183.22.0.253 is an example of a host on that network. In a Class B address, the first and second octets are the network portion and the remaining two octets are the host portion.

Another IP address that we cannot use as a host address is the *broadcast address*. The broadcast address is illustrated in Fig. 6.3. The address 194.216.4.255 will reach all network interfaces belonging to LAN A. The address 194.216.5.255 will reach all network interfaces belonging to LAN B. If data is sent to the broadcast address, it will go to all the hosts on the LAN. When a host sends data to all hosts on a network at once, this is called a *broadcast*. In binary, the host part of a broadcast address is all 1s. For example, the broadcast address for LAN A is 11000010. 11011000.00000100.11111111 in binary.

Table 6.2 ARP table

Internet address	Physical address
192.168.0.1	00-02-4a-8c-6c-00
192.168.0.6	00-06-5b-f1-c6-7e
192.168.0.7	00-02-44-37-60-fa

6.1.3   Address Resolution Protocol

For a TCP/IP packet to be able to reach its destination, it needs *both* an IP address and a MAC address. It follows that a network device that wants to send a packet needs both the IP and the MAC address of the destination. Network devices maintain address resolution protocol (ARP) tables, which contain the correspondences between the IP addresses and the MAC addresses of other devices on their LAN. ARP tables are kept in random access memory (RAM). Whenever a network device needs to transmit data, it consults its ARP table. A typical ARP table is shown in Table 6.2.

Once the sending device knows the IP address of the destination, it needs to know the MAC address too. It looks in its ARP table for this. If it finds an entry in the table for the destination IP address, it can look up the destination MAC address from there.

A network device builds its ARP table in two ways. First of all, it has to analyse the traffic on its Ethernet segment to find out whether data that has been sent out is for it. During this process, it writes the IP addresses of datagrams that it sees and their associated MAC addresses to the ARP table. But sometimes a computer wants to send a message to a station whose MAC address is not in its ARP table. In this case, it has to send out an *ARP request*.

The ARP request is a broadcast to all devices in the network. The ARP request packet contains the sender's hardware Ethernet address and its IP address. It also includes the target machine's IP address. All the network devices examine the ARP request packet that has been broadcast to them. If one of these finds that its own IP address is the target address, it will respond directly to the enquiring device with its Ethernet address. The sender now has the target's Ethernet address and can encapsulate its IP datagram inside an Ethernet frame and send it off. The ARP request and response is illustrated in Fig. 6.4.

6.1.4   Fragmentation

When an IP datagram arrives at a network device in a data-link frame, the receiver extracts the datagram and discards the frame header. Each network in an Internet (two or more interconnected networks) may be different at the data-link layer. Figure 6.5 shows what happens to an IP datagram at each stage of its journey across an Internet. Whenever it goes across a particular network, the datagram is encapsulated in the correct type of frame for this network.

Fig. 6.4 ARP request and response

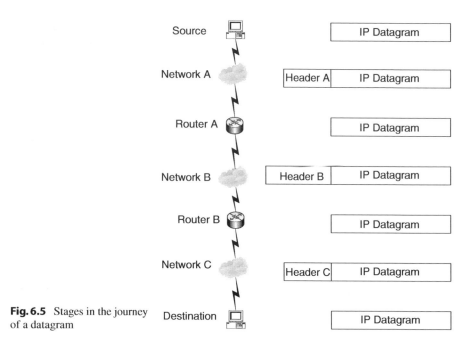

Fig. 6.5 Stages in the journey
of a datagram

Every network has a *maximum transmission unit* (MTU). For example, the standard
Ethernet MTU is 1,500 bytes and that of 16-Mbps Token Ring is 17,914 bytes,
but the standard MTU for the Internet is only 576 bytes. Therefore, it is quite possible that an IP datagram may be too large for a particular network across which it
has to travel. In this case the datagram has to be *fragmented* (divided up into smaller
pieces). When a router receives an IP datagram bigger than the MTU of the network
that it is going to be sent over, it divides the datagram into fragments. When the
datagram reaches the destination, it must be *reassembled* (put back together again).
Fragmentation and reassembly are illustrated in Fig. 6.6.

An IP datagram starts its journey on the left-hand side of Fig. 6.6, where it is in
a Token Ring LAN with a large MTU size. Since the next network is an Ethernet
LAN, the router that connects the two LANs together has to fragment the original
datagram into smaller pieces. The next router along knows that the data must now

Fig. 6.6 Fragmentation and reassembly

be put onto a WAN with an even smaller MTU size than the Ethernet LAN had, so it has to fragment again. The final router does not need to do any fragmentation, as the datagram is now moving to another Ethernet LAN, which has a larger MTU than the WAN network. Finally, the target computer reassembles the fragments using information that was put into their headers when the fragmentation happened.

6.1.4.1 Path MTU Discovery

Path MTU discovery is an alternative to expecting routers to fragment IP datagrams. The transmitting host finds out the largest datagram that it can send to the destination. It first sends a datagram of the MTU size of the first link in the chain of links that stretches to the destination. There is a flag in an IP header that instructs a router that receives it not to fragment the datagram under any circumstances.

This is called the *don't fragment* (DF) flag (please see a figure showing the IPv4 datagram header format in Appendix A). The transmitting host sets the DF flag so that the receiving router does not fragment the large datagram that it has received, even though it is necessary to do so for the datagram to be able to travel over the next link in the chain. If the datagram is too large, the router will throw it away and send an ICMP message back to the host that transmitted the datagram (see Sect. 6.1.8 for further details of ICMP). This message tells the host that fragmentation was needed and what the MTU is for the next link. When the host receives this ICMP message, it can adjust the size of the datagrams that it is sending out accordingly. This procedure may need to be carried out several times before the host finally knows the path MTU. The host can now use the path MTU as the maximum size for the datagrams that it is sending out. This will guarantee that the routers along the path will not need to do any fragmentation. The system is efficient because it cuts down the amount of work that routers have to do. Every now and then, the host will send out a large datagram to see if a new route has been found. Path MTU discovery is illustrated in Fig. 6.7.

6.1.5   Ways of Assigning IP Addresses

In addition to its MAC address, any host on an IP network needs an IP address. The ways of giving a host an IP address divide into static and dynamic assignment.

Fig. 6.7 Path MTU discovery

Fig. 6.8 Assigning a static address

In static assignment, the administrator of the network has to enter the host's IP address manually. If the network is small and does not change very often, static assignment is fine.

A screen for static address assignment in Microsoft® Windows® is shown in Fig. 6.8. In operating systems where no graphical user interface (GUI) is available, commands will be used to assign a static IP address. For example, the command 'IP address 192.168.0.1/24' gives an interface on a router that accepts Cisco-style commands an IP address and a subnet mask (see Sect. 6.1.6 for an explanation of subnet masks).

Fig. 6.9 DHCP

Alternatively, dynamic assignment can be used. There are three different mechanisms for dynamic address assignment. All of these involve a server that will dole out IP addresses on request. The first two mechanisms, reverse address resolution protocol (RARP) and the bootstrap protocol (BOOTP), are much less commonly used than the dynamic host configuration protocol (DHCP). Accordingly, we are going to concentrate on DHCP here. When setting up a Windows client PC to use DHCP to get an address, one will use the 'Obtain an address automatically' option instead of the 'Use the following IP address' option shown in Fig. 6.8. When the DHCP server receives a request from an unknown hardware address, it can assign an IP address from a pool of available addresses. These addresses can be recycled when they are released. The DHCP server can also configure other items automatically. For example, it can configure the subnet mask, the default gateway address (the address of the router that the computer will use to access another network by default) and the DNS address (see Sect. 7.2).

The DHCP system is illustrated in Fig. 6.9. The DHCP server 'leases' IP addresses to a client for a certain time, for example, 1 day. The sequence of events is as follows. The client computer broadcasts a request for the location of a DHCP server. All the local DHCP servers reply to the request by offering an IP address. If the client gets more than one offer, it selects the best, for example, the one with the longest lease. It sends out a broadcast asking to lease this IP address. The DHCP server that made the best offer responds, and all the other servers rescind their offers.

	Class	First address	Last address
Table 6.3 Private IP address ranges	A	10.0.0.0	10.255.255.255
	B	172.16.0.0	172.31.255.255
	C	192.168.0.0	192.168.255.255

Using an auto-configuration protocol such as DHCP is advantageous in large networks. This avoids having to configure a large number of machines by hand. New machines can be added to the network more easily. There is less chance of making errors (e.g. duplicate IP addresses being configured).

6.1.6   Shortage of IP Addresses

It is essential that all devices connected to public networks should have unique IP addresses. As the Internet rapidly grew bigger and bigger, a danger arose that there would be insufficient IP addresses available. The system of address classes (see Sect. 6.1.1) appears to be rather wasteful. For example, certain large organisations took all the Class A addresses long ago, even though they could not actually use all the 16 million plus host addresses that belong to each Class A network. There have been several partial solutions to the shortage of addresses. These include private IP addresses, network address translation (NAT), subnetting, variable-length subnet masks (VLSM) and classless interdomain routing. The ultimate solution, IPv6, is covered in Sect. 6.1.7.

6.1.6.1 Private IP Addresses
Certain ranges of IP addresses are reserved for use as private addresses. These can be used only within a private network and cannot be used on public networks. The ranges are shown in Table 6.3. The same private addresses can be used simultaneously in many different networks all over the world.

6.1.6.2 Network Address Translation
NAT can be used in conjunction with private IP addresses. The idea behind NAT is that internally a network can use different addresses from its external address, the address seen by devices on the Internet. NAT is usually performed by routers. NAT takes traffic from the internal network and presents it to the Internet as if it were coming from only one computer, which has only one IP address. An example of NAT is shown in Fig. 6.10. It can be seen in the figure that one of the interfaces of the router and all the other devices on the internal network have private addresses ranging from 192.168.0.1 to 192.168.0.5. The interface that is connected to the Internet has a completely different (public) address. The NAT router uses a *port-mapping table*, so that it knows which device on the internal network is sending or receiving data via the external address at any one time. (Port numbers are explained in Sect. 6.2.6.)

Fig. 6.10 Network address translation

Another advantage of NAT is that it hides the internal structure of the network from any potential attacker. The attacker is not given an idea of how many hosts there are on the internal network or how these are organised.

6.1.6.3 Subnetting

Subnetting is another technique that is used to make the most efficient use of IPv4 addresses. As part of the discussion, we will first investigate standard subnet masks. Any Internet device that is using IP needs to find out what IP network a given network device belongs to (including its own network interface). It does this by performing a logical AND operation on its address and subnet mask. Table 6.4 shows the standard subnet masks for the three address classes with two alternative ways of expressing the masks.

According to Table 6.4, the standard subnet mask for a Class C address is 255.255.255.0 or/24. Such a subnet mask indicates that the first three octets of the address are network bits, and the last octet is host bits. The reader can try for himself or herself to relate the masks for Classes A and B to the information on these address classes that is given in Sect. 6.1.1. In binary, the standard Class C subnet mask is 11111111.11111111.11111111.00000000. Let us now see what happens when a network device needs to know to which network a given Class C address, say

Table 6.4 Standard subnet masks

Class	Subnet mask	
A	255.0.0.0	(/8)
B	255.255.0.0	(/16)
C	255.255.255.0	(/24)

Fig. 6.11 Subnetting

Class C Network:
Subnet Mask 255.255.255.128

Network Address   Host
                         Number

192.168.0.2, belongs. It performs a bitwise logical AND operation between 192.168.0.2 and 255.255.255.0, the standard Class C subnet mask. In binary, this is as follows:

Address: 11000000.10101000.00000000.00000010
Subnet Mask: 11111111.11111111.11111111.00000000
Result: 11000000.10101000.00000000.00000000

The result of the AND-ing operation is that the network device now knows that the device with address 192.168.0.2 belongs to the 192.168.0.0 network. Although a human being can see this at a glance, a machine, having no intuition, has to work it out using a logical operation. Although this may seem to be a clumsy process, a computer can carry out logical operations of this sort extremely fast. When a router receives an IP datagram, it has to find out which network it belongs to by applying the appropriate subnet mask. It can then consult its routing table to find out which network to forward the datagram to.

So far, the reader will probably have received the impression that the system of address classes is inflexible. However, there is an alternative to using the standard subnet masks. It is possible to use custom subnet masks and ultimately to move the boundary between the network and host parts of the address almost at will. Part of the host field of the address can be used as part of the network field. This allows a network to be divided into interior networks (subnets). Externally, only one network address is sufficient to access the site. A great advantage of this system is that it keeps the size of external routing tables to a minimum. An example of a custom subnet mask is given in Fig. 6.11.

In Fig. 6.11, we see that the first host bit of the last octet has been 'borrowed' to become part of the network field. Whereas the standard Class C subnet mask (255.255.255.0) would give no subnets and 254 hosts, a subnet mask of 255.255.255.128 gives two subnets with 126 hosts on each subnet. Figure 6.12 shows the effect of various custom Class C subnet masks on the number of subnets and hosts that are available. We can see from the figure that as the number of subnets

255.255.255.0	0 subnets	254 hosts
255.255.255.128	2 subnets	126 hosts
255.255.255.192	4 subnets	62 hosts
255.255.255.224	8 subnets	30 hosts
255.255.255.240	16 subnets	14 hosts
255.255.255.248	32 subnets	6 hosts
255.255.255.252	64 subnets	2 hosts

Fig. 6.12 Effect of the subnet mask

increases, the number of hosts that are possible on each subnet decreases. The node number of a host on a given subnet is added to the subnet address to give the complete IP address for the node. For example, with a subnet mask of 255.255.255.128 and a network address of 193.78.142.128, host 1 on this network would have the IP address 193.78.142.129.

6.1.6.4 Variable-Length Subnet Masks

Some routing protocols (see Sect. 6.5 for a discussion of routing protocols) allow VLSM. With VLSM, an organisation can use more than one subnet mask inside the same network address space. In effect, VLSM allows the subnetting of a subnet.

6.1.6.5 Classless Interdomain Routing

Classless interdomain routing (CIDR, usually pronounced 'cider') gets round the problem of waste of addresses that is posed by the IP address classes. The 'classful' addressing system meant that any organisation that required more than 254 host addresses had to have a class B address, which gave over 65,000 addresses, the majority of which would be completely wasted. The owners of Class A addresses, with 16 million available host addresses, were even more profligate. CIDR was designed for Internet service providers (ISPs) so that they could put together contiguous blocks of addresses to give efficient addressing schemes. Using CIDR, a block of addresses can be represented by just one summary address. This is termed *route summarisation* or *aggregation* or *supernetting*.

For example, if an organisation needed about 1,000 addresses, four Class C networks of 250+ hosts each could be supernetted to represent approximately 1,000 hosts with a single summarised address. Figure 6.13 illustrates route aggregation. Four Class C routers with a 24-bit mask are summarised at the ISP router with a 22-bit mask. The Class C addresses are as follows.

Router 1: 194.200.128.0 (binary: 11000010.11001000.10000000.00000000)
Subnet mask: 255.255.255.0 (binary: 11111111.11111111.11111111.00000000)
Router 2: 194.200.129.0 (binary: 11000010.11001000.10000001.00000000)
Subnet mask: 255.255.255.0 (binary: 11111111.11111111.11111111.00000000)

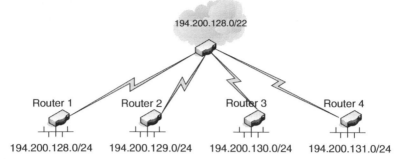

Fig. 6.13 Route aggregation

Router 3: 194.200.130.0 (binary: 11000010.11001000.10000010.00000000)
Subnet mask: 255.255.255.0 (binary: 11111111.11111111.11111111.00000000)
Router 4: 194.200.131.0 (binary: 11000010.11001000.10000011.00000000)
Subnet mask: 255.255.255.0 (binary: 11111111.11111111.11111111.00000000)

These are summarised as 194.200.128.0/22, which substantially reduces the size
of the ISP router's routing table.

Those routing protocols that support VLSM also support CIDR. Note that the
subnet masks in the diagrams (e.g. /24) are expressed using the CIDR format rather
than the older (255.255.255.0) format.

6.1.7   IP Version 6

IPv6 is the next generation of IP. It is designed to improve upon IPv4 in various
ways. It is easier to configure and more secure than IPv4. It is also designed to support
large-scale applications, peer-to-peer applications and mobile applications.
Diagrams showing the formats of the IPv6 datagram and the IPv6 base header can
be found in Appendix A.

6.1.7.1 Header Format
The format of the IPv6 header is rather different from that of IPv4. The basic IPv6
header (*base header*) is simpler, with fewer fields. Any additional information is stored
in optional *extension headers*. This header system is extensible, allowing new features
to be added more easily than with IPv4. The base header is always the same size: 40
octets. Since the header is only as large as it needs to be, we get greater efficiency.

Let us examine the fields of the IPv6 base header. As with IPv4, the *version* field
is 4 bits long. However, it contains 0110 (6) rather than 0100 (4). The *traffic class*
field is an 8-bit field that has a similar function to the type of service (TOS) field in
the IPv4 datagram header. It is used to specify priority. The *flow label* is a 20-bit
field that is used to label a set of packets that belong to the same flow. The flow label is
used to forward datagrams along a prearranged path so that demanding applications
such as audio and video can get the quality of service that they need. The 16 bits of

the *payload length* field indicate how many bytes there are in the data field following the 40-byte datagram header. The 8 bit *next header* field is similar to the IPv4 protocol field. It identifies the type of header that follows the base header. Usually, this will be TCP or UDP, but there are many other possibilities. The 8-bit *hop limit* field is decremented by one every time a node (normally a router) forwards the datagram. If the hop limit field is decremented to zero, the packet is thrown away. This field is similar to the IPv4 TTL field (see Sect. 6.1.8).

Some fields that are present in the IPv4 datagram are missing from the IPv6 datagram. Information about fragmentation is kept in a separate extension header. There is no options field. There is no checksum field in IPv6, unlike in IPv4. This is because error checking is normally done elsewhere in the protocol stack, for example, at the data-link layer and/or the transport layer. If faulty packets are going to be detected at these layers, then why duplicate the effort in the IP layer? If error checking has to be done by routers unnecessarily, then their speed is being seriously reduced for no good reason.

6.1.7.2 Addressing

The most obvious advantage of IPv6 is its addressing capacity. Every year, more and more IP addresses are needed in the world. For example, mobile phones and televisions did not use to need IP addresses but modern phones and TVs do. IPv6 uses 128-bit addressing instead of IPv4's 32-bit addressing. 128-bit addressing provides enough addresses (2^{128} or 3.4×10^{38}) to give every person alive today over a million addresses each. IPv6 has no need for NAT (RFC1918). When using IPv4, network administrators must devote a lot of effort to not wasting addresses. With IPv6 that is unnecessary because so many addresses are available.

There are no address classes in IPv6. The boundary between the network (subnet) prefix and host suffix (interface identifier) could fall anywhere, although it usually falls at the halfway point through the 128 bits. CIDR notation is used to show how many bits there are in the subnet prefix. Usually, the length of the subnet prefix is 64 bits, which is /64 in CIDR notation.

Dotted decimal notation would be unwieldy, and so 'colon hexadecimal' (colon hex) is used instead to represent the underlying binary. Colon hex consists of groups of 16-bit numbers (fields) in hexadecimal separated by colons, for example, 0ADC :8564:FFFF:FFFF:0000:1380:8E01:FFFF. Leading zeros in a field are optional, so the address given in the previous sentence could be written as ADC:8564:FFFF:FF FF:0:1380:8E01:FFFF. In addition, adjacent fields of zeros can be written as two colons ('::'), so the address 6ADC:8564:FFFF:0000:0000:1380:8E01:FFFF can be represented as 6ADC:8564:FFFF::1380:8E01:FFFF. This is a useful feature because it shortens most addresses considerably.

IPv6 *private addresses* all start with 'FE'. The next digit in a private address ranges from 8 up to B. Such addresses are called 'link local'. They are never used by routers for forwarding datagrams and are used on only one physical network. The IPv6 *loopback address* is ::1 (or 0:0:0:0:0:0:0:1). The IPv6 *unspecified address*, which a host uses when it does not know its own address, is :: (or 0:0:0:0:0:0:0:0).

Address auto-configuration is built into IPv6. StateLess Address Auto-Configuration (SLAAC) allows a large number of IP hosts to discover the network easily and to get new, globally unique addresses. This means that devices such as mobile phones, small handheld computers and various domestic appliances can be deployed on a 'plug-and-play' basis. There is no need for manual configuration as with IPv4. Duplicate address detection (DAD) is built in.

Interface identifiers (rather like the host part of an IPv4 address) identify interfaces on a link. These must be unique and are always 64 bits long. It is possible to obtain an interface identifier automatically from a MAC address.

Extended Unique Identifier-64 (EUI-64) provides a way of forming a 64-bit interface identifier from a MAC address. We first insert the hexadecimal sequence FFFE between the two halves of the MAC address. Then we invert the seventh bit. The result is the interface identifier. An example is given below.

For example, let us assume that the MAC address of an interface is 00 02 44 37 60 FA. On inserting FFFE between the two halves of this address, we get 00 02 44 FF FE 37 60 FA. We then invert the seventh bit to get 02 02 44 FF FE 37 60 FA. This is now the 64-bit interface identifier. The second hexadecimal digit changes to 2 because 00 hexadecimal is 00000000 in binary. When we invert the seventh bit, this becomes 00000010 in binary or 02 in hexadecimal. The seventh bit is termed the *local/universal flag*.

Another way of configuring IPv6 addresses is to use a special version of the DHCP protocol (DHCP is described above in Sect. 6.1.5). DHCPv6 allows a DHCP server to allocate IPv6 addresses and other configuration details to hosts. This is termed stateful address auto-configuration, which contrasts with the stateless method described above.

IPv6 uses multicasts instead of broadcasts for such purposes as router discovery and router solicitation requests (in which a host asks for a router). This saves network bandwidth and improves network efficiency. Address resolution is done in a similar fashion to ARP, but the traffic is carried by ICMPv6 (see Sect. 6.1.3 for an explanation of ARP and Sect. 6.1.8 for an explanation of ICMP). The IPv6 equivalent of an ARP request is called *neighbour solicitation,* and the equivalent of an ARP reply is *neighbour advertisement.*

6.1.7.3 Security

Security in IPv6 is better than in IPv4, in that the IP security protocol (IPSec) is mandatory in IPv6 but only optional in IPv4. (IPSec is explained in Sect. 8.2.1.) IPv6 makes encryption (scrambling data to keep it secure), authentication (finding out if someone or something is who or what he/she/it claims to be) and VPNs easier to implement. It offers access control, confidentiality and data integrity without needing extra firewalls (firewalls are described in Sect. 8.3).

6.1.7.4 Support for Mobile Computing

Mobile IP is part of IPv6. It allows mobile computers to keep their network connections while roaming about. A mobile node sends information about its point of attachment to a *home agent.* The home agent is a node on the home network that allows the mobile node to be reachable at its home address, regardless of where it is actually located. The home agent intercepts packets that are addressed to the mobile node. It then sends the packets directly to the mobile node's current location. Each IPv6 mobile node has two addresses: a home address and a care-of address.

Fig. 6.14 Dual stacking

Fig. 6.15 IPv6 tunnelling over IPv4

The care-of address is created whenever the mobile node attaches to the Internet from a fresh location. When the mobile node sends packets to another node, its care-of address is used as the source address.

6.1.7.5 Coexistence with IPv4

Some parts of the world, for example, Far Eastern countries such as China, were much more receptive to IPv6 early on than countries such as the USA. The fact that the USA had the lion's share of IPv4 addresses goes some way towards explaining this. In many countries, the move towards IPv6 has proceeded much more slowly than in the Far East.

IPv4 and IPv6 need to be able to coexist, and we need a mechanism that will allow this. The Internet is such that there cannot be a 'big bang', in which all IP-based communications suddenly switch from IPv4 to IPv6. The commonest strategy for transition from IPv4 to IPv6 is *dual stacking*. In dual stacking, a network node is connected to an IPv4 network and an IPv6 network at the same time. Two protocol stacks are operating on the node simultaneously. The node selects one stack or the other according to the destination address in the datagram that is being processed. Dual stacking is shown in Fig 6.14.

Tunnelling is an alternative to dual stacking. Here, IPv6 datagrams are encapsulated in IPv4 datagrams and sent over an IPv4 network. Tunnelling is illustrated in Fig. 6.15. The general principle is to use dual stacking wherever possible and to resort to tunnelling only where it cannot be avoided. The ultimate aim is to use IPv6 exclusively with no need for dual stacking or tunnelling at all.

6.1.8 Internet Control Message Protocol

IP provides so-called best-effort delivery. In other words, if there is a problem in delivering a datagram to the destination, it can be discarded. It is important that the source host knows about such problems, and so ICMP exists to provide an error-reporting mechanism. Various errors can be detected. One problem that might occur is that a packet's time to live (TTL) has expired. The TTL limits the number of routers that a datagram is allowed to pass through before it is discarded (see Fig. A.1 in Appendix A). The TTL is set when the source host sends the datagram. It is decremented by every router that it passes through on its journey. If the TTL ever gets down to zero, the datagram is thrown away. Another potential problem is that, for some reason, there is no route to the destination network. It may be impossible to deliver a datagram to the destination host because there was no reply to an ARP request. Errors of these kinds can be reported to the source host using ICMP. The router sends a message encapsulated in an IP datagram back to the source. This message carries information about the problem that has arisen.

As well as error messages, ICMP is also used to transmit informational messages. For example, it is used to discover a replacement router when a router has failed. *Ping*, a very useful utility program for testing reachability, makes use of ICMP echo request and echo reply. We shall now devote some space to an exploration of Ping.

6.1.8.1 Ping
If datagrams can be delivered from IP host B to host A, we can say that A is *reachable* from B. Ping tests reachability in the following way. Ping sends a datagram from B to A (ICMP echo request). Host A echoes this datagram back to B (ICMP echo reply). Here is an example in which a host is pinged from a Microsoft® Windows® computer. By default there are four pings (and, it is to be hoped, four replies) when using Windows.
ping bs47c.staffs.ac.uk
Pinging bs47c.staffs.ac.uk [193.60.1.15] with 32 bytes of data:
Reply from 193.60.1.15: bytes=32 time<10 ms TTL=63
Reply from 193.60.1.15: bytes=32 time=1 ms TTL=63
Reply from 193.60.1.15: bytes=32 time<10 ms TTL=63
Reply from 193.60.1.15: bytes=32 time<10 ms TTL=63
Ping statistics for 193.60.1.15:
    Packets: Sent=4, Received=4, Lost=0 (0% loss)
    Approximate round trip times in milli-seconds:
    Minimum=0 ms, Maximum=1 ms, Average=0 ms

6.1.8.2 Traceroute
ICMP echo messages are also used by another very useful utility program called *traceroute* (*tracert* in Windows). This can be employed to trace the complete route

from host X to host Y. The route is the list of all the routers along the path from X to Y. Host X sends out ICMP echo messages with an increasing TTL. Whenever a router decrements the TTL to 0, it sends back an ICMP message, including its own address as the source address. When the TTL is 1, the echo message only gets as far as the first router. The first router discards the echo message and sends back an ICMP message saying that the TTL was exceeded. When the TTL is 2, the message gets as far as the second router. The TTL is increased by 1 each time host X has another attempt at sending the echo message, until a message is received back from the destination host. Here is an example in which a route is traced from a Windows host.

tracert www.google.com

Tracing route to www.google.com [216.239.39.100] over a maximum of 30 hops:

1. 8 ms 8 ms 8 ms 10.33.0.1
2. 12 ms 6 ms 9 ms gsr01-du.blueyonder.co.uk [62.31.176.129]
3. 10 ms 10 ms 7 ms 172.18.4.37
4. 24 ms 33 ms 29 ms atm7-0-wol-hsd-gsr-linx.cableinet.net [194.117.158.130]
5. 27 ms 25 ms 24 ms e41-isp1-gw1-uk.cableinet.net [194.117.140.9]
6. 25 ms 25 ms 27 ms ibr01-g2-0.linx01.exodus.net [195.66.224.69]
7. 26 ms 25 ms 27 ms 212.62.2.209
8. 111 ms 10 ms 112 ms bbr02-p1-2.whkn01.exodus.net [209.185.249.133]
9. 104 ms 105 ms 112 ms bbr01-p3-0.stng02.exodus.net [209.185.9.102]
10. 105 ms 104 ms 106 ms dcr01-g2-0.stng02.exodus.net [216.109.66.1]
11. 106 ms 105 ms 111 ms csr11-ve241.stng02.exodus.net [216.109.66.90]
12. 103 ms 105 ms 106 ms 216.109.88.218
13. 108 ms 105 ms 105 ms dcbi1-gige-1-1.google.com [216.239.47.46]
14. 106 ms 103 ms 113 ms www.google.com [216.239.39.100]

6.2 The Transport Layer of TCP/IP

Transport-layer protocols (OSI Layer 4) work on top of IP to transport data from an application running on a source host to the same application running on a destination host. The most important of these protocols is TCP, which will be discussed in some detail. User datagram protocol (UDP), the second most important transport-layer protocol, will get less attention.

6.2.1 Introduction to Transmission Control Protocol

TCP has to transport data between the source and the destination accurately and reliably. It also has to regulate the flow of data. One of the most important services that it provides is data segmentation, in which the data is chopped up into segments. *Segment* is the special name that is used to refer to a packet of data at the transport layer. Other important functions performed by TCP are establishing and maintaining connections between two machines, as well as getting rid of these connections once they are no longer needed. TCP provides flow control using sliding windows.

It ensures that the transfer of data is reliable by using sequence numbers and acknowledgements (ACKs). A diagram showing the TCP segment format can be found in Appendix A.

6.2.2   Connection-Oriented and Connectionless Working

The terms connection oriented and connectionless describe different kinds of communication. In connection-oriented working, when devices communicate with each other, they first do *handshaking* to set up a connection from one end to the other. Handshaking is not done only at the transport layer. For example, modems also carry out quite a complex handshaking process to negotiate their communications parameters. Duplex communications are essential for connection-oriented working. TCP is a good example of a connection-oriented protocol.

In connectionless working, a dedicated end-to-end connection is not set up. Instead, the data is simply sent out in the hope that it will arrive at the destination. There is no checking whether the destination is ready to receive the data or even whether it still exists. A walkie-talkie radio is an example of connectionless communication. IP and UDP are examples of connectionless network protocols.

6.2.3   Flow Control

If the sending host were allowed to send data segments as quickly as it could, irrespective of all other considerations, the receiving host might not be able to cope with the flood of segments. Data could be lost if the receiver could not deal with the incoming bytes of information quickly enough. It might be forced to discard some of the data because there was not enough room in its buffers. TCP lets the sender and receiver negotiate with each other to find a data rate that is mutually acceptable.

6.2.4   Three-Way Handshake and Four-Way Tear Down

Before TCP data transfer can start, a connection-oriented session has to be established. The sender initiates a connection, and the receiver must accept this. Once the connection has been set up, the two sides keep checking that the data is being received with no errors. TCP uses a three-way handshake to open a connection and to synchronise both ends of the connection. During the open connection handshake sequence, beginning sequence numbers are exchanged. If any data subsequently gets lost, the sequence numbers make it possible to recover it. The open connection handshake sequence for two hosts, X and Y, is illustrated in Fig. 6.16. Note how the sequence numbers are incremented after each message is sent.

In Fig. 6.16, we can see that host X first requests synchronisation (SYN). In the second handshake, Y acknowledges the SYN request of X. The final handshake

Fig. 6.16 Three-way handshake

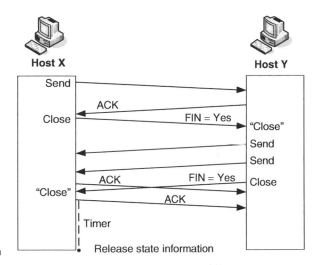

Fig. 6.17 Four-way teardown

acknowledges that both ends have reached agreement that a connection has been established. Data transfer can now commence.

Once the connection is finished with, the usual way of getting rid of it is with a four-way tear down. This sequence is shown in Fig. 6.17. Two FIN and two ACK segments are sent by each of the hosts. After these exchanges, the side that wishes to terminate waits for a timeout. When that occurs, the connection is finally closed.

6.2.5   Windowing

The receiver needs to get all the data segments in the same order as they were transmitted, undamaged and with no duplicate segments. One way to guarantee this is to

Fig. 6.18 Simple windowing system

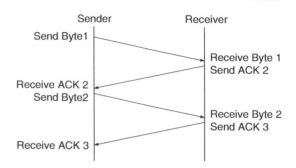

let the receiver acknowledge every data byte before the next one is transmitted. This scheme is illustrated in Fig. 6.18.

However, making the sender wait for an ACK before sending every byte is rather inefficient. Therefore, TCP, like most reliable connection-oriented protocols, lets there be more than one unacknowledged data byte in transit at a time. The number of outstanding, unacknowledged bytes is called *the window size*. (The reader is invited to relate this discussion to the discussion of ARQ mechanisms that was presented in Sect. 2.6.1.)

The ACKs that TCP uses are called 'expectational'. This means that the ACK number refers to the segment that is expected next. (The ACKs that are shown in Fig. 6.18 are of this kind.) If the receiver finds that a segment is missing from a sequence (i.e. there is a missing sequence number), the segment is sent again.

The TCP window size is not fixed, but is negotiated dynamically during a session. This windowing system is used for flow control. The sender and receiver may be working at different speeds, so the receiver needs to be able to tell the sender to stop sending any more data if its buffer is full. The receiver sends a *window advertisement*. The advertisement shows how much buffer space the receiver has available in terms of a number of bytes. The sender is allowed to send only as much data as the receiver has space for. As the data is received, the ACKs show a smaller and smaller window. When the window advertisement is 0, the sender must stop sending any more data. When the receiving application deals with some data, it sends an ACK with a new window size. The sender and the receiver have separate window sizes because they are communicating on a full-duplex basis. Figure 6.19 shows how the TCP sliding window operates. (In practice, the window sizes are likely to be somewhat larger than those shown in the figure.) There is also a congestion-control window, which is of the same size as the receiver's flow-control window most of the time. (Congestion is what happens when there is too much network traffic on a link or node for a good service to be maintained.)

6.2.6   Port Numbers

TCP uses *port numbers* to pass data to the upper protocol layers. The port numbers identify different conversations that are on the network simultaneously. For example,

Sender   Receiver

Advertise window size 250 bytes

Send bytes 1-100

Send bytes 101-200

Send bytes 201-250

ACK up to 100 bytes; window size = 150 bytes
ACK up to 200 bytes; window size = 50 bytes
ACK up to 250 bytes; window size = 0 bytes

Receive ACK for 100 bytes
Receive ACK for 200 bytes
Receive ACK for 250 bytes

Application deals with 200 bytes
ACK up to 250 bytes; window size = 200 bytes

Send bytes 251-350
Send bytes 351-450

ACK up to 350 bytes; window size = 100 bytes
ACK up to 450 bytes; window size = 0 bytes

Receive ACK for 350 bytes
Receive ACK for 450 bytes

Application deals with 100 bytes
ACK up to 450 bytes; window size = 100 bytes

Receive ACK for 450 bytes

Fig. 6.19 Sliding window

the client PC in Fig. 6.20 has two different Web browsers running. Each of the browsers is connected to a different Web server. The TCP software running on the PC is able to sort out which data is for which application by using the port numbers. It can do this because the two applications have set up their connections with different port numbers. Each of the conversations shown in Fig. 6.20 has its own full-duplex TCP connection. The complete address consists of an IP number plus port number. For example, in numerical form, the address for the connection to the Web server in the top right-hand corner of Fig. 6.20 is 64.86.203.2:1727. The portion before the colon is the IP address; the portion after the colon is the port number.

Well-known port numbers are low port numbers (below 1024) that are always used for standard TCP/IP applications. For example, Telnet (see Sect. 7.4) uses Port 23, while HTTP uses Port 80, as can be seen in Fig. 6.20. If a well-known port number is not involved, a random port number above 1023 is used. The client PC in Fig. 6.20 is using the originating source port numbers of 1727 and 1743.

Fig. 6.20   Port numbers

Fig. 6.21   HDLC frame

8	8	8	>= 0	16	8
Flag	Address	Control	Data	Checksum	Flag

6.2.7   User Datagram Protocol

UDP is a connectionless alternative to TCP in the TCP/IP protocol stack. Unlike TCP, it does not give ACKs, does not guarantee delivery and does not do windowing. It is an *unreliable* protocol, whereas TCP is *reliable*. When UDP is in use, any errors that occur or retransmissions that are needed must be dealt with by higher layer protocols. All UDP does is send and receive datagrams. The main difference between UDP and IP is that UDP adds port numbers, to indicate to which application the data belongs.

UDP is used wherever there is no need for sequences of segments that must be put together. Among the application-layer protocols that use UDP are DHCP, DNS, trivial file transfer protocol (TFTP) and simple network management protocol (SNMP). UDP is faster than TCP. When communications are time sensitive, UDP is often used. For example, it is used for VoIP (see Sect. 7.7.2), where speed is of the essence.

6.3   High-Level Data Link Control

When data needs to be sent out over a WAN link, it is passed from the network layer for delivery. The data-link layer *encapsulates* (builds up a frame round) the network layer data. Every time that a data frame reaches a router, the router strips off the frame information so that it can read the layer-3 address inside. When the router has found out, after consulting its routing table, where the data packet should be sent next, the data packet is re-encapsulated in the appropriate data-link frame for transmission on the next leg of the journey.

As its name would suggest, HDLC is a data-link layer protocol. It is used in WANs. HDLC and several other closely related layer-2 protocols use the frame that is shown in Fig. 6.21. The figures above the fields indicate the number of bits that each field occupies.

Fig. 6.22 Generic MPLS
label format

DLL	Label	NL	OL + D

DLL = Header for Data Link Layer
Label = MPLS Label
NL = Header for Network Layer
OL + D = Headers for Other Layers + Data

Every HDLC frame begins and ends with a Flag field. The distinctive bit pattern of this field is always 01111110. There is a possibility that this pattern might appear somewhere in the data field, which would confuse the receiving device. So, the sender always inserts an extra 0 bit after every five 1s in the data field. This is called *bit stuffing,* and it ensures that the flag sequence only ever occurs at the beginning and end of a frame. The receiver automatically removes the stuffed bits from the data.

The address field is normally superfluous, as most WAN links are point to point. The control field shows the type of frame. There are three types of frame. *Unnumbered* frames are for line set-up information. *Information* frames carry data. *Supervisory* frames deal with flow control and error control. A sophisticated windowing system, similar to that used by TCP, may be used for flow control.

The checksum field (FCS field) actually contains a CRC. The reader might wish to compare the above description of the HDLC frame with those of the Ethernet frames given in Sect. 4.2.2.

As mentioned above, HDLC is one of a family of closely related data-link layer protocols. Link access procedure balanced (LAPB) is used for X.25. Link access procedure for frame mode services (LAPF) is used in frame relay. Link access procedure D-channel (LAPD) is used in the ISDN D-channel.

6.4   Multiprotocol Label Switching

IP forwarding, described in the first paragraph of Sect. 6.3, is a laborious process. It can often work too slowly when routers try to deal with large traffic loads. The idea behind multiprotocol label switching (MPLS) is to supplement standard IP forwarding by add-ing a *label* to packets. This 4-byte label is added to the packets as they enter the MPLS network. The label is inserted into the layer-2 frame between the layer-2 header (e.g. Ethernet) and the IP header. Wherever possible, the routers then base their forwarding decisions on the value in the label. This is much simpler and more efficient for routers than having to look through large routing tables. The label acts as an index to the routing table and only needs one lookup (a lookup of the MPLS label) rather than the many more lookups that might be needed when using classical IP forwarding. When the pack-ets reach the destination network, the label is removed. MPLS can work only with rout-ers that are capable of understanding it, but it has many advantages. It increases speed and reduces delay and jitter. It offers guaranteed quality of service for voice and video. Virtual private LAN service (VPLS) securely connects two or more Ethernet LANs over an MPLS network. To the user, it is as if he or she is on a very large Ethernet segment. The details of MPLS are beyond the scope of this book but suffice it to say that it has become very widely used. The generic label format is shown in Fig. 6.22.

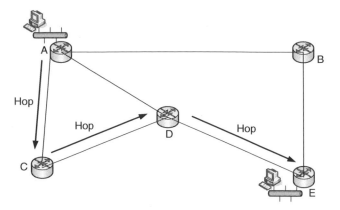

Fig. 6.23 Router hops

6.5   Routing Protocols

An administrator can configure a router by entering routes manually. In a large network where many changes are happening, maintaining the routing tables in this way could be very costly in terms of both time and money. Fortunately, routing protocols exist which can maintain routing tables automatically. Routing protocols let routers share information with each other about open paths through networks of which they have knowledge. It is important not to confuse routing protocols with the protocols that are routed. IP is a good example of a routed protocol. A packet belonging to a routed protocol contains an address that lets it be sent from one network device to another. Examples of routing protocols are Routing Information Protocol (RIP) and Open Shortest Path First (OSPF). Both of these are examples of open-standard protocols, but proprietary protocols also exist.

There was a description of routing tables in Sect. 5.9, and a sample routing table was given in Table 5.1. A routing protocol learns about routes. It finds out what the best routes are and puts these in the routing table. We say that an internetwork has *converged* when all the routers that belong to it possess the same knowledge of routes through it. The routers get to a state of convergence as a result of talking to each other and sharing their knowledge.

There are two types of routing protocols: distance vector and link state. A router that is using a *distance-vector* protocol regularly sends copies of its routing table to its neighbours. The name distance vector refers to the method that is used to measure the distance (or *metric*) from one network device to another. A common metric is *hop count*—a measure of the number of hops (links) between one router and another. Hops are illustrated in Fig. 6.23.

The route from router A to E going via routers C and D in Fig. 6.23 is three hops long. (The links from A to B, from B to E and from A to D are also hops, though not labelled as such in the diagram.) The RIP distance-vector protocol uses hop count as its metric. In Fig. 6.24, we see the exchange of routing tables. Router Y sends copies

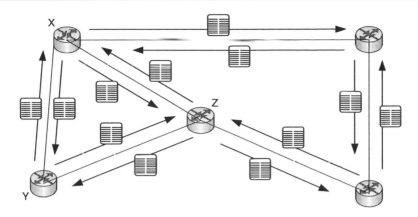

Fig. 6.24 Distance-vector routing

of its routing table to its neighbours, Routers X and Z. Routers X and Z send copies of their routing tables to their neighbours, which include router Y. The other routers in the internetwork also send their routing tables to their neighbours. This happens automatically every few seconds (every 30 s by default in the case of RIP).

Link-state routing protocols work in a manner rather different from distance-vector routing protocols. Each router in an internetwork keeps a map of the topology of the whole internetwork. The router is able to build this map because it broadcasts small packets called link-state advertisements (LSAs) to all the other routers in the internetwork whenever there is a change in the state of a link. It also receives broadcasts of LSAs from the other routers. The LSAs contain information on the status of a link between two routers (e.g. the link between router M and router N is up). The router uses the information from the LSAs to build its map of the topology of the internetwork. The router applies an algorithm called shortest path first (SPF) to its database of topological information. This produces a routing table in which the router doing the calculation is the source host.

Link-state routing protocols possess certain advantages over distance-vector protocols. Firstly, routing updates are sent only when there is a change in the topology. Distance-vector protocols send updates on a regular basis, whether or not any changes have happened. Convergence happens faster than with distance-vector routing. On the other hand, link-state protocols work the router's CPU harder and need more memory than distance-vector protocols.

6.6   Summary

This chapter has looked at various network protocols. The IP protocol, which carries all the traffic on the Internet, was described in some detail, including both versions 4 and 6. IP is responsible for moving packets from source to destination across networks. It supplies a connectionless, unreliable service. ICMP, which is used on TCP/IP networks to send error messages and informational messages of various kinds, was covered next. TCP received a lot of attention. It works on top of IP to give a reliable, connection-oriented service. It guarantees end-to-end delivery of packets. It corrects lost, corrupted, out-of-order and delayed packets. HDLC, a layer-2 protocol that is used in WANs, was described. Multiprotocol label switching, which permits highly efficient routing, was briefly covered. Finally, two different classes of routing protocols, distance vector and link state, were described. Routing protocols allow routers to inform each other about open paths through internetworks automatically.

6.7   Questions

1. What is *'dotted decimal'*?
2. To which IPv4 address class does the address 193.60.1.15 belong?
3. What is the purpose of a *'broadcast address'*?
4. What service does IP provide?
5. (a) What are the differences between IP addresses and data-link layer addresses?
   (b) Give an example of each kind of address.
   (c) When a message is sent from one computer to another, how is the destination IP address translated to a data-link layer address?
6. Describe the structure of IPv4 *address classes*.
7. Why might an IP datagram need to be *fragmented*?
8. Where are IP fragments *reassembled*?
9. Explain *path MTU discovery*.
10. What is a *default gateway*?
11. (a) How many subnets does the Class C subnet mask of 255.255.255.224 give?
    (b) How many hosts can there be on each subnet?
12. What is the purpose of the *TTL* field in the IP datagram structure?
13. Following *zero compression*, how does the IPv6 address FF0D:0:0:0:0:0:0:A1 appear?
    • FF0D:0:0:0:0:0:0:A1
    • FF0D::A1
    • FF::D::A1
    • FF0D:0::A1
14. Using *EUI-64*, form a 64-bit interface identifier from the MAC address 00 50 BF 44 E4 F9.
15. What is the *ping* utility program used for?
16. What is the purpose of the *traceroute* (tracert) utility program?
17. What functions does *TCP* perform?
18. Explain the differences between *connection-oriented* and *connectionless* working.
19. Explain the steps in the TCP *three-way handshake*.
20. What is the purpose of *port numbers*?
21. What is the smallest number of bits that there can be in an *HDLC* frame?
22. The following sequence of bits is to be sent out over a link in the user data field

of the HDLC protocol. Write down what the sequence will be after *bit stuffing* has taken place.

01111111010101011111011100000001111110101

23. Explain the differences between *distance-vector* and *link-state* routing protocols.

Internet Application-Layer Protocols

7

Abstract

In the previous chapter, we saw how IP packets carry TCP segments or UDP datagrams across networks. Now it is time to look at what happens in the top layer of a TCP/IP-based network, the application layer. This chapter starts with an explanation of client–server technology, which underlies most Internet activities. We examine the following applications in turn: the domain name system (DNS), the World Wide Web, remote access, file transfer, E-mail, the delivery of streamed content over the Internet and voice over IP (VoIP). We discuss the main protocols for each of these applications. The chapter ends with brief descriptions of peer-to-peer (P2P) file sharing, instant messaging (IM) and microblogging.

Note that all the applications described below depend on TCP/IP and the underlying network to deliver the data. If necessary, please refer back to Chap. 3 or to Sect. 7.4.1 for a reminder of the encapsulation process.

7.1 Client–Server Applications

Client–server technology is commonly used on networks. Examples of client–server applications are Web browsers, file transfer protocol (FTP) and e-mail. Such applications have two components: client and server. Typically, the local machine runs a client application, and the remote system supports the corresponding server application. The client requests services and the server provides services in response to the client's requests (Fig. 7.1).

In a client–server application, the following sequence is constantly repeated: client-request, server-response. For example, if a user wishes to access a certain Web page, the Web browser requests a special kind of address called a uniform resource locator (URL) from a remote Web server on behalf of the user (see Sect. 7.3.2 for further details of URLs). Once the Web server has found the address, it responds to the request. The client can then either request more information from

J. Cowley, *Communications and Networking: An Introduction*, Undergraduate Topics in Computer Science, DOI 10.1007/978-1-4471-4357-4_7,
© Springer-Verlag London 2012

Fig. 7.1 A client–server application

Fig. 7.2 Client–server request–response

the same Web server or can access another Web page from a different Web server
(Fig. 7.2). More details of this process are given in Sect. 7.3.

7.2 Domain Name System

7.2.1 Difficulties with Using Numerical IP Addresses

In the previous chapter, we saw that the Internet depends on IP, which uses either
a 32-bit numerical address, usually expressed in dotted decimal format (IPv4) or a
128-bit address, usually shown in hexadecimal (IPv6). It is possible to download a

Fig. 7.3   Using an IP address to retrieve a Web page

page from the Internet by specifying a numerical address, as shown in Fig. 7.3 (compare with Fig. 7.2).

However, it is not easy for human beings to remember numerical addresses for websites. The *DNS* allows us to use textual names instead of numeric addresses, which is a much more attractive idea.

A *domain* is a group of computers that belong together for some reason. For example, they may be located in the same place or belong to the same type of business. A *domain name* is a string of characters, usually a name or an abbreviation. This string of characters represents the numeric address of an Internet site. In Table 7.1, there is a list (not exhaustive) of generic top-level domains.

Many two-letter, country code top-level domains also exist. Examples include the following:

.uk – United Kingdom

.de – Germany (Deutschland)

7.2.2   Domain Name Server

A DNS server is a computer that responds to requests from client machines to translate domain names into numerical IP addresses. The DNS consists of a hierarchy of different levels of DNS servers. The complete system forms a worldwide distributed database of names and their corresponding IP addresses. Any application that uses domain names to represent IP addresses uses the DNS to translate names into

Table 7.1 Top-level domains

Domain	For use by
.aero	Air-transport industry
.biz	Businesses
.com	Companies
.coop	Cooperative associations
.edu	US educational institutions
.gov	US government
.info	For anyone
.int	International organisations
.mil	US military
.museum	Museums
.name	For registration by individuals
.net	Networks
.pro	Accountants, lawyers and doctors
.org	Non-commercial organisations

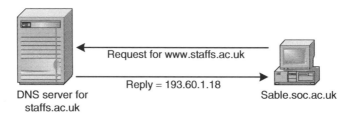

DNS server for staffs.ac.uk — Request for www.staffs.ac.uk — Reply = 193.60.1.18 — Sable.soc.ac.uk

Fig. 7.4 Direct DNS query

numerical IP address. Microsoft® Windows® Active Directory (a directory service that offers a way of managing the objects that make up network environments) also depends on DNS.

If the local DNS server is able to translate a domain name into its IP address, it does so and returns the result directly to the client. This is illustrated in Fig. 7.4.

If the local DNS server is not able to carry out the translation, it passes the request on to the next higher level DNS server. This server tries to translate the address. If it is able to translate the domain name, it returns the result to the client. If it cannot manage the translation, it sends the request to the next higher level DNS server. This carries on until either the domain name has been translated or the top-level DNS server has been reached. If the top-level DNS server cannot find out the answer, then an error is returned.

7.3   World Wide Web and HyperText Transfer Protocol

The World Wide Web is perhaps the best known service offered over the Internet. The Web has grown extremely fast, mainly because it allows very easy access to information.

This is an important heading.

This is a heading too, but not as important.

This is a paragraph. This is a link to another Web site.

A list follows below:

* list item 1
* list item 2

Here is a picture:

Fig. 7.5   A typical Web page

Fig. 7.6   HTML source for
Web page in Fig. 7.5

```
<h1>This is an important heading.</h1>
<h2>This is a heading too, but not as important.</h2>
<p>This is a paragraph. This is a link to <a
href="http://www.staffs.ac.uk">another Web site</a>.</p>
A list follows below:
<ul>
 <li>list item 1</li>

 <li>list item 2</li>
</ul>
Here is a picture:
<img src="book2003APicture.gif" width="180" height="162">
```

7.3.1   HyperText Markup Language

Web pages are usually composed with a markup language called HyperText Markup Language (HTML). HTML causes a Web page to appear on screen in a particular way. It uses *tags* such as <p> and </p> to structure the text into paragraphs, lists, hypertext links and so on. An example of a Web page and the HTML that specifies its content is shown in Figs. 7.5 and 7.6. By comparing Figs. 7.5 and 7.6, note the effects of the various tags. The HTML source text has been kept as simple as possible. Normally, more HTML would be included. Many people compose Web pages using a specialised HTML editor, but others just use a simple text editor.

There are several other varieties of markup language, such as Extensible HTML (XHTML) and Extensible Markup Language (XML), but these will not be discussed here.

7.3.2   Hyperlinks

In the Web page illustrated in Figs. 7.5 and 7.6, there is a hyperlink (http://www.staffs.ac.uk) to another website. This kind of address is called a URL. By clicking on such links, users can navigate around the Web very easily; this, indeed, is one of the Web's main attractions. In the URL http://www.staffs.ac.uk, the 'http://' part instructs the browser to use the HyperText Transfer Protocol (HTTP). The 'www' part is the name of the server that the browser must contact (the name 'www' is often used for the name of a Web server). The 'staffs.ac.uk' part identifies the domain entry of the website.

7.3.3   Web Browser

Commonly used Web browsers are Microsoft® Internet Explorer, Mozilla Firefox, Google Chrome, Safari and Opera. Though these differ in their details, quite radically in some respects, they are all based on the same principles. A Web browser (just like the other applications covered in this chapter) is a client–server application and has a client and a server component. A Web browser presents data in the form of Web pages. The pages are multimedia: not just text but also sound, still pictures and moving pictures. The page shown in Fig. 7.5 typifies this.

When the user starts a Web browser, the first thing that usually appears is the 'home' page. The URL of the home page was previously stored in the browser's configuration. To move away from the home page, there is the choice of clicking on a hyperlink or typing a URL in the browser's location bar. The Web browser then examines the protocol that is specified in the URL to find out if it needs to start another program and discovers the target Web server's IP address.

After that, the transport layer, network layer, data-link layer and physical layer start off a session with the Web server. The browser (client) sends the HTTP server data containing the directory name of the Web page location (and possibly also a specific file name for a particular page). If the browser does not supply such a name, then the server will use a default location.

The server's response to the browser's request will be to send all of the files specified in the HTML instructions. In the case of the page shown in Figs. 7.5 and 7.6, both a text file and a graphics file will be sent. The browser puts all the files together and displays the page. If the user then clicks on another page that is located on a different server, the whole sequence starts off again.

7.3.4   HyperText Transfer Protocol

Each type of application-layer program has its own application protocol or protocols. In the case of the World Wide Web, HTTP is the most important protocol, for it is the one that is used to transfer pages of information. In an HTTP transfer, a TCP/IP connection is established between the client and the server. The HTTP GET command is then used to retrieve a file from the server. In HTTP version 1.0, the original version, as soon as the server sent back its response, the TCP/IP connection was broken. This meant that a new TCP/IP connection had to be established for every file sent. However, HTTP 1.1, the current version, allows the TCP/IP connection to persist through multiple request–response sequences. This arrangement reduces the overhead of TCP/IP. The HTTP POST command can be used to transfer data from browser to server, but this is much less frequently used than GET. (There are also other HTTP commands, but these will not be mentioned in this text.)

7.3.4.1 Caching in Web Browsers

The above explanation of Web browsers ignores the fact that caching (pronounced like 'cashing') is usually used. Web browsers tend to reference pages frequently and a cache (temporary disk storage) is used to improve performance. A copy of items can be kept on the local disk for a certain time.

7.4 Remote Access and the Telnet Protocol

Being able to access a computer remotely is a very useful facility. Telnet (terminal emulation) permits logging into an Internet host and then executing commands. The Telnet client is called the local host and the server is called the remote host. The Telnet server software is called a *daemon* (pronounced like 'demon'). The relationship between a client and a server is illustrated in Fig. 7.7.

Figure 7.8 shows the initial window when the Microsoft® Telnet client is used to contact a remote machine.

Figure 7.9 shows a typical login prompt.

When you use Telnet, your computer acts as a dumb terminal with no processing power of its own. The keystrokes that you make are sent to the remote host and all the processing is done on the remote computer. Figure 7.10 shows a typical command-line prompt on a remote computer that has been logged into via Telnet.

7.4.1 Encapsulation of Telnet Commands

Telnet is a TCP/IP application-layer protocol, and it depends on TCP/IP to set up a session. (In terms of the OSI 7-layer model, the Telnet commands work at the application

Fig. 7.7 Telnet client and server

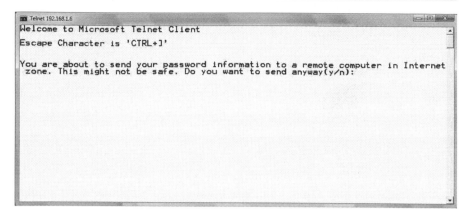

Fig. 7.8 Microsoft Telnet client initial window

Fig. 7.9 The Telnet login prompt

Fig. 7.10 Typical command-line prompt on a remote computer

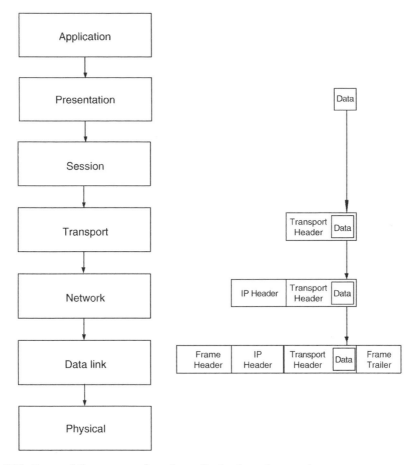

Fig. 7.11 Encapsulation sequence from the application layer downwards

layer, the formatting is done at the presentation layer and transmission is done at the session layer.) From the TCP/IP application layer, the data is passed to the transport layer. At the transport layer, it is divided up into segments, a port address is added and a checksum to detect errors is calculated. Next, at the network layer, the IP header is added, including the IP addresses of the source and destination. The data is then passed to the data-link layer. The packet is encapsulated in a frame that includes the MAC addresses of the source and destination and a frame trailer. (An ARP request may be needed to find out the MAC address of the destination.) The frame now travels over the physical medium (e.g. a copper cable) to the next device (e.g. a router). The encapsulation process is illustrated in Fig. 7.11.

At the final destination (the remote host computer), the data-link layer, network layer and transport layer put back together the original Telnet commands. The remote host computer carries out the commands and sends the results back to the local client computer. To do this, just the same process of encapsulation as was used to deliver the commands from the Telnet client is employed. The sequence of

Fig. 7.12 PuTTY SSH client being used to contact a SSH server

sending commands and receiving results is repeated until the local client has done whatever work it needed to. At that point, the client terminates the session.

It is important to note that Telnet is not regarded as a secure protocol (note the warning message that is visible on screen in Fig. 7.8). Since the user sends his or her password in unencrypted form over the network, it is not hard for an intruder to find out the password. The same is true of FTP (please see the next section for details). Secure Shell (SSH) is a protocol and program that includes all the functionality of Telnet but is secure because the password is encrypted. Figure 7.12 shows the PuTTY SSH client being used to contact a SSH server on a remote machine.

7.5   File Transfer and the File Transfer Protocol

FTP can be used to transfer files from or to an FTP server (*downloading* or *uploading*). Downloading means transferring files from a remote host (server) to the local host (client). Uploading means moving files from the local client to a remote server.

Fig. 7.13 File transfer between FTP server and client

An example of downloading is copying freeware programs from the Internet to install them on a home computer. An example of uploading is moving Web pages that one has prepared on one's home computer to a website so as to publish them on the Internet. Being able to move files around easily like this is one of the Internet's main advantages.

Like Telnet, FTP is a client–server application, which needs server software running on the remote computer that can be accessed by client software running on the local computer (Fig. 7.13).

FTP can be used in various ways. The user has the following choices of interface: command line, GUI based or Web browser based. The command-line version is the hardest to use of the three but is very flexible (see Fig. 7.14 for a screenshot of FTP being invoked from the command line). A sample of FTP commands is given in Table 7.2 (the list is not exhaustive).

A more secure way of doing file transfers, using the PuTTY Secure FTP (SFTP) client is shown in Fig. 7.15.

A typical GUI-based FTP client program is illustrated in Fig. 7.16. The FTP client shown in the figure is FileZilla, a free program (the FileZilla server application, also free, is being used in Fig. 7.14). Many alternative GUI-based FTP clients exist; FileZilla is not the only possible choice.

The third form of interface is a Web browser. Instead of entering 'http:' into the location bar as normally, the user enters 'ftp:' followed by a location (see Fig. 7.17). This instructs the browser to use FTP to download the file, rather than HTTP.

7.5.1   Anonymous FTP

Anonymous FTP services, where the user does not need an account on the remote host, are common on the Internet. The username that is used when logging in anonymously is 'anonymous', and the password is one's e-mail address. When using command-line FTP or a GUI-based client such as FileZilla, it is possible to log into an FTP server on which one has an account using one's own username and password. The user may then both download and upload files if the directory permissions are set to allow this.

```
Command Prompt - ftp 192.168.1.6
Microsoft Windows [Version 6.0.6002]
Copyright (c) 2006 Microsoft Corporation.  All rights reserved.

C:\Users\John>ftp 192.168.1.6
Connected to 192.168.1.6.
220-FileZilla Server version 0.9.39 beta
220-written by Tim Kosse (Tim.Kosse@gmx.de)
220 Please visit http://sourceforge.net/projects/filezilla/
User (192.168.1.6:(none)):
```

Fig. 7.14 Invoking FTP from the command prompt

Table 7.2 Some FTP commands

FTP command	What it does
open *remote machine*	Opens connection to remote machine
quit	Ends the FTP session
get *file*	Transfers (i.e. copies) a file from server to client
put *file*	Transfers (i.e. copies) a file from client to server

```
PSFTP
psftp: no hostname specified; use "open host.name" to connect
psftp> open 192.168.1.6
The server's host key is not cached in the registry. You
have no guarantee that the server is the computer you
think it is.
The server's rsa2 key fingerprint is:
ssh-rsa 1024 8b:cf:24:ca:16:1f:a2:bd:c9:59:24:c2:bd:72:8a:37
If you trust this host, enter "y" to add the key to
PuTTY's cache and carry on connecting.
If you want to carry on connecting just once, without
adding the key to the cache, enter "n".
If you do not trust this host, press Return to abandon the
connection.
Store key in cache? (y/n) y
login as: john
john@192.168.1.6's password:
```

Fig. 7.15 Invoking SFTP from the command prompt

7.5.2   TCP Control and Data Connections

An FTP session is established in the same way as a Telnet session. Just as with Telnet, the FTP session is maintained until the client terminates it or there is an error.

FTP uses a control connection, a TCP connection to a remote machine, to send commands. A second TCP connection is used for the data. The two connections are illustrated in Fig. 7.18. To avoid confusion between these two connections, different TCP port numbers are used for each.

Fig. 7.16 File transfer with FileZilla

Using the control connection, it is possible to manipulate directories and files on the server if one has sufficient privilege to do so.

7.5.3   FTP Transfer Modes

Data transfer can be done in ASCII or binary mode. Binary transfer produces an exact copy of the bits, whereas ASCII transfer preserves the formatting of text files. It is important to choose the correct mode, though Web browsers and GUI-based FTP clients are able to choose the appropriate mode automatically.

After file transfer is completed, the data connection terminates automatically. At the end of the session, the user logs out. This action closes the command link and ends the session.

7.6   Electronic Mail

Electronic mail (e-mail) allows messages to be sent between computers that are connected together over a network. E-mail has existed in some form for about 30 years. The first e-mail systems simply consisted of using file transfer protocols,

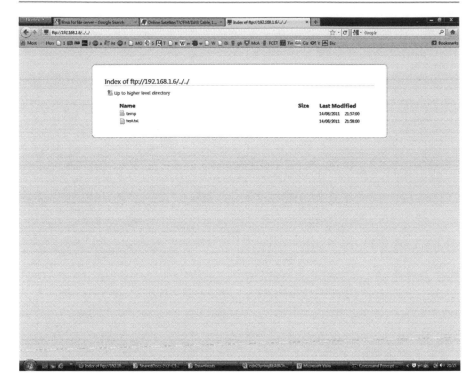

Fig. 7.17 Using FTP from a browser

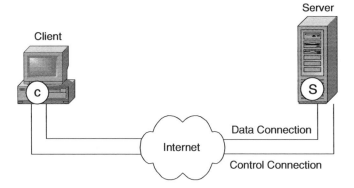

Fig. 7.18 FTP control and data connections

and there were several disadvantages to such an arrangement. There was no feedback to let the sender know that a message had arrived. It was not possible to send multimedia messages. In modern e-mail systems, these problems have been resolved, as we shall see.

Fig. 7.19 Sending an e-mail

Fig. 7.20 E-mail address

7.6.1 Transmitting a Message to an E-mail Server

When an e-mail message is sent, two separate processes have to be carried out. First, the e-mail is sent to the receiver's 'post office' (the technical name for the post office is *message transfer agent* (MTA)). Then, the e-mail has to be delivered from the post office to the receiver's e-mail client (the technical term for the e-mail client is *user agent* (UA)). These processes are illustrated in Fig. 7.19.

If an e-mail facility is available to you, try doing the following:

1. Start your e-mail client (e.g. Outlook, Thunderbird).
2. Type in the e-mail address of the person to whom you want to send a message.
3. Enter the subject of the message.
4. Compose the message.

The recipient's e-mail address will look something like this: a_person@yahoo. co.uk. The address comprises two parts: the name of the recipient and the address of the recipient's post office, separated by an @ sign. The post office address is a DNS name, which stands for the IP address of the recipient's post office server (Fig. 7.20).

```
Return-Path: <ssdesk@bighotel.com>
Received: from camcord2-smrly1.igtei.net (camcord2-smrly1.igtei.net
[128.23.173.4]) by mail.staffs.ac.uk (8.9.1/8.9.1) with ESMTP id
VAB18434 for <J.Cowley@staffs.ac.uk>; Sun, 13 May 2004 21:25:08 +0100
BST)
From: ssdesk@bighotel.com
Received: from ae1.travelweb.com (ae1.travel.com [207.248.14.24])by
camcord2-smrly1.gtei.net (Postfix) with ESMTP id 33E18481A for
<J.Cowley@staffs.ac.uk>; Sun, 13 May 2004 20:25:01 +0000 (GMT)
Received: from ae1 (localhost [127.0.0.1]) by ae1.travel.com
(8.9.3+Sun/8.9.3) with SMTP id NAB08430 for <J.Cowley@staffs.ac.uk>;
Sun, 13 May 2004 13:25:04 -0700 (MST)
Date: Sun, 13 May 2004 13:25:04 -0700 (MST)
To: J.Cowley@staffs.ac.uk
Subject: Confirmed Reservation Notification
Content-Type: text/plain
Content-Transfer-Encoding: 7bit
Mime-Version: 1.0
Message-ID: <23137631.989785505049.JavaMail.abc@af1>

THANK YOU FOR CHOOSING BIG HOTELS. WE LOOK FORWARD TO YOUR STAY WITH
US.
```

Fig. 7.21 Full e-mail message

This part of the address is what will be used to get the message as far as the post office. The recipient's name does not matter to the e-mail system at this stage.

7.6.2   E-mail Standards

The standard protocol for sending electronic mail over the Internet is the simple mail transfer protocol (SMTP). A different protocol, as we shall see later, is used to retrieve mail from a mailbox.

The format of e-mail messages is structured according to the standard RFC 822. The key idea is the distinction between the envelope of the message and what the envelope contains. The envelope encapsulates the message and contains the necessary information for transporting the message, such as the destination address, the priority of the message and so on. The MTAs use the envelope for routing, just as a postal service does with physical mail. The message content inside the envelope has two parts: the header, which contains control information for the user agents, and the envelope where the actual, meaningful message is placed.

A full e-mail message is shown in Fig. 7.21. The user does not normally see as many details as this. The forward path, which follows the SMTP command TO, is used to route the message to the destination. Note that a return path is also specified. This can be used to let the sender know that the message has arrived at the destination, to send any error messages to the sender and for the recipient to send a reply. The maximum message size for SMTP is only 64 K. In the example shown in Fig. 7.21, ESMTP (Extended SMTP, which allows much longer messages than normal SMTP) is used.

Fig. 7.22 E-mail client DNS request

7.6.2.1 Multipurpose Internet Mail Extensions

E-mail messages may be ASCII plain text, but sometimes we wish to send an attachment. There is a large variety of potential types of attachment, for example, a spreadsheet, a piece of music, a picture or a video. We need a standard way of encoding and decoding attachments that will be used at both ends of the communication. The commonest standard for e-mail attachments is Multipurpose Internet Mail Extensions (MIME). MIME also allows messages in languages that have different character sets from English, for example, Arabic and Chinese. The commonest standard method for encoding binary messages is Base64. In the Base64 scheme, groups of 24 bits (3 bytes) are broken up into four 6-bit units. Each of these units is sent over the network as an ASCII character. MIME file formats (MIME *types*) are also used by Web servers and Web browsers.

7.6.2.2 Use of DNS for E-mail

The DNS was explained in Sect. 7.2. It is crucial to the operation of an e-mail system, as a DNS server is needed to translate domain names to IP addresses. When the e-mail client sends a message, it has to ask a DNS server to find out what is the IP address that corresponds to the domain name part of the recipient's address. First, the local DNS server is queried (see Fig. 7.22). If it knows the answer, then it will

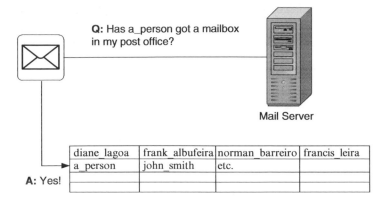

diane_lagoa	frank_albufeira	norman_barreiro	francis_leira
a_person	john_smith	etc.	

Fig. 7.23 Mail server checks for a matching mailbox

give the e-mail client the IP address of the recipient's post office. The message can then be segmented at the transport layer, passed on to the Internet layer (OSI network layer) and encapsulated for transmission. If that server does not know the answer, it may have to ask another DNS server. That server may in turn have to query another, etc.

Up to this point, the part of the e-mail address with the recipient's name has not been used. It now becomes important. The server checks whether the recipient belongs to the post office (Fig. 7.23). If the recipient does not belong, an error message and the original e-mail message are sent back to the sender. If the recipient does belong to the post office, the server stores the message. The e-mail is now ready for the recipient to download it from the server.

7.6.3 Fetching the E-mail from the Server

Now that the e-mail message has been transferred to the recipient's mailbox, the second stage of the e-mailing process can take place. The recipient can check whether there is a message in the mailbox, and if so, download it. The recipient's e-mail client asks the server whether there is any mail to download. To do this, it uses the post office address that was entered when the e-mail client was configured (see Fig. 7.24 for an example of an e-mail client configuration screen).

There has to be another DNS query to find the mail server's IP address. When the IP address has been discovered, the request to the mail server is divided into segments at the transport layer, put into IP packets at the Internet layer and finally encapsulated and sent over the Internet to the mail server. At the mail server, the packets comprising the request are put back together again in the correct order and checks for errors are carried out. The mail server then examines the request. If everything about the request is OK, it sends all of the recipient's e-mail messages to him or her. When an e-mail message arrives at the recipient's computer, it can be read. If the recipient replies to a message or forwards it, the whole sequence described above is repeated.

Fig. 7.24 Configuring an e-mail client

7.6.3.1 Protocols for Retrieving Mail

Post Office Protocol (POP) has been the most frequently used protocol for retrieving mail. POP allows users to connect to a mail server and download messages. POP version 3 (POP3) is the most recent version. The description of fetching e-mail from a server given above assumes the use of POP3.

The *Internet Message Access Protocol* (IMAP) is an alternative, rather more complex and more powerful, protocol to POP3. IMAP version 4 revision 1 (IMAP4rev1) is the latest version. IMAP provides the same service as POP3 but with a number of important improvements. It allows proper, secure authentication mechanisms, whereas POP3 is very insecure. IMAP allows multiple mailboxes to be managed at the same time and allows multiple mail commands to be executed concurrently, among other advantages. When IMAP is in use, the e-mail messages stay on the mail server. Users of IMAP are able to access and manipulate messages on the

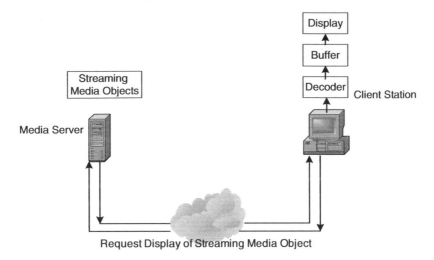

Fig. 7.25 Interaction of streaming media client and server

server remotely, whereas POP3 users have to download messages from the server to their own computer.

Web browser-based e-mail offers a third way of retrieving e-mail. With Web mail, HTTP is the protocol used to view messages, rather than POP or IMAP. HTTP is even used for sending messages as far as the mail server (beyond that point SMTP is used to send e-mail). The great advantage of this system is that mail can be checked from any Web browser anywhere. It is especially useful for mobile devices.

7.7   Delivery of Streamed Content over the Internet

From a technical point of view, delivering audio or video information over the Internet in timely fashion is a challenging problem. TCP/IP was not designed to perform such a feat, yet it has been adapted to do so with remarkable success. In this section, two different kinds of streamed content are considered: streaming audio and VoIP.

7.7.1   Streaming Audio

If an entire file had to be downloaded before it could be played, this might involve a long wait. Streaming audio avoids such a delay. The streaming client is a *media player*, for example, Winamp, RealPlayer or Microsoft® Windows® Media Player. The server is often a specialised *media server*, which is optimised to perform such a function. Real-time streaming protocol (RTSP), described in RFC 2326, is often used to control the delivery of streamed data over a network. It emulates the kind of commands that are used to control a CD or DVD player, for example, Play, Fast-forward, Fast-rewind, Pause and Stop. The interaction of client and server is shown in Fig. 7.25. The user selects a song to play by clicking on its title and a *metafile* is downloaded. The metafile carries just the name of the song and its location, for example, 'http://www.luvlymusik.com/audio/trk257k.rm'. The music starts playing even though only part of the file has been downloaded.

The music is usually transmitted by means of the real-time transport protocol (RTP), which is described in RFC 1889. RTP normally runs over UDP and offers neither error correction nor flow control. TCP, a connection-oriented protocol, would be unsuitable for streaming because it is too slow. RTP is designed to support multicasting of real-time data, but it can also be used for unicasting (communicating with a single receiver). RTP provides timestamping and sequence numbers, which allow samples to be played back at the destination in the right order, even if they arrive out of order. Timestamping also facilitates synchronisation of multiple streams, for example, an audio and a video stream that belong to the same Moving Picture Experts Group (MPEG) file. A payload type identifier indicates the format of the payload and the encoding algorithm, for example, MPEG-1 audio layer 3 (MP3). The receiving application can use this identifier to decide how to play the data. RTP can also be used for VoIP and video on demand. Secure RTP (SRTP) can be used to protect VoIP communications. It gives message authentication and confidentiality (see Chap. 8 for explanations of these terms), as well as a certain degree of protection against some forms of attack. RTP control protocol (RTCP) is a special control protocol, which works together with RTP.

7.7.2   Voice over IP

The terms VoIP and IP telephony are used to describe the employment of IP networks to carry voice traffic. The aims of VoIP are to save money and to facilitate *unified communications* (UC). Money is saved because circuits can be used more efficiently than when separate circuits are used for voice and data. Management costs are lower because users themselves can manage any moves, additions or changes that happen at a site. UC makes communications more efficient, which should lead to greater customer satisfaction. Without UC, for example, a customer contacting somebody at a company might send an e-mail and then make a call from either a mobile or a fixed-line phone. With UC, the various media are combined, and the customer needs to make only one call.

RTP is used over UDP and IP to transport encoded audio information between IP phones. Unfortunately, there are several contending protocol standards for call set-up and call management. There is not sufficient space here to consider all of these, so we shall concentrate on just one, session initiation protocol (SIP).

SIP is a TCP/IP application-layer protocol, which is described in RFC 3261. It is designed to work with other TCP/IP protocols, for example, RTP, UDP and IP. SIP can establish, modify and end multimedia sessions, including VoIP calls. SIP is responsible for establishing the IP addresses and port numbers that end systems use for sending/receiving data. The six core SIP methods are shown in Table 7.3.

For VoIP sessions, SIP works as follows. Callers and callees are identified by SIP addresses, which are URLs such as 'sip: 3221@staffs.ac.uk'. A SIP caller first locates a server and then sends a SIP request (an invitation). A SIP request may

Table 7.3 Core SIP methods

Method	Description
INVITE	Request that a session be created
ACK	Acknowledge that a session has been created
BYE	Request that a session be terminated
CANCEL	Cancel a request that is pending
REGISTER	Register a user's location (URL)
OPTIONS	Query a host to find out its capabilities

Fig. 7.26 Interaction between a SIP server and clients

reach the callee directly. Otherwise, it may be redirected or may start off a chain of new SIP requests, which are carried out by proxy servers (intermediary systems involved in call set-up). Users are able to register their location with SIP location servers. Interaction between a SIP server and clients is illustrated in Fig. 7.26.

7.8   P2P File Sharing

We first encountered the term *peer-to-peer* LAN in Sect. 4.1.1. This term is also used to refer to a system that allows people to transfer files over the Internet without a central server. By the end of 2004, 60% of the traffic on the Internet was P2P. P2P is often used for software distribution. Users who have downloaded a file can make it available for others to download from their own computer. Files are broken up into pieces, and the pieces can be downloaded from different places at the same time. If one host goes down, the file will still be able to be downloaded from other places. BitTorrent is an example of a P2P system. Unfortunately, P2P has also been used to transfer illegal copies of songs, films and so on. As a result, several P2P networks were shut down.

7.9   Instant Messaging

Communication by e-mail is not fast enough in all situations. One problem with e-mail is that when a message is sent out the sender cannot tell whether the addressee is on-line. Thus, the sender cannot tell how soon the message is likely to be received and replied to. IM systems allow users to maintain a list of people with whom they can exchange instant messages. There are several proprietary IM systems. Pidgin (formerly called Gaim) is free software that supports several systems (http://pidgin. im/pidgin/home/).

All IM systems work in roughly the same way. IM client software allows a service user to connect to the IM server and log in. The client sends the host computer's IP address and the port number that the client is using to the server. The server creates a file that contains this information as well as a list of *contacts* (or *buddies*). Having created the contact list, the server finds out whether any of our user's contacts are logged in. If it finds any, it sends the details to the IM client. The IM client can now present to the service user a list of all the contacts who are logged in. When the user clicks on the name of any contact that is shown as being on-line, he or she can send a message directly to the contact's computer, on a P2P basis, without the server's being involved.

7.10   Microblogging

A blog (formed from the words 'Web' and 'log') is a diary that is published on the World Wide Web. It often contains an individual's personal opinions and recounts events that have happened to him or her. Alternatively, the blog might contain information about a subject that the writer is interested in. Often, links to other sites are included. The blog is normally updated frequently.

As the name would suggest, a microblog is a very small blog. Microblog posts are restricted to a limited number of words. Twitter is an example of a microblogging site. Other social networking sites such as Facebook include a microblogging element termed 'status updates'. Social networking has supplanted e-mail for many people, particularly younger people. That is why social networks have become a major target for cybercriminals (see Sects. 8.12 and 8.14).

7.11   Summary

This chapter has looked at the application layer of TCP/IP-based networks. The chapter started with an explanation of client–server technology, which underlies most Internet activities. The following applications were examined in turn: the DNS, the World Wide Web, remote access, file transfer, e-mail, the delivery of streamed content over the Internet and VoIP. The main protocols for each of these applications were discussed. The chapter ended with brief descriptions of P2P file sharing, instant messaging and microblogging.

7.12   Questions

1. (a) Table 7.1 gives some examples of *top-level domains*. Find out some more examples of such domains by researching on the Internet and/or in books.

(b) Find out some more examples of *two-letter, country code top-level domains*, in addition to the examples given in Sect. 7.2.1.

2. (a) What is the difference between Internet *names* and Internet *addresses*?
   (b) Give an example of both.
   (c) How are names translated to addresses?

3. Find out what a *URI* is (not mentioned in this text). How does it differ from a *URL*?

4. The HTTP commands GET and POST were mentioned in Sect. 7.3.4. Find out what other HTTP commands exist and what their purpose is.

5. Look at the explanation of the encapsulation procedure for the Telnet protocol given in Sect. 7.4.1. Write down the encapsulation steps involved in transferring a file using *FTP*.

6. FileZilla, a free FTP client program, was mentioned in Sect. 7.5. Find out about alternative FTP client software.

7. What are *SMTP*, *POP3* and *IMAP* for?

8. Research the e-mail RFC 1939 (which describes POP3) and RFC 2060 (which describes IMAP) on the Internet and/or in books. Find out how many commands have the same name in the two standards.

9. Rashid Rasool Khan (e-mail address = Rashid_Rasool@mymail.com) is sending an e-mail message to Yiorgos Zacharias (e-mail address = Yiorgos_Zacharias@amblecote.com). The message has a graphics image attached (car.jpeg). Yiorgos Zacharias uses POP3 to access his e-mail account.
   The following information is also known:
   Rashid Rasool Khan's host address = 128.1.0.5
   Rashid Rasool Khan's default gateway address = 128.1.0.254
   Rashid Rasool Khan's DNS server address = 128.2.0.254
   Rashid Rasool Khan's mail server = mail.mymail.com
   Yiorgos Zacharias's host address = 192.4.5.6
   Yiorgos Zacharias's default gateway address = 192.4.5.254
   Yiorgos Zacharias's e-mail server = mail.amblecote.com
   Yiorgos Zacharias's DNS server address = 192.4.6.6
   Yiorgos Zacharias's POP3 username = Yiorgos_Zacharias
   Yiorgos Zacharias's password = 76!p4ab
   DNS table:
   mail.mymail.com 128.2.0.100
   mail.amblecote.com 192.4.8.100
   For this transaction, answer the following:
   (a) List and describe in brief all the protocol interactions (packet by packet) between Rashid Rasool Khan's computer and the network when sending the mail message.
   (b) List and describe in brief all the protocol interactions (packet by packet) between Yiorgos Zacharias's computer and the network when he downloads the message.

(c)   Describe the internal format of the message.
(NB: Remember to include packets from the following protocols: ARP, DNS, IP, TCP, POP3, SMTP and MIME.)

10. Why does the *real-time transport protocol (RTP)* offer neither error correction nor flow control?

11. Find out what the *common channel signalling system no. 7 (SS7)* protocol is for.

Network Security

8

Abstract

Network security is one of the tasks of network management, other aspects of which we deal with in the next chapter. However, network security is such an important issue that this chapter is devoted to it. The chapter starts with an explanation of several important security concepts and gives some security techniques related to these concepts. We examine the following aspects of network security in turn: virtual private networks (VPNs); firewalls; intrusion detection, intrusion prevention and unified threat management systems; various kinds of attacks that may be made on networks; viruses, worms and Trojan horses; rootkits; spam e-mail; spyware; phishing; social engineering; dynamic Web links; and physical security. Wireless networks receive detailed coverage in Chap. 10, but there is a section on wireless LAN security in this chapter. Finally, we consider the security of mobile devices.

8.1 Authentication, Authorisation, Confidentiality, Non-repudiation and Integrity

Unfortunately, distributed enterprise networks are much easier to attack than the centralised mainframe computers that preceded them. Five important issues in network security are authentication, authorisation, confidentiality, non-repudiation and integrity. We shall now examine these concepts one by one.

8.1.1 Authentication

Authentication (checking that someone or something is who or what he/she/it claims to be) is often done via a password. Unfortunately, passwords are not very secure. They can be guessed or stolen. Many people are unwise in their choice of password, using the word 'password' or the name of a member of their family as their password.

J. Cowley, *Communications and Networking: An Introduction*, Undergraduate Topics in Computer Science, DOI 10.1007/978-1-4471-4357-4_8,
© Springer-Verlag London 2012

Fig. 8.1 Time-synchronous authentication

Users even write down their passwords on Post-it® notes and stick them round the edge of their computer monitor. It is only necessary to have a single compromised password for a network to be rendered insecure. Certain TCP/IP application-layer protocols, such as Telnet (a terminal emulation protocol) and file transfer protocol (FTP), send the user's password across the network in the clear. 'Sniffer' programs can be used to capture these passwords easily.

A safer form of authentication is to use an intelligent token that generates a one-time password. This password is transmitted to a secure server that verifies it and allows the user to log in. Intelligent tokens are commonly used in Internet banking. There are two forms of intelligent token: time synchronous and challenge response. In a time-synchronous system, the token and the server have to be synchronised. A random number is generated roughly once per minute by both the server and the token. To log into a server, a user has to enter a personal identification number (PIN) plus the random number that the token is displaying. This is an example of *two-factor authentication*. Users have to combine something they have (the token) with something they know (their PIN number). The time-synchronous scheme is illustrated in Fig. 8.1.

In a challenge–response system, users have to supply an encrypted number that is the same as the one that the server has generated. Hardware tokens are in plan view about the same size as a credit card but are thicker. They can be either hand-held or designed to plug into a computer. Software tokens are easier to crack. The challenge–response scheme is illustrated in Fig. 8.2. Encryption is explained in Sect. 8.1.3.

Another approach to authentication uses *biometrics*. The idea here is to use something that you *are* for authentication. In other words, you use one of your physical characteristics such as your fingerprint or the pattern of the iris (the coloured part) of the eye. This can be used as one of the factors in a two-factor authentication system.

Fig. 8.2 Challenge–response authentication

One advantage of a biometric system is that users cannot forget their fingerprint or eye. The same is not true of a password, unfortunately. A disadvantage of biometric systems is that they tend to be rather expensive if deployed in large numbers.

8.1.2   Authorisation

Authorisation allows administrators to control who can have access to which network resources. For example, the sales department will be prevented from accessing the payroll records. *Secure single sign-on* lets users log into the network only once and thus get access to all the resources that they are allowed to use. Inevitably, this will involve a rather complex system. Without single sign-on, however, there is a large administrative load. The administrator will have to monitor the security mechanisms used by every piece of software that is being used on the enterprise network. Single sign-on systems can be either workstation based or server based.

Kerberos is an example of a server-based system. It is named after the three-headed dog that guarded the entrance to Hades, according to Ancient Greek mythology. It is free but there are also commercial versions. It is a flexible and extensible system. A full explanation of Kerberos is beyond the scope of this book, but here is a brief sketch. Kerberos has three parts: the client software, the authentication server computer (or security server) and the application server. The authentication server computer keeps the database of encrypted user identities. It is kept in a secure location. The application server (software) usually runs on the same computer as the application to which access is being allowed. Before a user is allowed to access an application, there are exchanges between the client computer and the security server computer and between the client and the application server. The client is given an encrypted *ticket*. This authenticates the client as an authorised user and it is able to get access

Fig. 8.3 Kerberos

Client

Authentication Server in Secure Location

Application Server

to authorised applications using the ticket. A very important point about Kerberos is that no passwords are sent over the network. This makes Kerberos very secure. Kerberos is illustrated in Fig. 8.3.

8.1.3   Confidentiality

Encryption is used to make sure that the information that is sent over a network can be read or altered only by authorised users. Encryption is performed by an encryption algorithm, which scrambles the data so that it cannot be read when it is travelling over the network. The encryption process turns the *plaintext* (the message in its initial form) into the *ciphertext* (the scrambled form of the message). A *key* (a value) is used to encode and decode a message. The encryption/decryption algorithm applies the key to the data.

Secret-key encryption (also known as private-key or symmetrical encryption) uses the same mathematical key for encryption and decryption. Secret-key encryption is illustrated in Fig. 8.4. The main advantage of secret-key encryption is that it is fast.

The key must be kept secret, which poses a problem. For how are we to transport the key from one place to the other, so that both ends can share it? We cannot simply pass it over the insecure network; it must be distributed 'out of band' instead. For example, we could hand it over face to face on a USB flash drive or send it by motorcycle courier. However, these methods will not work if we want to have secure communications from one side of the world to the other. The Advanced Encryption Standard (AES) is an example of a secret-key algorithm. This algorithm performs permutations and substitutions to transform the plaintext into the ciphertext. Permutations are rearrangements of the data; substitutions replace one piece of data with another.

Fig. 8.4 Secret-key encryption

Fig. 8.5 Public-key encryption

In *public-key encryption*, different keys are used for encryption and decryption. The encryption key is made available to everybody, whereas the decryption key is kept secret. Public-key encryption is illustrated in Fig. 8.5. For some reason, typical users of encryption systems are always called Alice and Bob. We shall follow that convention in this book. In Fig. 8.5, we see that Alice wants to send a message to

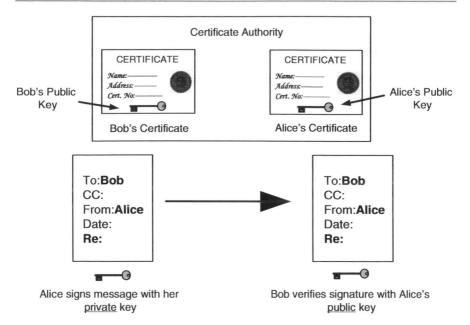

Fig. 8.6 Digital signature

Bob. She encrypts the message with Bob's public key, which is freely available to anybody who needs to use it. When Bob receives the message, he decrypts it with his private key, which only he possesses.

Public-key encryption is possible because the private and public keys are mathematically related. However, they are related in such a way that it is computationally infeasible to try to derive the one from the other, especially if long keys are used. It would take so long, even with a supercomputer, that it is just not worth attempting.

Public-key encryption may be supported by a public-key infrastructure (PKI). The PKI is the legal, organisational and technical framework that is used to support public-key cryptography. It provides a *digital certificate*, which contains the user's public key that has been digitally signed plus some other information. This signing guarantees the identity of the owner of the certificate. Without digital certificates, somebody could compromise the security of the public-key system by making available a false public key for a certain user. A *certificate authority* (CA) does the digital signing. There is a hierarchy of CAs. The root CA allows the authentication of individuals, organisations or other CAs. We see an explanation of digital signatures in Fig. 8.6. Alice wants to prove to Bob that the message that she is sending him is really from her. She signs the message with her private key. Bob uses Alice's public key to decrypt Alice's signature.

When the Secure Sockets Layer (SSL) protocol is in use for a secure Internet connection, an icon depicting a locked yellow padlock such as the one shown in Fig. 8.7 appears in the bottom right-hand corner of the Web browser window. (SSL is covered in Sect. 8.2.2.) If this yellow padlock is visible, then a digital certificate

Fig. 8.7 SSL padlock

Green Area in
Address Bar

Fig. 8.8 Green site identity button

that was signed by a CA somewhere on the Internet was almost certainly used to create the secure connection. The Web browser gets the digital certificate from the website and then checks if it is still valid by asking the CA about it. It checks whether the certificate has expired, whether the CA that issued it is genuine and so on. All that the user needs to know about this is whether he or she can see the yellow padlock. If the locked padlock can be seen, the connection is secure.

If the left-hand portion of the address bar (site identity button) has turned green, this indicates that Extended Validation SSL (EV SSL) encryption is present. This shows not only that the session is encrypted but also that the business behind the site is authenticated. An example is shown in Fig. 8.8.

We saw earlier that secret-key encryption is fast. Public-key encryption is slower but more secure than secret-key encryption. A common arrangement is to use public-key encryption to get a message containing an encrypted secret key from one side to the other. Once the secret key has been received, it can be used by both parties in the communication. This is more efficient than using public-key encryption only.

8.1.4   Message Digests

Digital signatures are produced by encrypting a *message digest* with a private key. The message digest is first created by means of a *one-way hash function*. The input to the hash algorithm is a long message. The output is a short value, the hash. The hash is called 'one way' because it is supposed to be as good as impossible for somebody who possesses only the hash value to turn it back into the original message.

Fig. 8.9 Use of message digest

Only the hash is used for a digital signature, not the complete message. Both the message and the digital signature are transmitted. The receiver applies the same hash function algorithm to the message as the sender used. If the result is the same as the value in the digital signature, the digital signature is considered to be valid. This is proof that the message has not been tampered with and that the sender is authentic. The use of a message digest is illustrated in Fig. 8.9.

8.1.5   Non-repudiation

Non-repudiation means preventing either the sender or the receiver of a message from denying that a message has been sent. One way of providing non-repudiation is to use a trusted third-party system usually called a *notary service*. The message is sent to the receiver via the notary service. A secure hash of the message is calculated. This secure hash is then passed to the notary service, which timestamps the message and keeps a copy of the secure hash. A notary service is illustrated in Fig. 8.10.

8.1.6   Message Integrity

We also need to be able to prove that the message has not been altered in transit. A digital signature can provide such proof.

8.1.7   Security Policy

A *security policy* is a document that gives rules for access, states how policies are enforced and explains the basic architecture of a security environment. It is usually

Fig. 8.10 Notary service

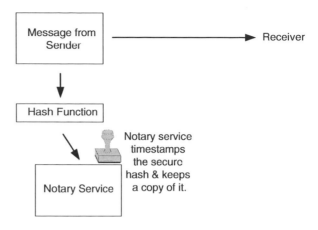

Table 8.1 Items that all security policies should cover

Item	Explanation
Identification and authentication	Employ passwords or other methods to ensure that users are authorised
Access control	Stop users reaching what they are not permitted to access, unless this is expressly allowed
Accountability	Make all activity on the network linked to a user identity
Audit trails	Keep an audit trail to help find out where and when there has been a breach of security
Object reuse	Make secure any resource that can be accessed by more than one user
Accuracy	Prevent security breaches happening by accident
Reliability	Prevent users monopolising resources
Data exchange	Ensure that all communications are secure

several pages long and written by a committee. The policy will give guidelines on such items as passwords, encryption, e-mail attachments, firewalls and so on. It must be easy to understand and stick to or users will ignore it. Templates for writing security policies are available. The IETF has even devised a special language, security policy specification language (SPSL), for writing security policies. A list of the items that all security policies should cover is given in Table 8.1.

8.2 Virtual Private Networks

Frame relay-based VPNs were mentioned in Sect. 5.3. However, other technologies are also used to provide VPNs. A VPN is a private, secure data network which runs over a public network, for example, the Internet. Only the communicating parties can read the data. The privacy results from security procedures of various kinds. VPNs can be classified into three types. A remote-access VPN lets home workers gain secure access to their company's network. A site-to-site VPN connects remote

Fig. 8.11 VPN

offices over the Internet. An extranet VPN allows a business to share some of its data with its partners, its suppliers, its customers and other businesses.

Figure 8.11 shows a VPN consisting of a secure, encrypted *tunnel* through the Internet. The tunnelling protocol encapsulates the data inside an additional header. This additional header contains sufficient routing information for the encapsulated packet to get through the Internet. When these packets reach the final point on the Internet, they are then decapsulated and sent on to their ultimate destination.

Non-IP-based VPNs, which use such technologies as leased lines, frame relay or ATM, can offer very high levels of quality of service (QoS). Obtaining the same levels of QoS is more difficult over the Internet, but IP-based VPNs can be just as secure and tend to be cheaper. The protocols in use for IP-based VPNs include IP security (IPSec), MPLS and secure sockets layer (SSL)/transport layer security (TLS). Since MPLS has already been covered in Sect. 6.4, we shall concentrate here on IPSec and SSL.

8.2.1 IP Security Protocol

IPSec (first mentioned in Sect. 6.1.7) is a framework of open security standards that was developed by the IETF. It allows data to be transmitted securely over public IP-based networks such as the Internet. IPSec protects IP datagrams that are being sent between network devices such as PCs, routers and firewalls. It provides confidentiality through the use of a standard encryption algorithm such as AES. IPSec provides integrity by means of a standard one-way secure hash algorithm. It also provides authentication via digital certificates.

IPSec can run on a router, a firewall or a VPN client machine depending on the particular situation. It uses two optional IP packet headers. The authentication header (AH) supports authentication and data integrity. The encapsulating security payload (ESP) offers privacy via encryption. ESP can also encapsulate the IP packet,

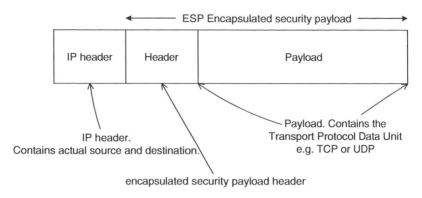

Fig. 8.12 IPSec transport mode

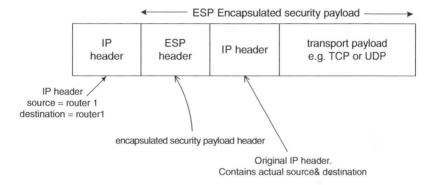

Fig. 8.13 IPSec tunnel mode

if desired. These two headers can be used either together or separately, depending on the functionality that the application needs. Internet Key Exchange (IKE) looks after transferring encryption keys. IPSec can work in transport mode or tunnel mode. In transport mode, routers use the original IP header, and so only layers higher than IP are protected, for example, TCP and UDP. In tunnel mode, the whole source packet, including the original header, is authenticated and encrypted and is given a new IP header. While the packet is traversing the Internet, both the source and the destination are kept secret. Transport mode is illustrated in Fig. 8.12. Tunnel mode is illustrated in Fig. 8.13.

8.2.2   SSL/TLS-Based VPNs

SSL/TLS-based VPNs are much simpler than IPSec. No special client software is necessary because all standard Web browsers and Web servers support this way of providing a VPN. SSL is a set of proprietary protocols that run on top of TCP. These provide encryption, authentication and integrity. The application runs above

SSL Handshake Protocol	SSL Change Cipher Spec Protocol	SSL Alert Protocol	HTTP	Other Application Layer Protocols
SSL Record Protocol				
TCP				
IP				

Fig. 8.14 SSL architecture

SSL. In OSI terms, SSL is at the session layer. Unlike IPSec, SSL encrypts only the application-layer data. TLS, an IETF open standard, is based on SSL and closely resembles it.

Normally, we access a Web page by specifying the HyperText Transfer Protocol (HTTP). So if, for example, we want to reach the IETF, we type into the browser's location bar 'http://www.ietf.org/'. If, on the other hand, we want to use SSL, instead of 'http' we type 'https'. This indicates that the data is going to have to be transferred using SSL (or TLS) via TCP Port 443 (rather than the standard HTTP Port 80).

SSL consists of two layers of protocols. The SSL record protocol provides security services for HTTP, among other TCP/IP application-layer protocols. It divides the application data into blocks of up to 16,384 bytes and encrypts it. Three SSL protocols work at the same level as HTTP: the handshake protocol, the change cipher spec protocol and the alert protocol. The SSL architecture is illustrated in Fig. 8.14. The handshake protocol negotiates various parameters to be used in the session and authenticates the remote machine. The change cipher spec protocol and the alert protocol are used during the session.

The sequence of events when SSL is in use is as follows. First of all, a TCP connection is set up between the client and the server on Port 443 using the normal three-way handshake. The client then sends a Hello message, which contains information about cipher suites that it knows about. The server responds to this with its own Hello message, which says which cipher suite will be used. The server next gives the client a copy of its certificate, which includes its public encryption key. It then sends a Hello Done message to the client. All exchanges up to this point are in clear text.

Now the client generates a secret session key, which it encrypts with the server's public key, and sends it to the server. This process is called the client key exchange. From this point on, everything that is sent is encrypted. The client sends a change cipher spec message to reconfirm which cipher suite (set of ciphers and keys) is going to be used. Each side next sends a Finished message showing that the SSL handshake is complete. A secure, encrypted tunnel has now been set up. This uses the secret key that has been negotiated. TLS works in a similar fashion.

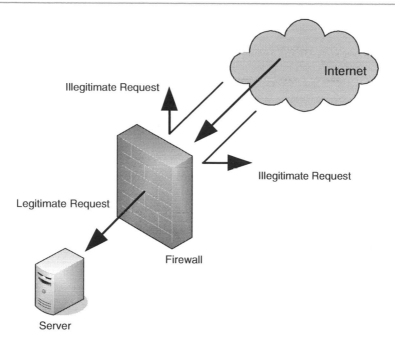

Fig. 8.15 Firewall

8.3 Firewalls

In cars, there is a barrier that stops fire spreading from the engine to the passenger compartment. This barrier is known as a *firewall*. In computer networks, firewalls protect vulnerable devices. They can be positioned between the internal network and the Web server computer or between the Web server computer and the Internet. Firewalls can be set up to control what traffic is permitted to leave the internal network, as well as what comes into it. They can be software only or a software/hardware combination. The capabilities of firewalls vary but all types protect a private network from intruders by controlling access to it. Many firewalls can hide the network addresses of individual users so that nobody from outside can find out what these are (that is, they have a NAT capability). They can log all traffic and can report suspicious events. Many firewalls can perform authentication on users. They may encrypt transmissions. Figure 8.15 shows how a firewall protects a server by refusing unwanted requests but letting through wanted requests.

A port on a firewall is sometimes used to provide a *demilitarised zone* (DMZ). The DMZ contains a device that must be accessible from the Internet. This device is usually a server computer of some kind, for example, a Web, FTP, mail or DNS server. The firewall offers the device or devices in the DMZ limited protection from attack but completely closes off the organisation's internal network from the Internet. A DMZ is illustrated in Fig. 8.16. An attacker could break into the Web server but

Fig. 8.16 Demilitarised zone

not into the trusted internal network. The use of the term 'DMZ' in this context derives from its use to describe a military buffer zone such as the one that was established between North and South Korea in 1948.

8.3.1 Packet-Filtering Firewall

The most basic kind of firewall is a packet-filtering firewall. Packet filtering is a task that routers can perform. Certain IP addresses, subnets or transport layer (TCP or UDP) port numbers can be blocked. This is done with an *access control list*. An access control list disallows all traffic that is not explicitly permitted. Here is an example of a router access control list.

access-list 1 permit 192.168.4.0 0.0.0.255

access-list 1 deny any

   The router interface to which this access list is applied will allow all incoming traffic from the 192.168.4.0 network but no other traffic. The group of dotted decimal

Fig. 8.17 Packet spoofing

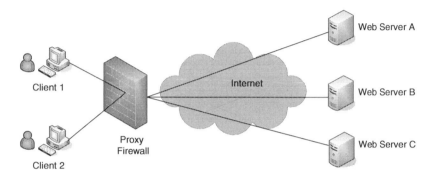

Fig. 8.18 Proxy firewall

numbers that follows the IP address looks something like a subnet mask, but it actually works in a different way. Called a *wildcard mask*, its bits indicate how the router should check the corresponding address bits. A zero means check; a one means ignore. In binary, the wildcard in the above access list is 00000000.00000000.0000 0000.11111111. This means that the router will ignore the host part of the address and will check only the bits in the first three octets.

Intruders are able to trick a packet-filtering firewall by *packet spoofing*. This involves constructing a packet with a false sender address. So other procedures in addition to packet filtering are needed. Packet spoofing is illustrated in Fig. 8.17.

8.3.2 Application Proxy Firewall

An application proxy firewall prevents network traffic from passing directly between external and internal networks. A client on one side of the firewall sets up a connection with the firewall. The firewall sets up a connection with the server on the other side. It acts on behalf of the client. The client believes that the proxy is the server; the server believes that the proxy is the client. A proxy firewall is shown in Fig. 8.18. Web server A, for example, thinks that it is communicating directly with client 1 and vice versa. In reality, as we can see, the proxy is pretending to be both the server and the client.

The proxy can inspect the data and check that a packet that is being sent out to the Web server really is an HTTP packet, as it is supposed to be. It can also check that the person who is sitting at the client machine is allowed to be surfing the Web. An application proxy firewall is so called because it has to be able to understand application-layer protocols, such as HTTP. The firewall needs a proxy for every protocol that it has to deal with.

8.3.3 Stateful Inspection Firewall

A third kind of firewall, the stateful inspection firewall, looks at the packets that come into it, as a packet-filtering firewall does. However, it goes further in that it can remember the port numbers that the connections use. When a connection closes, the firewall closes the port that it was using. It can do this because it has in memory a table where it keeps information about the connections. It inspects packets at all communication layers, looking at the bit patterns and comparing these to trusted packets. Typically, the stateful inspection firewall will pass all packets from the trusted network to the untrusted network by default. But it will deny all packets that are coming in from the untrusted network unless they are responding to outgoing traffic. A stateful inspection firewall is more complex than packet-filtering and application proxy firewalls.

8.3.4 Application Firewall

An application firewall is one that recognises applications, irrespective of the ports or protocols that they use. It knows exactly what the application's traffic ought to look like and is able to block any traffic that deviates from that pattern. This makes it capable of offering more features than other types of firewall, including the stateful inspection firewall. These additional features include URL filtering and malware scanning. However, the features that are desirable in a firewall will depend on what is required to put the company's security policy into practice.

8.4   Intrusion Detection and Prevention Systems

8.4.1 Intrusion Detection Systems

Intrusion detection systems (IDSs) monitor computer systems for suspected attempts at intrusion. They give an alarm if they detect anything untoward. IDSs can be network based or host based. In a *network-based IDS,* a sensor is placed on each network segment. This monitors all traffic on the segment. A central intrusion detection engine usually receives data from the remote sensors. This can log events and give alarms. Figure 8.19 shows a network-based IDS. As the name suggests, a *host-based IDS* is mounted on a host computer.

Fig. 8.19 Network-based IDS

Some IDSs look for specific events, while others look for changing patterns. An example of a sequence of events that might trigger an alarm is several failed attempts in a row at logging in. A system such as this depends on having a recently updated database of attack patterns. If an event is not in the database, there will be no alarm. An IDS that looks for changes in patterns is able to detect previously unknown forms of attack. It does not depend on a database of attack signatures. An example of a change of pattern is somebody logging into the network in the early hours of the morning, whereas previously this person has only ever logged in during standard working hours.

8.4.2 Intrusion Prevention Systems

An intrusion prevention system (IPS) is shown in Fig. 8.20. Unlike an intrusion detection system, an intrusion prevention system can respond so fast to an intrusion attempt that it can automatically block it. Rather than simply alert an administrator while the attempt at intrusion continues, the IPS responds automatically to attacks.

IPSs possess several advantages over IDSs. Because IPSs can block intrusion attempts in real time, any network downtime that is due to such attacks is reduced to a minimum. An IPS's active prevention system means that security costs and loss of data are reduced. Unfortunately, IPSs have the disadvantage that they can cause network performance to drop because of the amount of processing that they have to do before network traffic is allowed to pass through them. This is particularly true

Fig. 8.20 Intrusion prevention
system

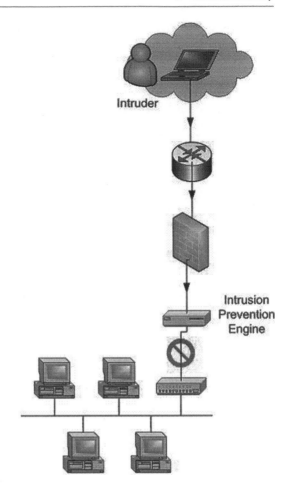

when an IPS has to deal with encrypted traffic, for example, in a VPN. IPSs alone
cannot be relied upon to stop every kind of attack, so they need to be used in combination with other defences.

One problem that bedevils both IDSs and IPSs is that of *false positives*. In other
words, the system identifies as suspicious activity that is totally innocent in reality.
This defect can be surmounted by using more than one detection method simultaneously. It is particularly important that an IPS gives accurate results, because false positives may block legitimate network activity. If too many of these occurred, they would
cause an organisation to lose business and would make users lose faith in the system.

8.5   Unified Threat Management

Unified threat management (UTM) systems integrate multiple security functions.
There is only one management console, so security threats can be dealt with from
one place. UTM systems can replace many separate threat management systems and

can reduce costs. They can offer firewall, intrusion detection/prevention, anti-virus, anti-malware, anti-spam (see Sect. 8.10 for a discussion of spam) and VPN functions in one box. Other features are often included, even routing and switching.

8.6 Denial of Service Attacks

The aim of a denial of service (DOS) attack is to stop an Internet server (usually a Web server) functioning. An attacker sends multiple connection requests so as to use up all the memory in the server computer or cripple its processing power. A variation on this theme is the *distributed denial of service* (DDOS) attack. Here, the attacker remotely installs a hidden program on several computers (often referred to as *zombies* or *bots*—short for 'robots'), unknown to their owners. The attacker then orchestrates a combined attack from all the machines that he or she has infiltrated. There are several types of DOS and DDOS attacks, and in this chapter, we shall discuss only a few of these.

Security is best regarded as a process rather than a finished product. New ways of exploiting vulnerabilities in software are constantly being devised. When a new exploit comes along, a *patch* (a software update) is issued. This often plugs the hole in the software but sometimes has the unfortunate effect of causing more holes. One way or the other, attackers always find new holes and exploit these sooner or later. Some attacks exploit vulnerabilities in operating systems, some take advantage of vulnerabilities in applications and others take advantage of vulnerabilities in people.

8.6.1 Ping of Death/Smurf Attack

The Ping utility program was described in Sect. 6.1.8. An attacker can abuse it by flooding a server computer with Ping packets. The machine is overwhelmed in trying to respond to a huge number of Pings.

The Smurf attack is a variation on the Ping of Death. The attacker does not send the Pings directly to the target device. Instead, the messages are sent out as a broadcast. The packets are forged and contain the source address of the target computer. Intermediary systems that receive these packets then bombard the target with Pings. A Smurf attack is shown in Fig. 8.21. There might be thousands of Pings sent from the bounce site to the victim host.

8.6.2 SYN Flooding Attack

The three-way handshake, which is used to set up a TCP connection, was described in Sect. 6.2.4. The reader will recall that when a TCP client connects to another host, the two ends have to synchronise the connection and exchange initial sequence numbers. In a SYN flooding attack, an attacking source host repeatedly sends forged SYN (SYNchronise) packets to the victim host. The sending address that these SYN packets contain does not exist. So when the victim sends a SYN ACK back to this

Fig. 8.21 Smurf attack

false address, there is never an acknowledgement of the SYN ACK. The result is
many half-open TCP connections, which build up to such a degree that the victim
host's connection queue gets full. At this point the host stops accepting all connection requests, whether legitimate or not. The attack has now crippled it. It could
even run out of memory completely, which would make it crash.

Below is an example of evidence that a SYN flood attack is in progress. The
operating-system command *netstat* (short for 'network statistics') can be used to
display information about TCP/IP network connections. The option being used below
(-n) makes *netstat* display the addresses and port numbers in numerical form.

C:\Users\John > netstat -n

Active connections

Proto	Local address	Foreign address	State
TCP	127.0.0.1:27015	127.0.0.1:49177	ESTABLISHED
TCP	127.0.0.1:49177	127.0.0.1:27015	ESTABLISHED
TCP	127.0.0.1:49522	127.0.0.1:49523	ESTABLISHED
TCP	127.0.0.1:49523	127.0.0.1:49522	ESTABLISHED

Proto	Local address	Foreign address	State
TCP	192.168.1.3:21	10.2.3.85:258	SYN_RECEIVED
TCP	192.168.1.3:21	10.2.3.85:259	SYN_RECEIVED
TCP	192.168.1.3:21	10.2.3.85:260	SYN_RECEIVED
TCP	192.168.1.3:21	10.2.3.85:261	SYN_RECEIVED
TCP	192.168.1.3:21	10.2.3.85:262	SYN_RECEIVED
TCP	192.168.1.3:21	10.2.3.85:263	SYN_RECEIVED
TCP	192.168.1.3:21	10.2.3.85:264	SYN_RECEIVED
TCP	192.168.1.3:21	10.2.3.85:265	SYN_RECEIVED
TCP	192.168.1.3:21	10.2.3.85:266	SYN_RECEIVED

C:\Users\John>

The entries that contain SYN_RECEIVED show that something has gone wrong with a TCP handshake and that the host is trying to contact a computer that cannot be accessed for some reason (it probably does not exist!). There are so many instances of SYN_RECEIVED that it is very likely that a SYN flood attack is happening.

8.6.3 Port Scanning

Port scanning is a method that an attacker can use to find out what TCP or UDP ports are open in a network device or a network. A port scanning tool connects to a series of ports one at a time. The response that the scan elicits shows whether a particular port is in use. The attacker can then focus his or her attack on the ports that have been found to be open and try to exploit any weaknesses to gain access.

8.7 Attacks on Databases via Web Application Servers

Web application servers are connected to databases which contain much information useful to criminals. This makes them popular targets for attack. Two of the methods used are described below.

8.7.1 Buffer Overflow

A buffer overflow attack happens when an attacker deliberately overloads the target system's temporary memory (buffer). Usually, the attacker includes instructions within the data that is used to make the buffer overflow. These instructions can cause the target system to make changes to data held within the database or send information back to the attacker. Buffer overflow attacks can be prevented by careful programming.

8.7.2   SQL Injection (SQLi)

In a SQLi attack, the attacker adds SQL commands to a database query so as to be able to misuse the database. Such an attack takes advantage of faulty input validation on a website. A SQL query is input via a search field in a Web form. The attacker can execute unauthorised database commands on a Web application database server. He or she is able to tamper with the data and steal it, change it or delete it from the database. The attacker might even manage to take total control of the system. One way of preventing SQLi attacks is to keep the logic of a query apart from its data. This will stop the execution of injected SQL commands.

8.8   Preventing Infection by Viruses, Worms and Trojan Horses

A *virus* spreads through networks by making copies of itself. In other words, it is self-replicating code that is attached to another file. A common means of transmission is an e-mail attachment. The exe, bat, pif, scr and cmd file types are particularly dangerous attachments. However, viruses are sometimes spread via removable disks or via download from the Internet. The virus program code runs only if the user opens a file. Once the virus has been activated, it can cause serious damage to the files stored on the computer where it is run. Viruses can carry out such harmful activities as formatting hard disk drives, erasing files, sending out e-mails and making attacks on other computers. The name derives from the way a biological virus attaches itself to a cell. A *polymorphic* virus is one that can change its form automatically, as often as every 20 min or so. This makes it more difficult to detect.

A *worm* spreads itself through networks automatically, copying itself from computer to computer. It is self-replicating code, but unlike a virus, it is not attached to another file. It takes advantage of vulnerabilities in systems. The aim is to infect as many computers as possible and as quickly as possible. The payload carried by worms varies. Worms can participate in DOS attacks, can deface websites and can delete, corrupt or steal data.

A *Trojan horse* hides itself within an apparently legitimate program. It is so named after the wooden horse in which, according to an Ancient Greek legend, Greek soldiers secreted themselves. When their enemies the Trojans brought the horse into their city, the Greek soldiers got out and opened the city gates to let the rest of their army in. A computer-software Trojan horse pretends to be a useful or interesting piece of software but is actually harmful. The gullible user is tricked into installing it. An example of a Trojan horse is a keystroke logger that captures passwords but appears to be an innocent login screen. Keystroke loggers can be defeated by asking the user to supply only part of the password (e.g. the third, fifth, seventh and tenth characters). Another way of combating keystroke loggers is to get the input via mouse clicks instead of the keyboard (the user selects the characters of the password from a menu). A *backdoor* Trojan enables an attacker to gain control of a computer.

8.8.1   Malware

All three of these types of program are *malware* (malicious software). Anti-virus software, as long as it is kept up to date, will help to protect a computer against viruses, worms and Trojan horses. Indeed, keeping *all* software up to date, particularly browser extensions and plug-ins, is an important precaution to take against malware. Common sense on the part of the user is also necessary. For example, it is unwise to open e-mail attachments unless one is sure that they contain nothing harmful. One should use a non-administrator account whenever possible, to limit the damage from malware if it tried to execute on one's PC.

The first malware was written for fun by people who wanted to infect as many computers as they could, simply to impress their peers. Some of this malware was definitely harmful, but attacks were not directed against individuals, just their hardware and their data. More recently, malware has been written by criminals who want to steal bank and credit card details. A further development is that malware has become stealthier. In this kind of attack, often termed an *advanced persistent threat* (APT), the aim is to penetrate a business using a variety of techniques and remain undetected for as long as possible, stealing the business's intellectual property. The information that is stolen is then used by competitors or even by foreign countries. Sometimes malware is used by political activists (*hacktivists*), perhaps to try to discredit the organisation that is being attacked.

8.9   Rootkits

A rootkit is a special form of remote-access Trojan horse. An intruder can use the software tools that a rootkit contains to gain complete control of a remote computer. The owner of the computer remains unaware that this has happened. *Root* is the system administrator in UNIX and UNIX-like operating systems such as Linux. A rootkit is so named because it allows the attacker to become the system administrator of the computer that he or she has infiltrated.

Software for detecting rootkits is available. This looks for hidden additions to files and changes made to the Windows registry (the database of binary files that contains system configuration information on Microsoft® Windows® computers). Unfortunately, the writers of rootkits are constantly refining their products to try to stay one step ahead of the defences against them.

8.10   Spam E-mail

Spam is unsolicited e-mail, much of which is caused by worms and viruses. One weapon that can be used against it is filtering. Filtering software examines the e-mail that comes into an organisation. It applies rules to the e-mail and tries to work out which e-mail is legitimate and which is not. It then filters out the e-mail that it has decided is spam. This filtering may be carried out at the company mail server.

Alternatively, an outside security service can be used to filter the mail before it even reaches the company network.

One kind of filter is a simple blacklist of names or IP addresses of known sources of spam. Another type of filter looks for keywords such as 'Viagra' that often appear in spam e-mail. In *adaptive* (or *Bayesian*) *filtering*, the filter categorises the words that appear in a user's e-mail as positive, negative or neutral. Positive words are those that are normally found in the user's legitimate e-mail. Neutral words are neither associated with the user nor with spam. Negative words are those likely to be found in spam. Unlike the first two methods, adaptive filtering adapts to changes in the nature of the user's e-mail over time. This makes it more effective than simpler types of filtering.

A rather different form of defence against spam is *challenge–response*. This involves a challenge being sent to a new sender of e-mail to confirm that he or she is bona fide. Once the new sender has done this, he or she is put on a *whitelist* of legitimate sources of e-mail. However, if too many users of e-mail in the world were to start using a challenge–response system, the number of messages might overwhelm the system. An alternative strategy would be to levy a small charge for sending an e-mail. The intended effect of this would be to make it too expensive to send spam.

Checking that the source IP address of an e-mail is not forged is another defence against spam. What makes this an effective measure is that spammers (those who produce spam) like to forge the 'from' address in their e-mail. This is done because it makes it difficult to find out who sent the spam. Filters can also be hoodwinked by this means. SMTP is also easily fooled.

Another measure that can be used against spam is signing legitimate e-mail with a digital signature. This also proves the integrity of the message. Sender and recipient both know that messages have not been tampered with en route.

8.11   Spyware

Spyware is software that gathers data about the way in which a computer is used. The program is installed without the user's knowledge and transmits over the Internet the information that it obtains. An example of relatively innocuous spyware is a record of visits to websites that is gathered for marketing purposes. An example of a rather more serious kind of spyware is that which captures personal information like credit card numbers. Anti-spyware software is available. Some anti-spyware programs prevent spyware being installed in the first place. Other programs simply scan for and remove it. Like anti-virus software, anti-spyware software needs to be updated on a regular basis to maintain its effectiveness.

8.12   Phishing

When phishing, a criminal sends out fake e-mails or makes a website that resembles a genuine site. The spoofed site might be an ISP, a bank or an online shop. The criminal is trying to trick people into handing over their access credentials (e.g. passwords) or financial information (e.g. credit card details). The victim might be asked to fill in a survey form to win a reward, which will prove that he or she is human. Phishing attacks sometimes concentrate on non-financial Web accounts, such as social networking sites. Once the attacker has the victim's credentials, he is betting on being able to use them for financial accounts. This is because many people unwisely use the same password for all sites.

Phishing has evolved as people have got more careful about which e-mails they click on. Banks moved on to two-factor log-ins using intelligent tokens like those described in Sect. 8.1.1. EV SSL (described in Sect. 8.1.3) is also of use in combating phishing attacks.

Phishing e-mails used always to be sent out indiscriminately, but criminals have progressed to targeting e-mails deliberately at individuals (termed *spear phishing*). They first try to find out as much information as they can about potential victims by doing Web searches. They then send the chosen victim a plausible e-mail that contains some of the information that they have found out. The victim's guard is down and he or she clicks on a malicious link in the message. Such an exploit that uses a URL in the body of an e-mail is termed a *blended threat*. A further level of phishing is sometimes jocularly referred to as *whaling*. This is spear phishing that is targeted at very important individuals.

8.13   Social Engineering

A simple example of social engineering is when a computer user is rung up by somebody pretending to work for the IT department. The social engineer, who is actually a criminal, obtains the user's password, perhaps on the pretext of making a few checks of the system. Social engineering is also used in network-based attacks, for example, in fake software updates. For example, a victim is keen to watch a short film that has been advertised (*malvertised*) on the Web. A message appears on the screen saying that it will be necessary to install a particular video codec to be able to watch the film. The software that the user has been tricked into installing contains malware.

Another example of the use of social engineering in a Web-based attack is installation of fake anti-virus software. The user is persuaded that his or her computer has been infected by a virus and that help is needed. The victim installs and pays for spurious anti-virus software that is supposed to remedy a problem that does not actually exist.

8.14   Dynamic Web Links

Most e-mail exploits now include dynamic Web links (as part of a blended threat). These links entice victims to click on them, offering a chance to buy a bargain or see an exciting video, for example. Dynamic Web links often make use of JavaScript and cascading style sheets (CSS). The content of the Web page changes according to what a user has clicked on.

Here is an example of how a dynamic Web link can be used by an attacker to deliver malware. The attacker has obtained the access credentials for a user of a social networking account. The attacker sends a message containing a dynamic link to all the user's 'friends'. The link appears to be to a picture which the user is impatient to view. But before the user can see the picture, he or she is asked to download and install a software update. If the user is trying to multi-task, perhaps using a mobile phone, he or she may impatiently click on through the update process without thinking, in his or her haste to see the picture. Unfortunately, some malware has now been delivered. Such an attack could also happen with a video, as in the example in Sect. 8.13 above, or some other form of digital media content.

Attackers using dynamic Web links take a lot of trouble to hide what they are doing. They use many layers of encryption. The lure and the payload are kept separate from each other and it is the dynamic link that connects these together. A tiny, invisible pixel is sometimes written to a Web page. The page looks harmless to the user, but it links to a site that launches an exploit. Another technique that attackers use is to truncate Web addresses, using a URL-shortening service. This makes a long, complicated and malicious URL look completely innocuous when viewed by the victim.

8.14.1 Defences Against Dynamic Web Links and Other Rapidly Evolving Malware

Traditional anti-virus software looks for a distinctive bit pattern (a *signature*) or a file hash value that will betray the presence of a virus. During the first few hours of a Web attack, standard anti-virus (AV) software is not very effective. Unknown, 'zero-day' malware will not be on a list of signatures or have a familiar file hash value. Heuristic filters are one defence that is used against zero-day threats. Making use of artificial intelligence, these look for patterns of behaviour that usually indicate malware.

Standard AV software has to compromise between speed of detection and security. If settings are turned up to the maximum, the AV software can be successful, but in that case it is likely to block activity that is innocent as well as genuine malware. AV software must be used in combination with firewalls, IDSs or IPSs, simple Web filtering and also special near real-time Web defences for protection against dynamic Web links during the first few hours of attacks.

8.14.1.1 Cloud-Based Security Services

Real-time Web defences are cloud based. They take advantage of a worldwide membership that can number millions of users. The protective software is delivered as a service (Security as a Service) via the Web on payment of a subscription. Web and e-mail traffic going into and coming out of the customer's network is sent to the service provider and scanned for malware. The provider removes anything harmful and then directs the traffic back to the customer. Information about dynamic Web links is collected automatically, and Web content is rated in real time. IP addresses,

Fig. 8.22 Security as a Service

traffic patterns, the modes of delivery, how the code behaves and how the malware is packaged can be analysed. At a central point, security experts can use this information to improve their defences. A typical cloud-based Web security and analysis centre belonging to a security as a service provider is shown in Fig. 8.22.

It is very difficult to protect nomadic users adequately without such defences. Even the infrastructure at the headquarters of a site may be much more fluid than in the past. The company will probably use virtualisation, where servers and switches which exist as software can be 'moved' about rapidly and can be instantly started and stopped just by clicking on a mouse. Security defences need to be able to cope with a mixture of virtual and physical infrastructure. They also need to be able to react quickly to sudden changes to that infrastructure. The development cycle of a Web defence is much faster than that of software for a fixed security appliance. This is important because of the speed of development of new Web-based exploits.

8.15   Physical Security

The most basic kind of DOS attack would be if an intruder were able to enter a server room and interfere with a power cable or network cable. Server computers must be locked safely away. Preferably, an electronic key card plus a biometric system will be used instead of just a combination lock. Routers and switches too should be physically secured. Well-placed security cameras can help to deter theft and vandalism.

All equipment should be protected from environmental damage caused by floods, heat and earthquakes. Computers should be positioned away from devices that produce electromagnetic interference. Data should be protected from harm by the use of a reliable backup/archiving system. RAID systems can help to prevent data loss. Fault tolerant systems should be used where necessary.

Fig. 8.23 Standby UPS

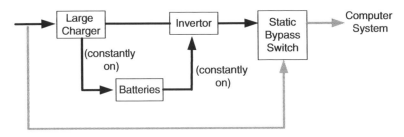

Fig. 8.24 Online UPS

The power to all vital network devices should be protected by an *uninterruptible power supply* (UPS). This contains a battery and an AC inverter which will provide power for some time after the mains supply has been cut off. An UPS will also condition the electricity supply to the computers and will protect against damaging power surges. There are various kinds of UPS, but the main ones are the standby and the online UPS. In the standby UPS (shown in Fig. 8.23), the battery is charged while the current is monitored. Power is coming straight from the mains electricity supply all the time, except when there is a power failure. If the power fails, the battery switches on automatically and restores power in 5 ms or less. The online UPS (shown in Fig. 8.24) uses its batteries to provide power all the time. The input power from the mains is used to charge the batteries while they are in use. This kind of UPS is usually more expensive than the standby variety.

8.16   Wireless LAN Security

Wireless LANs were first mentioned in Chap. 4 and are described in more detail in Chap. 10. Securing such networks is especially problematic. Since wireless transmissions are not confined inside a cable, it is very easy for an eavesdropper to listen in to them. The eavesdropper may even perpetrate a man-in-the-middle attack, in which the user's messages can be modified without his or her realising this. The man-in-the-middle attack is not limited to wireless networks only, but these networks are particularly vulnerable to such attacks. Figure 8.25 shows a man-in-the-middle attack on a WLAN. The attacker, who could be sitting in the company's car park or

Fig. 8.25 Man-in-the-middle attack

Access Point

Victim   Man in the Middle

a nearby building, is impersonating a legitimate access point (AP). All communication between the victim client and the network is going via the attacker, who is able to read and modify the messages at will.

The first security protocol that was used with WLANs was *wired equivalent privacy* (WEP). The intention was that WEP would offer the same level of privacy over a WLAN as could be expected with a wired network. Unfortunately, WEP used 40-bit static encryption keys that were too easy to break. WEP was replaced by *Wi-Fi protected access* (WPA). WPA uses a different key for every packet of data that is transmitted. It also checks for integrity and offers authentication of clients. WPA2, the second version of WPA, uses AES encryption and is part of IEEE 802.11i, the official WLAN security standard which was agreed after WPA2. 802.11i uses the *extensible authentication protocol* (EAP), which offers several different types of authentication. One of these types of authentication technology is EAP-TLS, which is PKI based. Also involved in 802.11i WLAN security is the 802.1X standard, which offers port-based network access control. In 802.1X, authentication is granted when a *supplicant* (usually a laptop or other portable computer) asks an *authenticator* (an AP) if it can be authenticated. The *authentication server* is the component that actually gives permission, though usually the AP performs this function as well as that of authenticator. The components of IEEE 802.1X authentication are illustrated in Fig. 8.26.

8.16.1 Practical Measures for Securing WLANs

A new WLAN AP has a default administration login name and password; it is not a good idea to continue to use these. The new password should be a strong one. The AP is usually able to restrict access to particular MAC addresses. This was once a very helpful security feature. Unfortunately, it has become too easy to spoof another PC's MAC address for this feature to remain very effective. There is often a built-in

Fig. 8.26   IEEE 802.1X
authentication

Authentication
Server

Authenticator

Supplicant

DHCP server, which can supply all clients, including any intruder, with an IP address. The DHCP server should be turned off. If a choice of security protocols is available, the best one should be used. WEP is of little use, but even the more modern security protocols such as WPA2 offer little resistance to cloud-based cracking tools.

By default, an AP broadcasts its service set identifier (SSID), which gives the network a name. Turning SSID broadcasts off was formerly a reasonable precaution to take but is not a very helpful defence against modern wireless sniffers. Some even argue in favour of using meaningful SSID names so that bona fide users will know what network they are connecting to.

It is best not to set up an AP and then just leave it alone for a long time. It is a good idea to check the logs now and again for repeated attempts to log in with the wrong password. It may be possible to configure the AP to send a message to the administrator whenever this happens.

There needs to be a security policy that defines the applications and protocols that are allowed to be used on the WLAN. Users should not be allowed to connect their own devices without supervision. It is a good idea to scan for open APs using the same free software that attackers use. The default access channel is usually 1, 6 or 11, and it is wise to change to a different channel. The AP should be positioned so that its signals have difficulty reaching outside the building. The middle of an office might be a better spot for the AP than an outside wall. The AP's management interface should be kept inaccessible from the WLAN. Finally, it is possible to protect a WLAN well by pretending that it is on the Internet. A firewall and a VPN can be used for maximum security.

8.17   Security of Mobile Devices

It is very important for all organisations that they safeguard their data. When data is held on a portable computer of any kind (such as a laptop or tablet computer or a mobile phone), it is particularly vulnerable. Since such devices are so easy to pick up and move, there is a great risk that they will be lost or stolen. Network administrators need to be able to take control of mobile devices, if need be. They need to be able to do a *remote wipe*, so that all the data can be removed from a device that has gone missing or is inactive for some reason. They need to be able to control what data users can access using their mobile device. They must oblige users to authenticate the device when it is switched on, for example, with a password. Whenever data is transmitted over the airwaves, it must be encrypted, for example, using SSL or TLS. The contents of any storage device on a mobile computer, for example a hard drive, should also be fully encrypted, in case it falls into the wrong hands. In addition, a mobile device must be configured to delete its data or cut off access to the company e-mail system if its user does not log into the network within a certain period of time. Any personal mobile device that joins the company network should be evaluated and blocked if it does not meet certain criteria. Workers often use their own mobile devices for work. There is a risk that they may use their device inappropriately, so a mobile device usage policy is necessary. If possible, the policy should be centrally enforced by the IT department.

Online application ('app') stores, where programmers are able to sell or give away software that they have produced, pose a risk from the point of view of security. Some of these may contain malware. A real-life example is an application that intercepted mobile phone short message service (SMS) text messages relating to financial transactions. In this way, the attacker was able to obtain credentials which gave him access to bank accounts.

Session hijacking is a great danger on unsecured public wireless networks. It is a way of taking over somebody else's Web session by getting hold of the session ID. The session ID is usually stored as a cookie. A cookie is a small text file that is stored on a user's computer when he or she visits a website for the first time. When a second visit to the site takes place, the information in the cookie is sent back to the site. Once the attacker has the session ID, he or she can pretend to be the victim and can do anything that the victim is allowed to do on the site. Software that facilitates session hijacking for portable computers of all kinds, including mobile phones, is readily available. Bluetooth and wireless fidelity (Wi-Fi) networks are both potential sources of danger.

There are other potential problems with public wireless networks. For example, criminals with a laptop computer might sit in or near a café. They might set up a fake Wi-Fi network and give it the same name as the café. This would lure unsuspecting customers into connecting to the fake network, which would be used to capture their credentials.

A mobile phone constantly searches for Wi-Fi networks to which it has previously connected. Using specialist equipment, a criminal who is sitting nearby can easily detect the Wi-Fi request signals that the phone sends out. The criminal can then imitate one of the Wi-Fi LANs that the victim's phone has previously connected to, so as to attract the phone to connect to it. The criminal has become the 'man in the middle' (see Sect. 8.16), and any data going from the phone and out to the Internet can then be captured.

8.18   Summary

This chapter has looked at various aspects of network security, which is an extremely important issue in today's networks. The chapter started with an explanation of several important security concepts and gave some security techniques related to these concepts. Further, the following aspects of network security were covered: VPNs; firewalls; intrusion detection, intrusion prevention and unified threat management systems; various kinds of attacks that may be made on networks; viruses, worms and Trojan horses; rootkits; spam e-mail; spyware; phishing; social engineering; dynamic Web links; physical security; the security of wireless networks; and the security of mobile devices.

8.19   Questions

1. When *AES* was devised, a competition was held to find the best encryption algorithm. Find out what criteria were used to select the winning algorithm, Rijndael. (This information is not included in this book.)
2. Why was *public-key encryption* developed?
3. If *SSL/TLS* is in use, how confident can a customer using a credit card to pay for goods from a website be that the transaction is secure?
4. Explain how a *digital signature* is produced.
5. Find two different *security policy templates* on the Internet and compare them. Relate their features to the list given in Table 8.1.
6. Explain the difference between the IPSec *transport* and *tunnel* modes.
7. What are the advantages of SSL/TLS-based VPNs over IPSec-based VPNs?
8. Draw a labelled diagram illustrating the exchanges that take place between client and server during the setting up of a secure, encrypted SSL *tunnel*.
9. The following is a router access control list:
   access-list 1 permit 172.16.0.0 0.0.255.255
   access-list 1 deny any
What does it mean?
10. Explain how an *FTP application proxy firewall* works.
11. How do *intrusion prevention systems* differ from *intrusion detection systems*?
12. What is a *DDOS* attack?
13. What is a *rootkit*?
14. What is a *man-in-the-middle* attack?
15. What can be done to secure wireless LANs?

Network Management

9

Abstract

This chapter begins with a description of the network management functional areas of the ISO network management model, which cover configuration management, fault management, performance management, accounting management and security management. Next comes a description of some hardware and software tools that are used for network management. We then look at some ways of troubleshooting networks. We investigate the important simple network management protocol (SNMP), a TCP/IP application-layer protocol that makes it easy for management information to be exchanged between network devices. We also take a look at the equally important variant of SNMP, remote monitor (RMON). In the next section, the value of good network documentation is stressed. The chapter ends with a short section on LAN server administration.

As networks become more and more complex, they can become more and more difficult to maintain. The users of a network tend to rely on it heavily and will suffer if it is not running efficiently or if certain applications are unavailable when needed. So the network manager must manage the network proactively, using all the management facilities at his or her disposal.

9.1 ISO Network Management Model

One major goal of network management is to keep the number of problems in the network to a minimum. The other major goals are to prevent those problems that do occur causing too much inconvenience and to stop any damage spreading. ISO provides five network management functional areas to help achieve these goals. These functional areas are configuration management, fault management, performance management, accounting management and security management. We shall now examine each of the first four of these in turn. Security was dealt with in the previous chapter. The functional areas for network management are shown in Fig. 9.1.

J. Cowley, *Communications and Networking: An Introduction*, Undergraduate Topics in Computer Science, DOI 10.1007/978-1-4471-4357-4_9,
© Springer-Verlag London 2012

Fig. 9.1 ISO functional areas for network management

9.1.1   Configuration Management

Configuration management is concerned with monitoring and controlling normal operations in a network. When doing configuration management, network administrators attempt to understand and control how the network is configured. The administrators need to know that the components of the network exist and what their names and addresses are, as well as routing details. They need to know what the relationships between these components are and what their operational characteristics are. In order to obtain such knowledge, network managers have to collect configuration data.

9.1.2   Fault Management

Fault management is concerned with abnormal network behaviour. Fault conditions must be detected, logged, isolated and dealt with. There are three main areas of fault management: error detection, error diagnosis and error recovery. There are several ways in which errors may be detected. Ordinary users of the network may discover faults during the normal course of operations. Alternatively, special reliability tests that are carried out by network administrators may reveal faults. Error diagnosis is performed by analysing logs and running diagnostic programs. There are various ways of carrying out error recovery. The most drastic form of recovery consists of replacing faulty items of hardware or software, but, fortunately, it is not always necessary to go as far as that.

9.1.3   Performance Management

Performance management is concerned with the performance of various components of the network. It analyses and controls network performance. Throughput, utilisation and error rates of various components of the network are measured, analysed and controlled. The aim is to make the network perform optimally. SNMP plays an important part in performance management. SNMP is described in Sect. 9.4.

9.1.3.1 Establishing Baselines
So as to be able to carry out performance management, the network administrator needs first to establish baselines for the various measures of performance. A baseline

Table 9.1 Hardware device record sheet

Hardware device documentation		
Type of equipment:		
Serial no.:		
Date purchased:		
Warranty expiration data:	Vendor:	Phone:
Service contract:	Vendor:	Phone:
Problems:		
Date:	Problem:	Solution:

sets the acceptable level of performance of the network. Without a baseline, it will not be possible to tell whether performance is improving or declining. And as the network is expanded or updated, the baseline itself will need to be updated.

Baselining involves measuring and recording how a network operates over a certain period of time. It can be used to find out how the network is performing currently and what the future needs are.

When performing a baseline study, the administrator has to get information on all the network devices, including workstations, server computers, hubs, switches and routers. Model numbers, serial numbers, NIC and IP addresses, protocols and network applications in use will all need to be recorded. A simple record sheet such as the one shown in Table 9.1 may be utilised, but alternatively software can be used to record the data. The manager will also need to record such figures as the average and peak network utilisation, the average and peak frame size, the average and peak number of frames per second, the number of broadcasts, the number of collisions per second, the number of CRC errors and the number of illegally short and long frames (runts and jabbers).

9.1.3.2 Useful Figures for Performance Management

Certain figures can be very useful for demonstrating current system demands and predicting future needs. Here, we shall look at *mean time between failures* (MTBF), *mean time to repair* (MTTR) and *availability*.

Networks have a large number of components. If a vital component fails, it is possible that the whole network will be disrupted. The likelihood of a component failure may be known, often as the MTBF. The MTBF is the mean (average) time a device or system will operate before it fails. The MTTR is the average time necessary to repair a failure within the computer system. The availability of a component or system is the probability that the component or system will be available during a fixed time period. If we know the MTBF and the MTTR, then we can calculate availability. The formula for availability is given below.

$$\text{Availability} = \frac{\text{MTBF}}{\text{MTBF} + \text{MTTR}}$$

For example, suppose that we want to calculate the availability of a network component that has an MTBF of 5,000 h and an MTTR of 20 h.

$$\text{Availability} = \frac{5,000}{5,000+20} = 99.6\%$$

If we want to know the availability of a whole system (such as a network), we will have to take into account the availability of each of its components. We must multiply the availability figures for all of the components together. Thus, if the availability of a system is A_{system}, the availability of device 1 is A_1, the availability of device 2 is A_2 and the availability of device n is A_n, then the formula for availability of the system is

$$A_{\text{system}} = A_1 \times A_2 \times \cdots \times A_n$$

For example, if a network sub-system consists of five components each with an availability of 0.96, what is the availability of the sub-system?

$$A_{\text{sub-system}} = 0.96 \times 0.96 \times 0.96 \times 0.96 \times 0.96 = 0.815$$

9.1.4   Accounting Management

Accounting management allows the network manager to collect data on how resources are being consumed by users and devices. From this data, the manager can work out how much to charge internal cost centres for the network services that they are using. Even if the organisation does not use a cost-centre system, accounting management is still useful because it will facilitate the analysis of current network capacity and trends. Accounting management deals with such items as adding and deleting users, setting their usage quotas and granting them privileges to access resources.

9.2   Tools for Network Management

We will now examine some of the tools that are used by network managers. Many of these tools are shown in Fig. 9.2. In the physical layer, *cable testers* are widely used. These vary in sophistication from a purely hardware *breakout box*, in which a light-emitting diode (LED) lights up if a wire of a copper cable has a good connection, to complex handheld computers. Cable faults are the commonest source of errors on networks, so cable testing is very important. Testers are also available for fibre-optic cable and wireless.

Cable testers use *time-domain reflectometry* (TDR) to measure the distance along a cable to an open or shorted end. TDR works rather like radar. A pulse of energy is sent along the cable. When the pulse reaches the end of the cable or the place where there is a fault, the energy of the pulse is reflected back to the cable tester. The instrument measures the time taken for the signal to go along the cable and then be reflected back from the end. From the time taken, the tester works out the distance and displays it. The calculated position of the fault depends on the known propagation

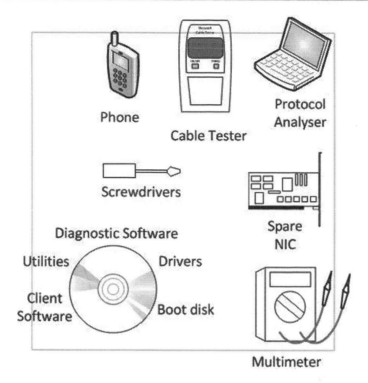

Fig. 9.2 Network toolkit

speed of a pulse in the cable. Each type of cable has its own propagation speed, which is a fraction of c, the free-space speed of light. Prior to transmitting the pulse, the TDR can be configured with the right propagation speed.

The distance to a cable fault is calculated using the following formula:

$$\text{distance} = \frac{1}{2} \times \text{propagation speed} \times \text{time for reflected pulse to return}$$

Here is a worked example:

Assuming that the propagation speed of CAT 5e UTP cable is 0.65, and that a reflected pulse from a TDR takes 500 ns to arrive, how far away is the fault?

$$\text{distance} = \frac{1}{2} \times (0.65 \times 3.0 \times 10^8) \times (500 \times 10^{-9}) = 49.5 \text{ m}$$

(Because the speed of light in a vacuum is approximately 300,000,000 m/s, or 3×10^8 m/s.)

Some network cable testers measure crosstalk by applying a signal to an 'aggressor' pair of wires and then measuring the induced signal on the 'victim' pair. This procedure is illustrated in Fig. 9.3.

Fig. 9.3 Measuring crosstalk

Fig. 9.4 Use of network monitors

Network *monitors* (or *probes*) can be mounted on each segment of a network. The monitors observe and record events on the network and detect problems. They run round the clock throughout the year without human intervention. The information that the monitors provide from their captures of network traffic can be viewed from a central point. The monitors count how much the network is utilised, how many frames are sent and received by each network device and so on. Network monitors are often a part of an integrated network management system (INMS). The use of network monitors is illustrated in Fig. 9.4. These generally use remote monitor (RMON) monitoring (see Sect. 9.4.5).

Fig. 9.5 Wireless protocol analyser

An INMS allows the network administrator to monitor and control the corporate internetwork from a central point. The INMS covers all five of the ISO network management functional areas. The administrator views the system via a graphical user interface (GUI). Software running on remote network devices gathers information that the INMS can use. SNMP (see Sect. 9.4) is often used in INMSs.

A *protocol analyser* (or *packet sniffer*) is able to capture and interpret network frames and packets. The protocol analyser may come in the relatively expensive form of a specialised portable computer, such as a tablet PC, with built-in software. A specialised (and expensive) laptop wireless protocol analyser is illustrated in Fig. 9.5. Alternatively, the analyser may be software only and designed to run on a cheap, general-purpose computer. There are several protocol analysis software packages. Wireshark (available from http://www.wireshark.org/) is an example of free protocol analysis software.

9.3 Network Troubleshooting

Troubleshooting involves finding out what is causing a problem on the network and sorting it out. The tools mentioned in the previous section can be used for this, along with other tools and techniques.

9.3.1 A Systematic Method for Troubleshooting

When troubleshooting, the network administrator should use a systematic method for finding out the cause of problems on a network and dealing with them. Troubleshooting is both an art and a science. On the one hand, the troubleshooter needs a thorough technical knowledge of the systems and sub-systems that constitute the network. He or she also needs to understand the relationship between symptom and cause, just as a scientist does. On the other hand, troubleshooting demands intuition, intelligence and skill in applying the knowledge that the troubleshooter possesses.

We will now describe one systematic approach to troubleshooting, though it must be pointed out that this method is not the only possible one. First, the network administrator should get all the information about the symptoms of the problem together and analyse it. The problem should then be narrowed down to a particular area, for instance, a network segment or a network device. Is the problem confined to a single computer or to all the workstations that are connected to a particular server computer? Or does it extend to all the stations in a building?

Next, the problem should be narrowed down still further, for example, to an item of software or hardware within a troublesome network device. The administrator makes a hypothesis. Is the problem due to hardware failure, to a configuration error, to incompatibilities between hardware and software or simply to an increase in network traffic?

Next, we test the hypothesis. Trying to reproduce the problem elsewhere in the network can be a useful tactic. Hardware components should be replaced one at a time. If there have been recent upgrades or changes in configuration, it may be worth rolling these back to the previous state to see if that improves matters.

When the exact nature of the problem has been discovered, we are in a position to correct it. The administrator takes whatever action seems to be necessary to repair the fault. We may have to replace or repair faulty components. We may have to implement configuration changes. We may need to obtain and install patches from software vendors. We may need to install new components.

After this attempt to remedy the situation, the network administrator must check that the problem really has been solved. Finally, the administrator must document both the problem and what the solution to it was. All members of the network support team must be aware of what other team members have done in order to sort out the problem. The solution must be documented so the team will know what to do if a similar problem occurs again. A systematic approach to troubleshooting is shown in Fig. 9.6.

9.3.2   Procedures for Troubleshooting

Network testing should start with layer 1 (physical layer) of the OSI 7-layer model and then proceed as far up through the other layers of the protocol stack as necessary. Possible errors at layer 1 include disconnected or broken cables and cables that are plugged into the wrong port on a hub, switch or router. Less easy to spot are the errors caused by intermittent cable faults or by the selection of the wrong type of cable, for example, a crossover instead of a straight-through cable or vice versa. A NIC, a router, a switch or a CSU/DSU might be faulty. The most fundamental error at layer 1 is that a device is either not plugged into the mains or has been switched off. It is advisable to check for basic faults such as this before trying more sophisticated troubleshooting.

Still not
right.

Symptoms?

Test the hypothesis

Right!

Person
Make a hypothesis.

Remedy the problem.

Fig. 9.6 Systematic troubleshooting

When troubleshooting at layer 1, there will be indicator lights that should be checked. For example, if a NIC is physically connected and working, a green light may be visible. There may also be lights that show network transmission or reception. If no green light is visible, this may be a symptom of a cable problem. On the other hand, the cause might be that the NIC is loose in its socket.

Potential problems at layer 2 include wrongly configured Ethernet or WAN interfaces. For example, the wrong kind of layer-2 encapsulation may have been chosen on one of the router's WAN interfaces. In the case of frame relay, the wrong DLCI (permanent virtual circuit number) may have been set. A layer-2 fault that can cause problems at layer 3 is one or more erroneous associations between MAC and IP addresses. Purging (emptying) the ARP cache may remedy this. If a layer-2 switch is in use, VLANs may have been wrongly configured, preventing communication between members of different VLANs.

There are several causes of layer-3 errors. The most common of these is an addressing error of some kind. For example, an interface on a device may have been configured with the wrong IP address or perhaps the subnet mask is wrong. For this reason, it is prudent to make sure that the addresses of router interfaces are correct before doing any further configuration. Routing protocols too can cause problems at layer 3. No routing protocol (such as RIP) may have been enabled. Or perhaps a routing protocol has been enabled but it is the wrong one.

The *Ping* utility program (described in Sect. 6.1.8) is a very useful tool for trouble-shooting layer-3 problems. It can be used to test network connectivity over IP-based networks. The output from Ping shows the minimum, average and maximum round-trip time for a test datagram to reach the target address and be sent back to the source. From this output, the network administrator can tell whether the target host

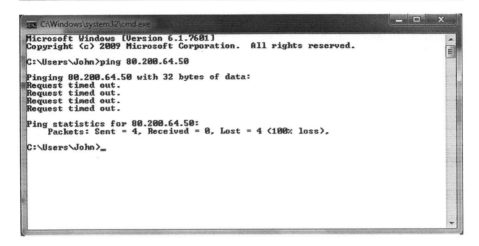

Fig. 9.7 Unsuccessful Ping

can be reached, what the delays over the path to the host are and how reliable the path is. In the example given in Sect. 6.1.8, the ping target 193.60.1.15 replies to all four datagrams sent to it. An unsuccessful attempt at pinging a target host is shown in Fig. 9.7. This display shows that the target host is unreachable, as none of the test datagrams got to the address that they were trying to reach.

For troubleshooting at layer 7, the *Telnet* utility can be useful. Telnet, a virtual terminal protocol that works at the application layer of TCP/IP, was described in Sect. 7.4. When used for troubleshooting, Telnet allows an administrator to check that at least one application works over a TCP/IP connection between the source and the destination. If Telnet functions OK, it shows that the whole protocol stack from Telnet downwards is working correctly. If it is not possible to Telnet to a server computer from a particular host, it might be worth trying from a router or some other device. If using the name of the server does not give a login prompt, it might be possible to get a successful result by using the server's IP address instead. The IP address may be able to be obtained by using the *nslookup* command (see below for an example). If one can still not get a response from the server, it is possible that the Telnet service is not running or that, for some reason, it has been moved from the normal port (23).

Here is an example of the nslookup utility being used to look up the IP address(es) of www.google.co.uk. In the first line, the command is issued from the prompt on a UNIX computer called bsussoc1. The output is from the second line onwards:

bsussoc1 > nslookup www.google.co.uk

Server: bsus.staffs.ac.uk

Address: 193.60.1.17

Non-authoritative answer:

Name: www.l.google.com

Addresses: 66.102.9.147, 66.102.9.99, 66.102.9.104

Aliases: www.google.co.uk, www.google.com

The *traceroute* utility was described in Sect. 6.1.8. This can be employed to trace the complete route from host X to host Y. The output shows a list of all the routers that were reached. If there is a failure anywhere along the path from X to Y, traceroute will show where this occurred. An attempt at tracing a route that ends in failure is shown below. An asterisk in the output indicates failure.

Tracing route to bs47c.staffs.ac.uk [193.60.1.15] over a maximum of 30 hops:
1. 12 ms 9 ms 29 ms 10.33.0.1
2. 10 ms 18 ms 11 ms gsr01-du.blueyonder.co.uk [62.31.176.129]
3. 17 ms 47 ms 19 ms 172.18.4.33
4. 39 ms 16 ms 19 ms 194.117.136.134
5. 17 ms 28 ms 39 ms 194.117.136.146
6. 16 ms 15 ms 16 ms 194.117.136.162
7. 16 ms 37 ms 19 ms janet-telewest-pvtpeer.telewest.net [194.117.147.30]
8. 18 ms 17 ms 30 ms po2-3.lond-scr4.ja.net [146.97.35.233]
9. 17 ms 33 ms 17 ms po1-0.read-scr.ja.net [146.97.33.26]
10. 24 ms 20 ms 20 ms po3-0.warr-scr.ja.net [146.97.33.54]
11. 22 ms 22 ms 21 ms po1-0.manchester-bar.ja.net [146.97.35.166]
12. 33 ms 22 ms 24 ms gw-nnw.core.netnw.net.uk [146.97.40.202]
13. 25 ms 24 ms 41 ms gw-staff.core.netnw.net.uk [194.66.25.94]
14. * * * Request timed out.
15. * * * Request timed out.
16. * * * Request timed out.
17. * * * Request timed out.
18. * * * Request timed out.
19. * * * Request timed out.
[etc.]

If the network manager compares the output from traceroute to a diagram of the internetwork concerned, he or she can find out where the problem area is. (In the traceroute attempt shown above, the reason for the request timing out is that the computer called bs47c.staffs.ac.uk is not directly connected to the Internet.) Traceroute also gives an approximate figure for the time taken to send an ICMP echo request and receive a response on each link. ICMP messages are sometimes filtered out by routers or firewalls at the target site, so ping and traceroute will not always work as expected.

9.4 SNMP and RMON

SNMP is used to manage networks. It was designed for use with TCP/IP, although it can work over other network protocols. SNMP has four parts. The SNMP *manager* runs on a network management station. It can query SNMP agents, get responses from these and make changes to variables by means of SNMP commands. The

Fig. 9.8 SNMP in the
protocol stack

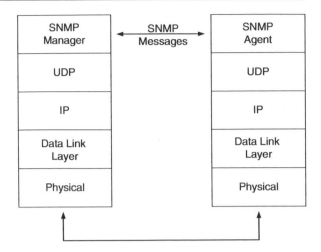

SNMP *agent* runs on a managed network device. It stores management data and
responds to requests from the manager. The *management information base* (MIB) is
a database of objects (variables). These can be accessed by agents and can have
changes made to them using SNMP. The SNMP protocol is a TCP/IP application-
layer protocol that is used to query agents and make changes to objects. Figure 9.8
shows where the SNMP manager and agent sit in the TCP/IP stack.

9.4.1 SNMP Manager

The SNMP manager is an SNMP client program that runs on a host workstation
(the management station). It can access the database of information that agents
keep. For example, an SNMP agent running on a router may store totals of the number
of datagrams sent and received. The SNMP manager can get these figures from the
agent and compare them. By doing this, it will be able to tell whether the router is
experiencing congestion. The SNMP manager can also send commands to a network
device by changing values in an agent's database. For example, the SNMP manager
can change the device's IP address or switch a certain port on or off.

9.4.2 SNMP Agent

The agent is the SNMP server program which runs on a managed network device
such as a hub, switch or router. Besides responding to the manager, it can also send
out a warning (called a *trap*) to the manager about an anomalous situation. The
agent's management information is stored in its MIB. The agent keeps information
on various items. Examples of these items include how many virtual circuits exist
and what their state is, broadcasts, error messages and so on. If the SNMP manager

needs to interrogate or send commands to a proprietary (non-SNMP) agent, this can be done by making use of a proxy agent, which translates between SNMP and the proprietary software.

9.4.3 SNMP MIB

Each agent has a database (the MIB) consisting of a range of objects (variables) that can be measured, monitored or controlled. Each agent must hold a set of standard MIB objects. The MIB may also contain so-called enterprise objects, which are specific to a particular vendor. The SNMP manager holds MIBs that correspond to those of all the agents on the network. Thus equipped, the SNMP manager and the agent can communicate with each other using the SNMP command set. A large number of MIBs exist. All MIBs have a hierarchical structure, in which the managed objects are the leaf nodes (the parts of the tree at the bottom of the hierarchy). Each managed object has a numerical identifier. The object identifiers are described using a language called Abstract Syntax Notation (ASN.1). The details of public-domain objects can be seen at http://www.ietf.org.

9.4.4 Simple Network Management Protocol

The SNMP protocol uses UDP on ports 161 and 162. SNMP is called 'simple' because it works by exchanging a limited number of types of message. The three main message types are *get*, *set* and *trap*. Get lets the SNMP manager retrieve MIB object values from the SNMP agent. Set allows the SNMP manager to set MIB object values at the agent. Trap lets the agent tell the SNMP manager about significant occurrences. Get and set work behind the scenes when a network manager clicks on an icon in the management station's GUI. A trap might cause an icon to turn red if, say, a connection has failed. Figure 9.9 shows the flow of SNMP messages between the manager and agent.

SNMP has evolved since it was first devised. Security was a concern in SNMPv1 and SNMPv2 because the 'community string', a field in the SNMP packet that acted as a password restricting access to managed devices, was transmitted in clear text form. The possibility of an attacker being able to control an organisation's network devices using SNMP was very worrying, so SNMPv3 supports authenticated and encrypted passwords.

When used over a WAN, SNMP traffic can slow down the response time for the normal network traffic. Further, when network devices are being interrogated using SNMP, they require extra processing. For these reasons, it is better not to poll network devices more frequently than is strictly necessary. Sometimes, a dedicated, separate network is used so that management traffic can be carried 'out of band', where it does not impede the passage of business data. One reason why the RMON MIB (see next section) was developed was to deal with the problem of monitoring network devices from a long distance away over a WAN.

Fig. 9.9 Flow of SNMP
messages between manager
and agent

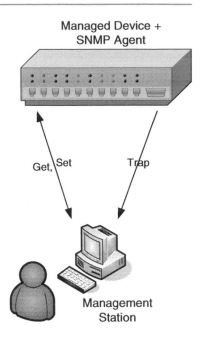

Managed Device +
SNMP Agent

Get, Set   Trap

Management
Station

9.4.5   Remote Monitor

RMON is an extension to the SNMP MIB. It was developed to facilitate the monitoring
of remote sites from a central point. RMON has two parts: the hardware or software
agent, usually called a *probe*, at the remote site and the client (the manager) that
displays and reports the information that the probe has collected. The probe sits on
the network building up a MIB that can be sent to the manager. The probe can be
either self-contained or a module on another device such as a switch. The first version of RMON worked only at the data link layer. RMON 2 added support for OSI
layers 3–7, giving the network administrator more information about the network
than SNMP on its own can provide. RMON can help the network administrator to
identify such items as where the most traffic on the organisation's internetwork is
generated and which are the most heavily used routes. It makes it easier for the
administrator to discover if a user is making database queries that are crippling the
network or spending a lot of time downloading large files. RMON can allow the
administrator to discover subtle changes that are occurring in the behaviour of a network. It can help the administrator to decide where to place server computers and
how to configure routers in the most efficient manner. Figure 9.4 (in Sect. 9.2) shows
a network manager using RMON to monitor a network's traffic from a long distance
away. Switch monitoring (SMON) facilitates the management of network switches.

9.4.5.1 RMON MIB Groups
RMON has nine more MIB groups (statistical tables) than SNMP. The statistics
group details Ethernet statistics, such as collisions and multicasts. The history group

can be used to take snapshots of the network. The alarm group will set off an alarm if preset parameters are exceeded. The host group gathers information about certain hosts. HostTopN lists the top network hosts rated according to a base statistic specified by the network management system. The filter group can be used to configure the probe to select individual packets for observation. The matrix group keeps tables of statistics about the number of packets, bytes and errors sent between two addresses, thus providing information about network traffic between users. The packet capture group is used to copy packets from the filter group into buffer memory. The event group allows a network administrator to define events for a probe, enabling it to log these events or send an SNMP trap. The advantage that this offers is that it becomes unnecessary to poll distant network devices over a WAN to discover faults. In RMON 2, 10 more groups were added. These enable the troubleshooting of applications across the network, whereas RMON 1 was restricted to viewing a single network segment at a time.

9.5   Documentation

Keeping up-to-date records of the network is of crucial importance. Unfortunately, since many people find maintaining their documentation rather tedious, they tend to forget to do it. There are many different kinds of documents that need to be kept. Some of these have been mentioned above (e.g. the importance of documenting solutions to network problems was mentioned in Sect. 9.3.1).

General-purpose computer OSs such as Microsoft® Windows® have pieces of software that can be used for network management purposes built into them. Figure 9.10 shows some typical output from the msinfo32.exe program. Such information can be used to document the configuration of a workstation. Other kinds of documentation that are needed are cut sheet diagrams, wiring closet layouts and details of the software that is installed.

A cut sheet diagram indicates the path of network cables. It indicates the type of cable, the length of each cable and how it is terminated. The diagram shows where the patch panels and wall sockets are located. It also indicates the cable-labelling scheme that is in use. Diagrams of the layouts of all wiring closets should include the location of equipment racks and the equipment that is mounted in them. They should also show the configuration details of the equipment. The details of all the software installed on each computer should be recorded. This will include the standard software configuration and details of the operating system.

9.6   LAN Server Administration

If a client–server LAN (see Sect. 4.1.1) is in use, the network administrator has useful capabilities for control and management. The network operating system allows the administrator to set the rights that individual users or groups of users have to access particular network resources. Users can be granted such permissions as read, write,

Fig. 9.10 Typical output from msinfo32.exe program

delete, print, copy and execute. The network administrator is also able to control the time periods when users or groups can access resources. The administrator can set up *profiles*, which facilitate customising of the user interface. Once set up, the profile can be used no matter which LAN workstation the user connects to the network from.

9.7   Summary

This chapter began with a description of the ISO network management model, which divides network management into configuration management, fault management, performance management, accounting management and security management. Some hardware and software tools that are used for network management were then discussed. Next, some ways of troubleshooting networks were mentioned. SNMP (a TCP/IP application-layer protocol that makes it easy for management information to be exchanged between network devices) was then described, along with its equally important variant RMON. In the next section, the value of good network documentation was stressed. The chapter finished with a short section on LAN server administration.

9.8   Questions

1. Match the functional areas of the *ISO network management model* to the facts about them.
   Functional areas
   (a) Configuration management
   (b) Fault management
   (c) Performance management
   (d) Accounting management
   (e) Security management
   Facts
   (a) Concerned with abnormal network behaviour
   (b) Analyses and controls network performance
   (c) Concerned with monitoring and controlling normal operations in a network
   (d) Concerned with access control, authentication and encryption
   (e) Allows the network administrator to collect data on how resources are being consumed by users and devices
2. A network component has an *MTBF* of 10,000 h and an *MTTR* of 12 h. What is its *availability*?
3. A network sub-system consists of four components each with an availability of 0.98. What is the *availability* of this sub-system?
4. Explain *time-domain reflectometry*.
5. Assuming that the propagation speed of a twisted-pair cable is 0.70, and that a reflected pulse from a TDR takes 400 ns to arrive, how far away is the fault?
6. You are a network administrator. Your staff have asked for a dedicated laptop protocol analyser which is so expensive that it exceeds your budget. What reasons could you give your line manager to persuade him or her to make available enough money to buy the analyser?
7. What is an *integrated network management system*?
8. What network utility program can be used to find out an IP address from a network name and vice versa?
9. What are the parts of *SNMP* and what is their function?
10. Explain what the SNMP message types *get*, *set* and *trap* do.
11. Find out from books or the Internet what security algorithms are used with *SNMPv3*.
12. Look up the details of the standard RMON MIB objects in RFC 2819 (available from the Internet). According to this RFC, what does a probe have to do in order to implement the MIB?

Wireless Networks

10

Abstract

Wireless networks have become more and more popular in business and industrial environments, in the home and in hotspots in public places such as airports and hotels. We can classify wireless networks in a variety of ways. In this chapter, we classify them as follows: personal area networks (PANs), home area networks (HANs), wireless LANs (WLANs), cellular radio networks (for mobile phones) and wireless technologies for replacing the wired analogue local loop. We start with a mention of some technical aspects of transmission. The chapter finishes with short discussions of mobile ad hoc networks, radio frequency identification (RFID), near field communication and the global positioning system.

Certain aspects of WLANs were covered in previous chapters, and the reader is encouraged to refer back to these. Infrared and microwave transmission (including satellites) were mentioned in Sect. 2.10.3. The WLAN access point and radio (the wireless NIC) were described in Sect. 4.1.3. The particular security problems posed by WLANs were covered in Sect. 8.16.

10.1 Spread Spectrum Wireless Transmission

This book is not the place to go into a detailed explanation of radio transmission. However, it is worth mentioning two related examples of transmission techniques that are commonly used in wireless networks. As we saw in Sect. 8.16, wireless networks pose a security problem. Direct sequence spread spectrum (DSSS) and frequency hopping spread spectrum (FHSS) are two transmission techniques that are used to help to alleviate this. In DSSS, each data bit is encoded as a group of bits that are transmitted simultaneously on a number of different frequencies. The individual transmissions are at such a low power level that an intruder has difficulty distinguishing them from the normal background noise. The IEEE 802.11b WLAN is an example of a wireless network that uses DSSS transmission.

J. Cowley, *Communications and Networking: An Introduction*, Undergraduate Topics in Computer Science, DOI 10.1007/978-1-4471-4357-4_10,
© Springer-Verlag London 2012

FHSS uses more powerful signals that are transmitted in a pseudo-random sequence on several different frequencies. The receiver has to ensure that it is on the same frequency as the transmitter at exactly the same time. Bluetooth is an example of a wireless technology that uses FHSS transmission over a very short range.

10.2   Personal Area Networks

PANs, or *piconets* as they are sometimes called, permit communication between devices that belong to a single owner. The distances involved are very short, about 10 m or less. The devices that are connected together can include mobile phones, portable computers, printers, televisions and so on. PANs resemble small-scale WLANs. The most important PAN standard is Bluetooth.

10.2.1 Bluetooth

Bluetooth (IEEE 802.15.1) uses microwave radio to communicate. Infrared transmission (see Sect. 2.10.3) would be unsuitable because it is highly directional and cannot pass through most solid objects. Bluetooth uses FHSS transmission in the same frequency band (2.4 GHz) as microwave ovens and many WLANs. It avoids interfering with the signals sent by other systems by transmitting at very low power levels. Nevertheless, the signals are still able to travel through the interior walls of a house. FHSS helps Bluetooth devices resist interference from other devices that use the same frequency band. Because the frequency changes regularly, any interference only affects a small part of the data. This small part is sent again if there was interference.

Bluetooth devices communicate with each other automatically whenever they come within range of each other. The devices arrange themselves into a piconet consisting of one master device and one or more slaves. The master has a clock that gives timing for the piconet. The slaves use this clock signal to synchronise with the frequency hopping sequence of the master. The piconet might be as simple as a mobile phone communicating with a headset or a more complex arrangement such as that illustrated in Fig. 10.1.

10.2.2 Wireless USB and Ultra-Wideband

The aim of wireless USB (WUSB) is to provide a wireless replacement for wired USB. WUSB is based on ultra-wideband (UWB). UWB transmits streams of very short pulses of energy (about 0.5 ns), which are spread over many frequencies simultaneously. It needs only very low power levels and resists interference well. It works well inside buildings. It can support data rates of several hundreds of megabits per second. Security is good because the energy pulses are so short that they are

Fig. 10.1 Bluetooth piconet

difficult to intercept. The range is short (potentially up to 100 m, but usually less), but this is not a problem if it is used to replace wired USB.

10.3 Home Area Networks

A house may have in it several remotely controlled devices. It would be convenient if the multiple remotes (remote control handsets) that are needed could be replaced by just one. A device that did not need a line of sight would also be convenient. ZigBee offers remote control of this nature.

10.3.1 ZigBee

ZigBee is based on the IEEE 802.15.4 standard and was designed to be used in wireless control and sensing networks. It uses DSSS transmission and can operate in the unlicensed 2.4-GHz band, like Bluetooth and some Wi-Fi networks. The data rate is low (up to 250 Kbps) and the range is limited (up to 30 m). As a consequence, power consumption is very low. Batteries will last for years, rather than just a few hours, as with IEEE 802.11x WLANs or Bluetooth devices. ZigBee can link up to 65,536 nodes together. It can be used in other applications besides home automation. For example, it can be used in toys as well as in industrial automation and building control.

10.4   WLANs

The aim of a WLAN is to provide exactly the same features as a wired LAN does but without the impediment of cables. WLANs can completely replace a conventional LAN or can be used to extend one. Figure 4.3 shows how wireless PCs can be integrated into a wired LAN. In all wireless networks, the atmosphere is the medium through which the signal travels. It would be possible to use infrared transmission (see Sect. 2.10.3), but using radio is popular because it offers greater range and higher data rates. The 2.4- and 5-GHz frequency bands are used because these do not need a licence in most parts of the world.

10.4.1 Benefits of WLANs

Although the data rate offered by WLANs tends to be lower than that of wired LANs, they possess many advantages. WLANs offer the possibility of users and devices being able to move about much more freely than is the case with wired LANs (*roaming* capability). Another advantage that WLANs possess over wired LANs is that it is possible to expand them fast and easily. The fact that there is no cabling to put in also means that WLANs are much easier and quicker to install in the first place. WLANs offer a much more flexible system than conventional LANs.

10.4.2 Drawbacks of WLANs

Security is very problematic (see Sects. 8.16 and 8.17). Data rates are often lower than can be obtained with a wired LAN. As we will see in the following section, the data rates that vendors claim for WLANs tend to be exaggerated. Though WLANs are easy to install, they will not necessarily perform reliably on a long-term basis. Since businesses need reliability, an expensive site survey is needed prior to installation, so as to ensure optimal performance. Line-of-sight obstructions, such as a metal cabinet or a partition in an open-plan office, can obscure the radio signals. Signals can also be reflected by walls and furniture. Another disadvantage of WLANs is that there is some concern that microwave radiation from transmitting WLAN devices may be harmful to humans.

10.4.3 802.11x WLAN Standards

The main standards for WLANs belong to the IEEE 802.11x family. 802.11x is a generic term that is used to refer to the whole family. An alternative name for 802.11x is Wi-Fi. The first really popular WLAN standard was IEEE 802.11b. This offered a nominal data rate of 11 Mbps in the 2.4-GHz band. The IEEE 802.11g standard provides a nominal 54 Mbps in the same frequency band. 802.11n is claimed to be about five to seven times as fast as 802.11g. 802.11n uses multiple input, multiple output (MIMO) aerial technology. Each 802.11n device has several aerials, and each of these aerials is connected to a separate transceiver (transmitter/

receiver). This means that multiple signal paths can carry multiple, independent streams of data, thus increasing the overall data rate.

The IEEE 802.11ac standard builds on 802.11n concepts to give still better performance. 802.11ac uses the 5-GHz band with up to eight MIMO streams, wider frequency bands and faster processing than 802.11n. As a result, 802.11ac offers roughly three times the speed of 802.11n, with better range and greater reliability. The IEEE 802.11ad standard offers higher data rates (claimed to be approaching 7 Gbps) over shorter ranges than IEEE 802.11ac. It uses the 60-GHz band.

Unfortunately, the claimed data rates for 802.11x WLANs are never reached in practice. For example, an 802.11b WLAN usually gives about half its claimed 11 Mbps. Also, the collision avoidance system used in Wi-Fi can cause the network to degrade dramatically if there are 'hidden nodes'.

10.4.3.1 The 802.11x Media Access Control Protocol
Wi-Fi networks have to use a different MAC protocol from wired Ethernet networks to be able to deal with collisions. The reason is that a wireless node cannot simultaneously listen to the network and transmit, as a standard Ethernet NIC does. So before the wireless node sends out any data in earnest, it listens to the channel. If all seems to be clear, it sends off the data frame. If the wireless node does not sense that the channel is clear, it backs off for a random period. If the node senses that the channel is busy while it is counting down for its random period, it suspends the countdown, ready to continue with it when the channel becomes free again. When the countdown is finished, the node sends its data frame and waits for it to be acknowledged. If no acknowledgement is received, the node backs off again using a longer random time period. This protocol is called carrier sense multiple access/ collision avoidance (CSMA/CA).

10.4.3.2 The Hidden Node Problem
The hidden node problem is illustrated in Fig. 10.2. The situation is as follows. Two nodes in a Wi-Fi network can connect to an access point or wireless router, but not to each other because they are too far apart. Neither can detect the other on the medium, and it is possible that they will transmit simultaneously. In Fig. 10.2, signals from nodes A and B can reach the wireless router, but they cannot reach each other. Node A cannot detect node B and vice versa. If both nodes transmit at the same time, an undetected collision occurs. Node C, which is located between A and B, will not be able to make sense of either transmission because of the collision.

10.4.4 WLANs Between Buildings

Figure 2.37 shows how an optical link can be made between LANs in two buildings. Microwave wireless bridges can be used in a similar way to extend a WLAN between buildings or even to join together LANs that are several miles apart. This kind of solution usually works out much more cheaply than using a leased line.

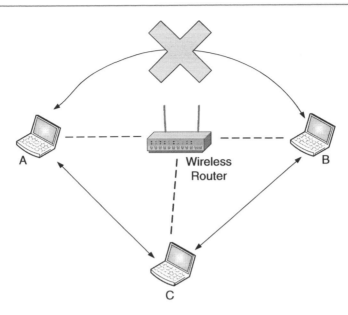

Fig. 10.2 Hidden node

10.5   Cellular Radio Networks

Mobile telephone networks use cellular radio. As can be seen in Fig. 10.3, the mobile unit (whether a phone or a computer) communicates with a *base station*. The base station is the equivalent of the access point in a WLAN and consists of a transceiver (transmitter/receiver) and a base station controller. The coverage area of a base station is called a *cell*. In reality, cells are somewhat misshapen, as shown in Fig. 10.4, but in network diagrams are usually shown as hexagonal, as in Fig. 10.3, or as perfectly circular. In city centres, the cells are much smaller (because of the denser population that they have to serve) than cells in rural locations. There are many base stations in a cellular network. Fibre-optic or point-to-point wireless links connect the base stations to a *mobile switching centre* (MSC)—a special telephone exchange for mobile applications. The MSC connects calls from fixed-line phones to mobile phones and switches calls between cells as the mobile devices move from one cell to another (*handoff* or *handover*). The same radio frequency can be used in more than one cell, as long as those cells are not next to each other. Reusing frequencies in this fashion increases the capacity of the phone network without causing interference between cells.

10.5.1 Mobile Telephone Technologies

It is possible to classify mobile telephone technologies by comparing the ways in which the medium is shared out among users. Both frequency division multiplexing (see Sect. 2.8.2) and time division multiplexing (see Sect. 2.8.1) have been used for

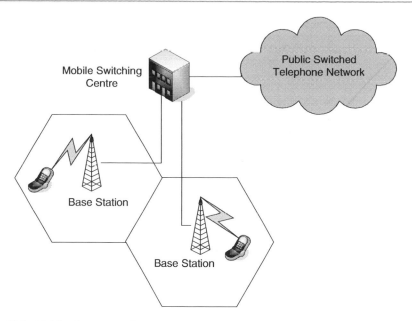

Fig. 10.3 Mobile phone network

Fig. 10.4 A real cell

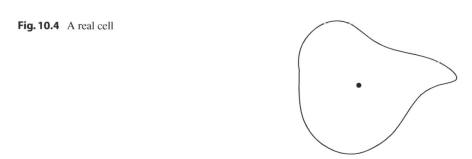

mobile phone systems. The first cellular mobile telephone networks were analogue. These used frequency division multiple access (FDMA). The cells were divided into separate channels, and different users used different frequencies for their calls.

A popular way to classify mobile phone technologies is to refer to them loosely as 'generations', although this is not the official name for any standard. So-called second-generation (2G) mobile phone networks use time division multiple access (TDMA). In these systems, different users are given different time slots on a channel. Global System for Mobiles (GSM) is the most widely used kind of 2G mobile phone system.

General packet radio services (GPRS)—sometimes referred to as 2.5G—is based on GSM. However, the data is chopped up into packets instead of a continuous stream of bits being sent down a switched circuit as in GSM. GPRS gives an 'always on' service, in which the user appears to be constantly connected to the network. It also offers higher data rates than does GSM.

10.5.1.1 The Third Generation

Third-generation (3G) mobile phone systems generally use some form of code division multiple access (CDMA). This is very different from FDMA and TDMA, where the bandwidth is divided into many narrow channels. In CDMA, in contrast, every station constantly transmits over the whole frequency spectrum. A transmission channel can carry many signals from different users at the same time without interference between the users because different users are allocated different codes to provide access to the system. The signal that carries the information is multiplied with another signal that is faster and has a wider bandwidth—a pseudo-noise (PN) sequence. The resulting, mixed signal closely resembles a noise signal. The receiver extracts the information by using the same PN sequence as the transmitter did. Signals from different users are distinguished by their use of different PN sequences. A good analogy for CDMA is a room that contains many people who are communicating in many different languages at the same time. The overall volume of noise is high, but one can still easily pick out someone speaking in the same language as oneself. CDMA is based on the DSSS transmission method (see Sect. 10.1). Wideband CDMA (WCDMA) is a variant of CDMA that can support multimedia communications at higher speeds than were previously possible. This is used in universal mobile telecommunications system (UMTS) 3G networks. High-speed downlink packet access (HSDPA) and high-speed uplink packet access (HSUPA) are add-ons to the standard 3G infrastructure that support faster data rates. Use of MIMO increases data rates further.

10.5.1.2 The Fourth Generation

Fourth-generation (4G) mobile phone systems offer still faster data rates. The term that the International Telecommunication Union Radio-communication Sector (ITU-R) standards body uses to refer to 4G is international mobile telecommunications-advanced (IMT-Advanced). IMT-Advanced specifies data rates of 100 Mbps for high mobility and 1 Gbps for low mobility. Such data rates will support advanced services and applications, such as interactive TV, mobile video blogging and advanced games. The technologies long-term evolution-advanced (LTE-Advanced) and the WirelessMAN-Advanced part of WiMAX 2 (IEEE 802.16m, explained in Sect. 10.6.2 below) are both official 4G standards. LTE is the most popular way to provide 4G by far, however, so we are going to focus our attention on that technology here. Time Division LTE (TD-LTE) is a variant of LTE that uses a different part of the wireless spectrum but is very similar to LTE.

LTE can use a large number of different frequency bands, which helps to make it very flexible. This is necessary because the same areas of radio spectrum are not available all over the world. In addition, LTE supports both frequency division duplex (FDD) and time division duplex (TDD) modes. In FDD networks, one separate carrier is used for the downlink and another one for the uplink. In TDD, there is only one carrier, shared by the uplink and downlink (TD-LTE uses TDD).

The modulation method that is used in LTE is called orthogonal frequency division multiplexing (OFDM). The high-speed data that is being transmitted is split into many lower-speed signals in narrow frequency bands (called *subcarriers*). There is no need to leave gaps between these frequency bands because each one is modulated to fit a particular waveform. This means that little radio spectrum is wasted. By design, the signals of the subcarriers are independent of each other (orthogonal) and so produce an overall signal that is fairly free from interference. Powerful computer chips are used to perform the fast Fourier transform calculations which are necessary to separate the subcarriers. OFDM is also used in other technologies besides LTE (see Sect. 10.6.2).

MIMO aerial technology is used in LTE. In LTE-Advanced, a refinement of simple LTE, up to eight aerials per handset and eight transmission layers can be used.

Increasing the density of base stations and using higher frequencies increases the data rates that are possible. However, the speed that the consumer actually gets depends on several factors. These include how many people are using the cell simultaneously, whether the user is stationary or mobile, whether the user is indoors or not, whether the user is near the mast or closer to the edge of the cell and weather conditions.

LTE-Advanced modules can be included in a wide range of terminals, not just phones per se. For example, laptops, tablet computers and games systems can all be equipped with LTE-Advanced. However, mobile phones—small, powerful, hand-held computers which can perform many different functions in addition to making voice calls—are the commonest place to find LTE-Advanced.

10.5.2 Integration Between Wi-Fi and Mobile Phone Networks

A service that integrates Wi-Fi and a mobile phone network is possible. When a subscriber to such a service moves within the range of a Wi-Fi hotspot, he or she may be switched over from the cellular radio network to the WLAN automatically. The advantage of this is that the WLAN provides a bandwidth greater than the phone network and is likely to be cheaper to use. Similarly, if a laptop computer is equipped with a suitable PC-card, it can switch between a mobile phone network and a WLAN when occasion demands.

10.6 Wireless Local Loop

As we saw in Sect. 5.2, the local loop is the telephone line between the customer's premises and the local exchange. It is usually composed of twisted-pair copper cable and is normally analogue. The local loop is a bottleneck for data communications. DSL (see Sect. 5.6) is one technology that has been used to speed up the local loop. There are also several wireless technologies that may be used to replace the copper local loop.

10.6.1 Satellite

A brief description of satellite technology was given in Sect. 2.10.3. With a satellite service, there is always more latency (delay) than with other options for replacing the local loop. This is caused by the distance the satellite is from the earth's surface.

Fig. 10.5 WiMAX

The data rates offered by satellite services tend to be high. So satellites are good for downloading large files (because of the high data rate) but not at all good for VoIP (because of the high latency). A two-way satellite system, where the dish on the customer's premises can transmit as well as receive, can be used for both upstream and downstream communication. If the system is only one way, some other technology (e.g. a phone line) is necessary for the uplink.

10.6.2 Worldwide Interoperability for Microwave Access

Worldwide interoperability for microwave access (WiMAX) is a microwave radio-based technology that can be used to replace the local loop. A base station offers about 70 Mbps, though that bandwidth has to be shared out among all the users of the base station. The coverage of a base station is a radius of 2–10 km. A base station can reach a broadcast tower up to 48 km away if there is a line of sight.

WiMAX uses the OFDM transmission technique (see Sect. 10.5.1 for an explanation of OFDM). OFDM, which is also used in 802.11a WLANs, 802.11g WLANs and elsewhere, reduces the need for a line of sight. Without a line of sight, the range of WiMAX is reduced. In addition, the further the signal has to travel, the lower the data rate that can be achieved.

The fixed wireless WiMAX standard is IEEE 802.16-2004. There is also a standard for mobile WiMAX, 802.16-2005. IEEE 802.16m, or WiMAX 2, offers better performance. WiMAX offers QoS guarantees for users. As can be seen in Fig. 10.5, the uses of WiMAX are not limited to local loop replacement.

10.7   IEEE 802.20

The aim of IEEE 802.20, which also uses OFDM transmission, is to facilitate a wireless network with data rates high enough to provide Internet access about as good as that available from cable modems. The result is rather like a high-speed mobile phone service, in that users can access it from almost anywhere while travelling at even high speeds. However, the network is accessible by portable computers such as laptops as well as mobile phones. So far, despite much promise, IEEE 802.20 has not proved very popular.

10.8   Mobile Ad Hoc Network

A mobile ad hoc network (MANET) is a self-configuring, mobile, mesh network that can be used for communication between moving users. When a mobile host that is part of a MANET transmits, all hosts that are within range receive the transmission. If any two hosts are out of range, other hosts in the network can forward their messages to them. Because any host may move anywhere at any time and may be turned on or off without warning other hosts, each host needs to be able to act autonomously. A specialised routing mechanism is necessary. An example of a MANET that is connected to the Internet is shown in Fig. 10.6. MANETS have many possible uses, including military applications, sensor networks (used to gather information in so-called 'smart' environments), Internet connection sharing and conferences. A variation on the MANET theme is the vehicular ad hoc network (VANET), in which vehicles are networked together.

10.9   Radio Frequency Identification

RFID is a form of automatic identification technology. In an RFID system, an ID number is transmitted wirelessly by an RFID *tag* (or *transponder*). A tag can be interrogated remotely about the information that it contains. Various radio technologies can be used to communicate with the tag, but it will normally consist of a microchip and a miniature radio aerial inside a mounting of some kind. Tags can be attached to items in supermarkets, factories or warehouses. The movements of such items can then be tracked. *Passive* tags need no internal power source, but *active* tags do need a power source. *Battery-assisted passive* (BAP) RFID tags need an external power source to activate them but have a greater range than ordinary passive tags.

10.10   Near Field Communication

Near field communication (NFC) makes use of RFID standards to provide two-way communication between devices. A special chip inside a mobile phone is activated by radio signals when it is placed near an NFC reader (either touching it or just a

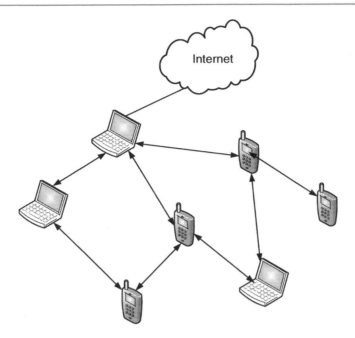

Fig. 10.6 MANET

few centimetres away from it). Thus equipped, the phone can act as a virtual credit or debit card. An NFC-enabled phone can even allow a customer in a shop to scan a product and pay for it directly without having to go to the checkout. There are many other possible applications for NFC. For example, an NFC smart card can be used to control access to a building or to pay for transport.

10.11 The Global Positioning System (GPS)

The GPS evolved from previous military aircraft tracking systems. It is based on a constellation of over 30 active MEO satellites, and in addition there are several spares. The orbits are arranged so that nine satellites are usually visible to a GPS receiver, though the receiver needs to be able to see only four satellites at any one time. People on the ground can find out accurately where they are (to within 1 m if using a specialised military receiver). The system provides 3D information, can operate in any type of weather and offers fast response times for speed information. The satellites have very accurate atomic clocks on board, as well as a computer and a radio. The clocks have to be resynchronised with a master clock at the ground control centre every 4 h. The satellites constantly broadcast their position and the time. By triangulation, a GPS receiver on the ground can find out its own longitude and latitude. It can also work out its altitude, speed and direction of travel.

GPS receivers are commonly built into mobile phones. Thus equipped, a phone may be used for *geolocation*. It can act as a satellite navigation device (Sat Nav) that can be used to plan routes or find out information on businesses that are nearby, for example.

If the phone is out of range of a GPS signal, it can still perform a less accurate form of geolocation by using information from cellular base stations. There are many other applications of GPS technology besides geolocation in mobile phones. For example, GPS facilitates some forms of *augmented reality*. In augmented reality applications, pieces of information, such as text or video, are overlaid onto the phone user's view of the real world.

10.12 Summary

This chapter started with a mention of some technical aspects of transmission. We investigated various kinds of wireless networks, both fixed and mobile. We saw how PANs can be set up, using such technologies as Bluetooth or WUSB. We looked at ZigBee, a HAN technology. We explored some aspects of WLANs that were not covered in Chap. 4. Various types of cellular radio networks for mobile phones were described. We found that satellite networks, WiMAX and IEEE 802.20 are all technologies that can replace the wired analogue local loop, although this is not the only possible use for these. The chapter finished with short discussions of mobile ad hoc networks, RFID, near field communication and the global positioning system.

10.13 Questions

1. Explain the differences between the *DSSS* and *FHSS* wireless transmission techniques.
2. In *UWB* transmission, extremely short pulses of energy are spread over many frequencies simultaneously. What is a potential problem with such a transmission method?
3. Discuss the advantages and disadvantages of *WLANs*.
4. How can users of 802.11x LANs be authenticated? (You may find it helpful to refer back to Sect. 8.16.)
5. Ethernet LANs do not use acknowledgements but 802.11x LANs do. Why is this?
6. A wireless access point (AP) has been set up as follows:
   SSID = 24HillSt
   Channel = 6
   SSID Broadcast = enabled
   Security = WEP
   Comment on what changes to the above configuration may be advisable.
   (You may need to refer to Sect. 8.16 as well as this chapter to answer this question.)
7. In what circumstances is wireless transmission required? (This question is an opportunity for reflection; a complete answer cannot be derived from this text only.)
8. Explain the role of *base stations* in a mobile phone network.

Appendix A

This appendix contains diagrams illustrating some TCP/IP packet formats. Figure A.1 shows the format of the IPv4 datagram header. Figure A.2 shows the IPv6 datagram format. Figure A.3 shows the IPv6 base header format. Figure A.4 shows the TCP segment format.

Ver	IHL	TOS	Total Length	
Identification			Flags	Frag Offset
TTL		Protocol	Header Checksum	
Source Address				
Destination Address				
Options				Pad

Fig. A.1 IPv4 datagram header format

Fig. A.2 IPv6 datagram format

J. Cowley, *Communications and Networking: An Introduction*, Undergraduate Topics in Computer Science, DOI 10.1007/978-1-4471-4357-4,

Fig. A.3 IPv6 base header
format

Ver	Traffic Class	Flow Label	
Payload Length		Next Hdr	Hop Limit
Source Address			
Destination Address			

Fig. A.4 TCP segment
format

Source Port		Destination Port	
Sequence Number			
Acknowledgment Number			
Offset	Unused	Flags	Window
Checksum		Urgent Pointer	
Options			Pad
TCP Data			

Appendix B: Glossary

2G See second-generation mobile phone network.

2.5G See GPRS.

3G See third-generation mobile phone network.

4G See fourth-generation mobile phone network.

10-Gb E See 10-gigabit Ethernet.

10GBASE-ER A 10-Gb E Ethernet variant.

10-Gigabit Ethernet Ethernet standard offering a nominal data rate of 10,000 Mbps.

40-Gb E See 40-gigabit Ethernet.

40-Gigabit Ethernet Ethernet standard offering a nominal data rate of 40,000 Mbps.

100-Gb E See 100-gigabit Ethernet.

100-Gigabit Ethernet Ethernet standard offering a nominal data rate of 100,000 Mbps.

ABR See available bit rate.

abstract syntax notation A formal language mainly used to specify data used in protocols.

access control list In networking, a packet filter that controls traffic in and out of a router interface.

access point Hardware or software that allows users of wireless devices to connect to a wired LAN.

accounting management An ISO network management functional area.

ACK See positive acknowledgement.

acknowledgement A signal that informs a transmitting device whether the receiver has successfully received data or not.

Active Directory The Microsoft® Windows® directory service that offers a way of managing the objects that make up network environments.

active RFID tag An RFID tag that needs an internal power source.

ad hoc See peer-to-peer.

adaptive filtering An e-mail filter that adapts to changes in the nature of the user's e-mail over time.

address resolution protocol A protocol that allows a source host to discover the data-link address of the destination.

J. Cowley, *Communications and Networking: An Introduction*, Undergraduate Topics in Computer Science, DOI 10.1007/978-1-4471-4357-4, © Springer-Verlag London 2012

address A unique value that identifies a computer.

ADSL See asymmetric DSL.

advanced encryption standard A secret-key encryption algorithm.

advanced persistent threat An exploit in which the attacker penetrates the target using a variety of techniques and remains undetected for as long as possible.

AES See advanced encryption standard.

aggregation See route summarisation.

AH See authentication header.

always on A service where the user is constantly connected to a network.

AM See amplitude modulation.

American National Standards Institute The organisation that administers and coordinates the US standardisation and conformity assessment system.

amplitude modulation A technique for encoding digital information by manipulating the amplitude of an analogue carrier signal.

analogue leased line A leased line that uses analogue signalling.

analogue network A network that uses analogue signalling.

analogue signalling Signalling that uses continuously varying electrical waves.

analogue transmission Transmission that uses continuously varying electrical waves.

anonymous FTP An FTP service for which the user does not need an account on the remote host.

ANSI See American National Standards Institute.

anti-spyware software Software that combats spyware.

anti-virus software Software that combats viruses.

AP See access point.

API See application programming interface.

application firewall A firewall that recognises applications, irrespective of the ports or protocols that they use.

application layer The highest layer in the OSI 7-layer model; the environment where user programs operate and communicate. Also the highest layer of TCP/IP.

application programming interface An interface that an application provides so as to allow other applications to request its services and to allow data to be exchanged.

application proxy firewall A firewall that prevents network traffic from passing directly between external and internal networks.

APT See advanced persistent threat.

ARP request A broadcast to all devices in a network.

ARP table A table that contains correspondences between IP and MAC addresses of devices on a network.

ARP See address resolution protocol.

ARQ See automatic repeat request.

ASCII transfer mode The mode of operation used in FTP to transfer plain text files.

ASN.1 See abstract syntax notation.

asymmetric DSL A form of DSL in which the downstream data rate is greater than the upstream data rate.

asynchronous transfer mode A point-to-point, switch-based and cell-based network technology, which was designed to be suitable for multimedia traffic.

asynchronous transmission Transmission where the unit of transfer is a single character and no clock signal is supplied to the terminal.

at command set A language for controlling modems developed by the Hayes modem company.

ATM See asynchronous transfer mode.

attenuation The weakening of a signal.

augmented reality Computer-generated information is overlaid onto a view of the real world.

authentication header An IPSec packet header that supports authentication and data integrity.

authentication server (security server) In Kerberos, the server that keeps the database of encrypted user identities.

authentication server In 802.1X, a server that authenticates supplicant devices.

authentication A procedure for checking that someone or something is who or what he, she or it claims to be.

authenticator In 802.1X, a component that grants authentication.

authorisation A procedure that allows network managers to control who can have access to which network resources.

automatic repeat request A procedure in which a receiver automatically asks for a retransmission of any erroneous data block.

availability The probability that a component or system will be available during a fixed time period.

available bit rate An ATM class of service that gives minimal bandwidth guarantees.

B channel See bearer channel.

backdoor Trojan A Trojan horse that enables an attacker to gain control of a computer.

bandwidth (analogue) The difference between the highest and lowest frequencies contained in a signal.

bandwidth (digital) See data rate.

BAP RFID tag See battery-assisted passive RFID tag.

base header The basic IPv6 header.

base station controller The element that provides the intelligence for a base station.

base station An element of a mobile phone network that consists of a transceiver and a base station controller and covers a cell.

base64 The commonest standard method for encoding binary e-mail messages.

baseband transmission Transmission that uses just one unmultiplexed channel.

baseline Sets the acceptable level of performance of a network.

basic rate interface An ISDN service that provides two 64-kbps B channels and a 16-kbps D channel.

battery-assisted passive RFID tag An RFID tag that needs an external power source to activate it but has a greater range than an ordinary passive tag.

Bayesian filtering See adaptive filtering.

bearer channel A 64-kbps ISDN channel that can carry voice or data traffic.

best-effort delivery A form of packet delivery in which the network tries its best to deliver the data but does not guarantee that it will be delivered.

binary exponential backoff algorithm The algorithm that computers on a CSMA/CD Ethernet network use after a collision has occurred.

binary transfer mode The mode used in FTP to transfer binary files.

biometrics The use of a physical characteristic such as a fingerprint to authenticate a user.

bit stuffing A process in HDLC which ensures that the flag bit pattern is not transmitted inside a data frame.

blacklist A kind of anti-spam filter.

blended threat An attack that employs a URL in the body of an e-mail.

blog (Weblog) A diary that is published on the World Wide Web.

Bluetooth A microwave transmission standard for PANs.

bonding A mechanism for combining two ISDN B channels.

BOOTP See bootstrap protocol.

bootstrap protocol A mechanism for IP address assignment.

bot See zombie.

breakout box Test equipment used for diagnosing cabling problems.

BRI See basic rate interface.

bridge A device that can be used to connect LAN segments.

broadband The use of a wide band of frequencies to transmit signals over more than one channel at the same time.

broadcast address The address used to send data to all hosts on a network at once.

broadcast A transmission sent to all hosts on a network at once.

buddy list See contact list.

buffer overflow attack The attacker deliberately overloads the target system's temporary memory (buffer), usually including instructions within the data that is used to make the buffer overflow.

burst error A consecutive sequence of erroneous bits.

bus A single piece of cable to which all the computers in a bus network are attached.

CA See certificate authority.

cable modem Device that modulates and demodulates computer data for transmission and reception over a cable TV system.

cable tester A device used to check the electrical connections in a cable.

caching Temporarily storing Web pages.

care-of address The IPv6 care-of address is created whenever a mobile node attaches to the Internet from a fresh location. When the mobile node sends packets to another node, its care-of address is used as the source address.

carrier Ethernet A service that uses Ethernet technology to provide long-haul links that offer the same performance and availability as standard WAN services.

carrier sense multiple access/collision avoidance The MAC protocol used in Wi-Fi networks.

carrier sense multiple access/collision detection The MAC protocol that non-switched variants of Ethernet use.

carrier signal A signal that is sent across a network and is manipulated to encode data.

carrier A telecommunications company that provides long-distance links.

CAT 5e See category 5e.

category 5e A form of UTP copper cable.

CBR See constant bit rate.

CCITT See Consultative Committee on International Telegraph and Telephone.

CDMA See code division multiple access.

cell A short, fixed-length packet (used in ATM).

cell The coverage area of a wireless base station.

cellular radio Provides a mobile telephone service by using a network of cells.

certificate authority Issues digital certificates.

challenge–response A defence against spam e-mail in which a challenge is sent to a new sender of e-mail to confirm that he or she is bona fide.

challenge–response system An authentication system in which users have to supply an encrypted number that is the same as the one that a server has generated.

channel service unit/data service unit DCE device that connects to a digital leased line; performs conversion between LAN and WAN data frames.

checksum A method for detecting transmission errors by adding up the bytes of the message.

CIDR See classless interdomain routing.

ciphertext encrypted text.

CIR See committed information rate.

circuit switching Communication in which a dedicated circuit is established for as long as the transmission lasts.

cladding Material that surrounds the core of a fibre-optic cable.

classful addressing The original Internet addressing scheme, using address classes A, B, C, D and E.

classless interdomain routing An addressing scheme for the Internet which is more efficient than the older, classful scheme.

client–server LAN A LAN that consists of one or more server computers (where shared files and programs are kept) and many client workstations.

client–server scheme A scheme in which the client requests services and the server provides services in response to the client's requests.

cloud computing The offering of information technology services over the Internet.

cloud See network cloud.

cloud-based security services Protective software is delivered as a service via the Web, on payment of a subscription.

cluster A set of computers that are coupled together using some kind of fast LAN, working as if they were one computer.

coaxial cable A kind of cable formerly used in Ethernet networks.

code division multiple access A mobile telephone technology.

collision What happens on a CSMA/CD Ethernet network when two computers try to transmit at the same time.

colon hex See colon hexadecimal.

colon hexadecimal The standard notation used for IPv6 addresses.

committed information rate The guaranteed data rate that a carrier commits to provide to a customer.

compact flash A small, removable, flash-based storage device.

confidentiality The process of ensuring that information can be accessed only by those authorised to have access to it.

configuration management An ISO network management functional area.

congestion What happens when there is too much network traffic on a link or a node.

connectionless working A form of working where no dedicated end-to-end connection is set up; data is simply sent out in the hope that it will arrive at the destination.

connection-oriented working A form of working in which when devices need to communicate with each other, they must first set up a connection.

constant bit rate An ATM class of service.

Consultative Committee on International Telegraph and Telephone The former name of the ITU-T.

contact list A list of people (contacts) with whom one wants to exchange instant messages and who are logged into the instant messaging system.

continuous RQ An ARQ scheme in which the sender can continue to transmit data blocks, even though no acknowledgements may have been received for previously transmitted blocks.

control field In an HDLC frame, indicates the type of frame.

convergence The state of an internetwork when all the routers that belong to it possess the same knowledge of routes through it.

cookie a small text file that is stored on a user's computer when he or she visits a Web site for the first time.

core The innermost region of a fibre-optic cable.

CRC See cyclic redundancy check.

crossover cable Λ cable that is used to connect two computers directly to each other without a hub or switch.

crosstalk Electromagnetic interference between the signals carried on adjacent wires of a copper cable.

CSMA/CA See carrier sense multiple access/collision avoidance.

CSMA/CD See carrier sense multiple access/collision detection.

CSU/DSU See channel service unit/data service unit.

custom subnet mask A mask that is used for subnetting.

cut sheet A record sheet that indicates the path of network cables.

cut-through mode A mode of operation of a layer-2 switch.

cyclic redundancy check An efficient error detection method.

D channel See delta channel.

DAD See duplicate address detection.

daemon A UNIX process that runs in the background without human intervention.

data circuit terminating equipment Communication equipment that connects to a carrier's network, for example, a modem.

data compression A technique that enables devices to transmit the same amount of data using fewer bits than without compression.

data over cable service interface specification Defines the standards for transferring data using a cable modem system.

data rate The amount of data transferred per second.

data terminal equipment A computer that connects to a network.

datagram packet switching A form of packet switching in which each packet contains the destination address.

datagram A packet which has no guarantees of its delivery, arrival time or order of arrival.

data-link connection identifier The virtual circuit identifier in a frame relay frame.

data-link layer The OSI layer that transforms the raw transmission facility provided by the physical layer into a communication channel that appears to be free of errors.

DCE See data circuit terminating equipment.

DDOS See distributed denial of service.

de facto standard A standard supported by more than one vendor but with no official status.

DECnet Network architecture of the Digital Equipment Corporation (now defunct).

decryption The inverse of encryption.

dedicated link A link provided for the exclusive use of an organisation.

default gateway address The address of the router that a computer will use to access another network by default.

delta channel The ISDN signalling channel.

demilitarised zone A network area between an organisation's trusted internal network and an external network such as the Internet.

denial of service An attack with the aim of stopping an Internet server (usually a Web server) functioning.

dense wavelength division multiplexing Similar to ordinary wavelength division multiplexing but offers greater data rates.

destination address An address that identifies the receiving computer.

destination The receiving computer.

deterministic network A network technology which guarantees that the maximum waiting time before gaining access to the network will not be above a certain figure.

DF flag See don't fragment flag.

DHCP See dynamic host configuration protocol.

DHCPv6 See dynamic host configuration protocol version 6.

dial-up modem A modem used with the analogue PSTN.

digital certificate A user's public key plus some other information that has been digitally signed.

digital subscriber line A technology which offers high data rates over ordinary copper telephone lines.

direct sequence spread spectrum A wireless transmission technique in which each data bit is encoded as a group of bits that are transmitted simultaneously on a number of different frequencies.

distance-vector routing protocol A routing protocol in which a router regularly sends copies of its routing table to its neighbours.

distributed denial of service A DOS attack mounted from many computers at once.

distributed system A system consisting of many processors linked together and acting as one computer, under the control of one copy of the operating system.

DIX The original Ethernet standard, developed by the Digital, Intel and Xerox companies.

DLCI See data-link connection identifier.

DMZ See demilitarised zone.

DNS server See domain name server.

DNS See domain name system.

DOCSIS See data over cable service interface specification.

DOD The US government Department of Defense.

domain name server A computer that responds to requests from client machines to translate domain names into numerical IP addresses.

domain name system The system that automatically translates domain names into IP addresses.

domain A group of computers that belong together for some reason.

Don't fragment flag A bit in an IP datagram that if set tells a receiving router not to fragment the datagram.

DOS See denial of service.

dotted decimal The standard notation for IPv4 addresses.

download To transfer files from a remote host (server) to the local host (client).

DSL access multiplexer A device that allows multiple subscriber lines to be multiplexed together for long-distance transmission over a high-speed leased line.

DSL See digital subscriber line.

DSLAM See DSL access multiplexer.

DSSS See direct sequence spread spectrum.

DTE See data terminal equipment.

dual stacking A network node is connected to an IPv4 network and an IPv6 network at the same time, with both protocol stacks operating on the node simultaneously.

dumb terminal A terminal with no processing power.

duplicate address detection A mechanism for detecting duplicate IP addresses.

DWDM See dense wavelength division multiplexing.

dynamic address assignment A system in which a server can give a host an IP address on request.

dynamic host configuration protocol version 6 The version of the dynamic host configuration protocol for use with IPv6.

dynamic host configuration protocol A protocol used for automatic address assignment.

dynamic Web link A Web link where the content changes according to what a user has clicked on.

E3 A digital leased line standard that offers a data rate of 34.368 Mbps.

EAP See extensible authentication protocol.

EAP-TLS An authentication protocol.

E-carrier A digital leased line service available in Europe and much of the rest of the world.

echo cancellation Techniques used to detect and remove echo from a telephone conversation.

echo message A type of ICMP message.

echo reply A type of ICMP message.

echo request A type of ICMP message.

EIA See Electronic Industries Alliance.

EIA/TIA-232 A physical-layer protocol.

Electronic Industries Alliance A standards body.

e-mail filtering E-mail is scanned before it reaches the addressee and deflected if it appears to be harmful.

encapsulating security payload An IPSec header that offers privacy using encryption.

encapsulation The packaging of data into a suitable form to be transmitted over a network.

encryption The process of encoding data so as to make it unreadable by anybody except the intended receiver of the data.

envelope A part of an e-mail message that encapsulates the message itself and contains the necessary information for transporting the message.

error control Error detection and error correction.

error correction Error control that allows a receiver to correct a message that has been corrupted during transmission.

error detection Error control that allows a receiver to detect errors in a message that it has received.

ESMTP See extended SMTP.

ESP See encapsulating security payload.

Ethernet address The address of an Ethernet NIC.

Ethernet II A synonym for DIX Ethernet.

Ethernet interface An Ethernet NIC.

Ethernet switch A layer-2 switch used on an Ethernet network.

Ethernet A type of LAN.

ETSI See European Telecommunications Standards Institute.

EUI-64 See extended unique identifier-64.

European Telecommunications Standards Institute A standards body.

EV SSL See extended validation SSL.

even parity A parity bit added to a character to make the number of 1 bits an even number.

extended SMTP Allows much longer messages than normal SMTP.

extended unique identifier-64 Provides a way of forming a 64-bit interface identifier from a MAC address.

extended validation SSL Offers improved validation of SSL Web sites.

extensible authentication protocol An authentication protocol used on WLANs.

extensible HyperText markup language A markup language similar to HTML but with a more tightly defined syntax.

extensible markup language A markup language used to describe many different kinds of data.

extension header An optional IPv6 header.

extranet VPN A VPN that allows a business to share data with partners, suppliers, customers and other businesses.

false positive The misidentification by an IDS or IPS of innocent activity as suspicious activity.

fault management An ISO network management functional area.

FCoE See fibre channel over Ethernet.

FCS See frame check sequence.

FDD See frequency division duplex.

FDDI See fibre-distributed data interface.

FDM See frequency division multiplexing.

FDMA See frequency division multiple access.

FEC See forward error correction.

FHSS See frequency hopping spread spectrum.

fibre channel over Ethernet A networking technology that can be used in storage area networks.

fibre channel A high-speed fibre-optic network technology.

fibre-distributed data interface A large-scale, ring-based token passing system, with built-in fault tolerance.

fibre-optic cable A glass (or plastic) fibre that carries a beam of light.

file transfer protocol A protocol used to transfer files to or from an FTP server.

firewall Software or hardware that restricts access to an organisation's computers.

fixed wireless A term referring to the use of wireless technologies with devices that do not move.

flag field The field that delimits an HDLC frame.

flow control A mechanism for speeding up or slowing down the rate at which a source is sending data, according to how much buffer space the receiver has available.

flow label A field in the IPv6 base header used to forward datagrams along a prearranged path.

FM See frequency modulation.

formal standard A standard issued by an official standards body.

forward error correction An error control mechanism that allows a receiver to correct errors without having to ask for a retransmission.

fourth-generation mobile phone network A mobile phone system offering high data rates.

four-way tear down A procedure used to get rid of a TCP connection once it is finished with.

FRAD See frame relay access device.

fragmentation An IP mechanism for dividing a large datagram into smaller ones.

fragment-free mode A mode of operation of a layer-2 switch.

frame check sequence The CRC field in a data-link layer frame.

frame relay access device A device that allows access to a frame relay network.

frame relay A WAN technology which uses virtual circuits.

frame trailer Extra data placed at the end of a frame.

frame The data-link layer protocol data unit.

free space optics The use of lasers for computer communications through free space (without a cable).

frequency division duplex A mode of LTE where one separate carrier is used for the downlink and another one for the uplink.

frequency division multiple access A technique used in analogue mobile phone systems for sharing out bandwidth.

frequency division multiplexing A technique for dividing up an analogue link into several frequency bands, with each frequency band carrying one channel.

frequency hopping spread spectrum A microwave wireless transmission technique in which signals are transmitted in a pseudo-random sequence on several different frequencies.

frequency modulation A modulation technique, involving manipulation of the frequency of the carrier signal, that can be used in modems.

frequency The number of times a wave goes up and down per second (measured in Hertz).

FSO See free space optics

FTP See file transfer protocol.

full duplex A form of working in which data is transmitted in two directions at the same time.

Galileo European alternative to GPS.

general packet radio services A mobile phone service in which the data is transmitted in packets.

geosynchronous orbit The usual orbit for communications satellites, synchronised with the rotation of the earth.

gigabit Ethernet The 1,000 Mbps version of Ethernet.

GLObal NAvigation Satellite System Russian alternative to GPS.

global positioning system A satellite navigation system that gives location and time information worldwide.

global system for mobiles The most widely used kind of 2G mobile phone system.

GLONASS See GLObal NAvigation Satellite System.

go-back-N An ARQ retransmission scheme in which all blocks from the erroneous block onwards are retransmitted.

GPRS See general packet radio services.

GPS See global positioning system.

grid computing A form of distributed computing in which multiple computers are networked together to give the equivalent of a very powerful supercomputer.

GSM See global system for mobiles.

hacktivist An activist who mounts cyber attacks on organisations for political reasons.

half duplex A form of working in which data can be transmitted in two directions but not in both directions at the same time.

HAN See home area network.

handoff The transfer of a mobile device from one base station to another as the device moves from one cell to another.

handover See handoff.

handshake An exchange between sender and receiver used to negotiate the parameters of a communication.

hashing algorithm An algorithm to which the input is a long message and the output is a short binary string.

Hayes A modem company (defunct).

HDLC See high-level data-link control.

head-end The place where a cable company is connected to the Internet and where it receives television channels.

header In an e-mail, contains control information such as sender, recipient, subject, etc.

header The information that precedes the data in a packet.

Hertz A unit used to measure frequency (cycles per second).

hidden node A potential problem in Wi-Fi networks, when two nodes are too far apart to detect each other.

hierarchical topology An alternative term for a tree topology.

high-level data link control A data-link protocol used in WANs.

high-speed downlink packet access An add-on to the standard 3G infrastructure that supports faster downlink data rates.

high-speed uplink packet access An add-on to the standard 3G infrastructure that supports faster uplink data rates.

home agent The home agent is a node on the home IPv6 network that allows a mobile node to be reachable at its home address, regardless of where it is actually located.

home area network A network for devices in the home.

home page The site a Web browser first goes to when it is started (can also signify the main page of a Web site).

HomePlug AV A HomePlug standard.

HomePlug AV2 The updated HomePlug standard.

HomePlug A power-line communication system that sends Ethernet signals over the mains electricity cables in a building.

hop count A measure of the number of hops (networks) between one router and another.

hop limit field A field in the IPv6 base header that is decremented by one every time a node forwards the datagram (similar to the hop count field in IPv4).

host field That part of an IP address which indicates an individual host on a network.

host A computer that is connected to a network.

host-based IDS An IDS that is mounted on a host computer.

HSDPA See high-speed downlink packet access.

HSUPA See high-speed uplink packet access.

HTML See HyperText markup language.

HTTP GET command A command used to download data from a Web server to a browser.

HTTP POST command A command that can be used to upload data to a Web server from a browser.

HTTP PUT command A command that can be used to upload data to a Web server from a browser.

HTTP See HyperText transfer protocol.

hub A central device that can be used to connect all the computers in a network.

hybrid cloud A mixture of private and public clouds.

hyperlink An element (e.g. a word or an image) in an electronic document (e.g. a Web page) that you can click on to reach a new document or a new place in the same document.

HyperText markup language A markup language used to make Web pages and cause them to appear on screen in a particular way.

HyperText transfer protocol A protocol used to transfer pages on the World Wide Web.

IaaS See infrastructure as a service.

ICMP echo reply The reply to an ICMP echo request.

ICMP echo request A message that sends a packet of data to a host and expects the data to be sent back in an echo reply (underlies the ping utility).

ICMP See Internet control message protocol.

idle RQ An ARQ scheme in which the sender waits for the receiver to acknowledge receipt of a data block before sending the next block.

IDS See intrusion detection system.

IEEE 1000BASE-T A twisted-pair variant of gigabit Ethernet.

IEEE 100BASE-T A twisted-pair variant of 100-Mbps Ethernet.

IEEE 1901.2010 Standard for HomePlug networks.

IEEE 802.11a A 54-Mbps wireless LAN standard.

IEEE 802.11ac A newer and faster wireless LAN standard than 802.11n.

IEEE 802.11ad A faster wireless LAN standard than 802.11ac, but with a shorter range.

IEEE 802.11b An 11-Mbps wireless LAN standard.

IEEE 802.11g A 54-Mbps wireless LAN standard.

IEEE 802.11i An official WLAN security standard which was agreed after WPA2.

IEEE 802.11n A high-speed wireless LAN standard that uses MIMO technology.

IEEE 802.11x A generic term used to refer to the 802.11 family of WLAN standards.

IEEE 802.15.1 The Bluetooth standard.

IEEE 802.15.4 The standard that ZigBee is based on.

IEEE 802.16-2004 A fixed wireless WiMAX standard.

IEEE 802.16-2005 A standard for mobile WiMAX.

IEEE 802.16e A standard for mobile WiMAX.

IEEE 802.16m The WiMAX 2 standard.

IEEE 802.1p A prioritisation standard for IP telephony.

IEEE 802.1q A standard that supports virtual LANs.

IEEE 802.1X An authentication standard for LANs.

IEEE 802.20 A high-speed mobile wireless standard.

IEEE 802.3 An Ethernet standard.

IEEE 802.3af-2003 The original power over Ethernet standard.

IEEE 802.3at-2009 The improved power over Ethernet standard.

IEEE 802.5 The Token Ring standard.

IEEE A standards body. See Institute of Electrical and Electronics Engineers.

IETF See Internet Engineering Task Force.

IKE See Internet key exchange.

IM See instant messaging.

IMAP See Internet message access protocol.

IMT-Advanced See international mobile telecommunications-advanced.

information frame An HDLC frame that carries data.

infrared A part of the electromagnetic spectrum that can be used for short-distance wireless communications.

infrastructure as a service Computing infrastructure (not including an operating system) is made available to customers over a network, normally the Internet.

INMS See integrated network management system.

instant messaging A form of messaging that allows real-time written communications over the Internet.

Institute of Electrical and Electronics Engineers A US standards body.

integrated network management system A system that allows a network manager to monitor and control the corporate internetwork from a central point.

integrated services digital network An all-digital telephone network that can offer integrated services of various kinds.

interface identifier Used in IPv6 to identify an interface on a link (like the host part of an IPv4 address).

intermediate system-to-intermediate system A routing protocol.

international mobile telecommunications-advanced Official ITU-R term for 4G mobile phone systems.

International Organisation for Standardisation A standards body.

International Telecommunication Union Radio-communication Sector A standards body. The sector of the ITU that is responsible for radio communication.

International Telecommunication Union Telecommunication Standardisation Sector A standards body.

Internet control message protocol The protocol that IP uses to report errors and carry informational messages.

Internet Engineering Task Force A standards body.

Internet key exchange A protocol that is responsible for transfer of encryption keys in IPSec.

Internet layer The TCP/IP equivalent of the OSI network layer.

Internet message access protocol A protocol for retrieving e-mail from a server.

Internet protocol A layer-3 protocol used on all TCP/IP networks, including the Internet.

Internet service provider A company or organisation that offers access to the Internet.

Internet small computer system interface A protocol that carries SCSI commands over an IP-based Ethernet SAN.

Internet telephony See voice over IP.

Internet A global internetwork that uses TCP/IP protocols.

internetwork Two or more computer networks connected together.

interoperability The ability of software and hardware on different computers from different manufacturers to share data.

intrusion detection system A system that automatically detects intrusion attempts.

intrusion prevention system A system that automatically prevents intrusion attempts.

IP address A layer-3 32-bit (IPv4) or 128-bit (IPv6) address given to a computer that uses TCP/IP.

IP security A framework of open security standards that was developed by the IETF.

IP telephony See voice over IP.

IP version 4 Version 4 of IP; uses 32-bit addresses.

IP version 6 Version 6 of IP; designed to improve upon IPv4 in various ways.

IP See Internet protocol.

IPS See intrusion prevention system.

IPSec transport mode An IPSec mode in which routers use the original IP header.

IPSec tunnel mode An IPSec mode in which the whole source packet, including the original header, is authenticated and encrypted and is given a new IP header.

IPSec See IP security.

IPv4 See IP Version 4.

IPv6 tunnelling IPv6 datagrams are encapsulated in IPv4 datagrams and sent over an IPv4 network.

IPv6 See IP Version 6.

iSCSI See Internet small computer system interface.

ISDN B channel See bearer channel.

ISDN D channel See delta channel.

ISDN See integrated services digital network.

IS-IS See intermediate system-to-intermediate system.

ISO See International Organisation for Standardisation.

ISP See Internet service provider.

ITU-R See International Telecommunication Union Radio-communication Sector.

ITU-T See International Telecommunication Union Telecommunication Standardisation Sector.

jabber An illegally long Ethernet frame (alternatively, a malfunctioning device).

jack A socket into which a plug fits.

jitter Variation in delay.

jumbo frame A large Ethernet frame.

Kerberos A server-based authentication system.

key A value used to encrypt and decrypt a message.

keystroke logger Software that captures a user's keystrokes.

label An extra 4 bytes added to packets as they enter an MPLS network (see flow label also).

LAN See local area network.

LAPB See link access procedure balanced.

LAPD See link access procedure D-channel.

LAPF See link access procedure for frame mode services.

laser diode A semiconductor-based laser (light-emitting device).

latency Delay.

layer-2 switch An internetworking device used to connect network segments.

layering The organisation of networks as a series of layers or levels.

leased line A permanent, dedicated, point-to-point link that is leased from a telecommunications carrier.

length field The field in an IEEE 802.3 frame that contains the length of the data.

LEO See low earth orbit.

line filter A device that can be used instead of an ADSL splitter.

link access procedure balanced An HDLC-type protocol used in X.25.

link access procedure D-channel An HDLC-type protocol used in the ISDN D channel.

link access procedure for frame mode services An HDLC-type protocol used in frame relay.

link-state advertisement In link-state routing, a small packet that is broadcast to all the other routers in the internetwork whenever there is a change in the state of a link.

link-state routing protocol A routing protocol in which each router in an internetwork keeps a map of the topology of the whole internetwork.

LLC field The field for logical link control in IEEE 802.3.

local area network A network spanning a small geographical area.

local loop The telephone line between the customer's premises and the local exchange.

localhost An alternative term for loopback address.

location bar The place where a Web browser shows the URL of the Web page that is being viewed.

logical connection An alternative term for a virtual circuit.

logical link control The upper sub-layer of IEEE 802 LAN protocols; controls the setting up of a link using an HDLC-type protocol.

logical topology How the transmission medium can be accessed by the computers on the network.

long-term evolution-advanced One of the official ITU-R standards for 4G mobile phone systems.

loopback address The address 127.0.0.1 (in IPv4), used for testing IP software.

low earth orbit An alternative orbit to the geosynchronous orbit.

LSA See link-state advertisement.

LTE-Advanced See long-term evolution-advanced.

MAC address The unique hardware address of an NIC.

MAC See media access control.

malvertising Advertising used in a malware attack.

malware Malicious software.

MAN See metropolitan area network.

management information base The database of objects (variables) used in SNMP.

Manchester encoding An encoding scheme used in 10-Mbps Ethernet.

MANET See mobile ad hoc network.

man-in-the-middle attack An attack in which a user gets between a sender and receiver and is able to read and modify the messages passing over the network at will.

maximum transmission unit The largest packet that can be sent over a network.

mean time between failures The mean time for which a device or system will operate before it fails.

mean time to repair The average time necessary to repair a failure within a computer system.

media access control Control of access to the network medium (e.g. a cable).

media player A streaming audio and/or video client.

media server A streaming audio and/or video server.

media The plural form of medium.

medium earth orbit An alternative orbit to the geosynchronous orbit.

medium The path along which data travels (often a cable).

MEO See medium earth orbit.

mesh topology A topology in which every computer is directly connected to every other one.

message digest The output from a one-way hash function.

message integrity Proof that a message has not been altered in transit.

message switching The switching of complete messages from router to router.

message transfer agent Software that transfers e-mail messages from one computer to another.

metafile A file that contains data describing another file.

metric A way of measuring how good routes are.

metropolitan area network A network that can span an entire city and its suburbs.

MIB See management information base.

microblog A very small blog, restricted to a limited number of words.

microwave radio The commonest form of wireless transmission; consists of ultra-high, super-high or extremely high-frequency radio waves.

MIME See multipurpose Internet mail extensions.

MIMO See multiple input, multiple output.

mobile ad hoc network A self-configuring, mobile, mesh network that can be used for communication between moving users.

mobile IP A feature of IPv6; allows mobile computers to keep their network connections while roaming.

mobile switching centre A special telephone exchange for mobile applications.

modem MOdulator/DEModulator; encodes digital information so that it can be carried over an analogue system.

modulation Refers to ways of encoding information onto a carrier signal—amplitude, frequency or phase modulation.

modulo-2 arithmetic A kind of arithmetic in which there are no carries and no borrows and there is no difference between addition and subtraction.

monitor See probe.

Moving Picture Experts Group A working group that develops video and audio encoding standards.

MP3 See MPEG-1 audio layer 3.

MPEG See Moving Picture Experts Group.

MPEG-1 audio layer 3 An encoding and compression format for digital audio.

MPLS See multiprotocol label switching.

MSC See mobile switching centre.

MTA See message transfer agent.

MTBF See mean time between failures.

MTTR See mean time to repair.

MTU See maximum transmission unit.

multicast The same message sent to a group of hosts.

multimode fibre Optical fibre in which multiple wavelengths of light take multiple paths through the fibre core.

multiple input, multiple output A microwave wireless technology that uses several aerials (antennae) at once.

multiplexer A communications device that combines several signals for transmission over a single line.

multiport repeater A repeater with several ports (a hub).

multiprotocol label switching An efficient way of doing routing, based upon a 4-byte label.

multipurpose Internet mail extensions A standard way of encoding and decoding non-text e-mail attachments.

NAK See negative acknowledgement.

NAT See network address translation.

near field communication Makes use of RFID standards to provide two-way communication between devices.

negative acknowledgement A signal that informs a transmitting device that the receiver has not successfully received data.

neighbour advertisement (neighbor advertisement) The IPv6 equivalent of an ARP reply.

neighbour solicitation (neighbor solicitation) The IPv6 equivalent of an ARP request.

netstat (network statistics) An operating-system command that can be used to display information about TCP/IP network connections.

network access layer A layer in the TCP/IP model that carries out the functions of the OSI data-link and physical layers.

network adaptor See network interface card.

network address translation A technique that allows many devices on an internal network to use only one external IP address.

network architecture A set of layers and protocols that work together.

network cloud A term that is often used to refer to a WAN when we are not interested in its internal details.

network interface card A circuit board that lets a computer connect into a network.

network layer The OSI layer that is concerned with the routing of packets across a network.

network operating system The operating system that runs on the server computer in a client–server LAN.

network troubleshooting The process of finding out what is causing a problem on a network and sorting it out.

network Consists of a number of interconnected, autonomous computers.

network-based IDS An IDS in which sensors monitor traffic on each network segment.

next header field A field in the IPv6 base header that identifies the type of header that follows the base header.

NFC See near field communication.

NIC See network interface card.

node A device connected to a computer network.

noise Interference (usually electromagnetic).

non-deterministic network The inverse of a deterministic network.

non-repudiation A procedure for preventing the sender or receiver of a message from denying that the message has been sent.

non-return-to-zero A digital encoding scheme.

NOS See network operating system.

notary service A trusted third-party system that provides non-repudiation.

NRZ See non-return-to-zero.

nslookup A network utility program that can be used to look up the IP address corresponding to a URL or vice versa.

OC-192 Optical carrier level 192: a SONET standard for transmission over optical fibre.

octet A group of 8 bits (a byte).

odd parity A parity bit added to a character to make the number of 1 bits an odd number.

OFDM See orthogonal frequency division multiplexing.

on-line UPS An UPS that uses its batteries to provide power all the time.

open shortest path first A link-state routing protocol.

open systems interconnection A network architecture devised by ISO.

optical fibre Glass (or plastic) fibre used to connect devices in a network.

orthogonal frequency division multiplexing A microwave transmission technique.

OSI 7-layer reference model See open systems interconnection.

OSI See open systems interconnection.

OSPF See open shortest path first.

P2P See peer-to-peer.

PaaS See platform as a service.

packet sniffer See protocol analyser.

packet spoofing The constructing of a packet with a false sender address by an attacker.

packet switching A technology in which messages are divided into packets before they are transmitted; the packets are then sent individually, possibly reaching the destination via different routes.

packet A unit of information suitable for travelling between one computer and another.

packet-filtering firewall A kind of firewall in which a router blocks certain IP addresses, subnets or TCP or UDP port numbers by means of access control lists.

PAN See personal area network.

parallel data transfer A procedure in which multiple wires are used to transfer whole units of data simultaneously.

parity An error detection technique in which an additional bit is appended to a character to give either an even or an odd number of 1 bits.

passive RFID tag An RFID tag that does not need an internal power source.

patch panel A piece of hardware that acts like a small switchboard and is a convenient means of connecting various pieces of networking equipment together.

patch A software update.

path MTU discovery A technique for finding out the maximum size of data that can be sent all the way from source to destination in one packet.

payload length field A 16-bit field in the IPv6 base header that indicates how many bytes there are in the data field.

PC-card A standard for 16-bit add-on cards for laptop computers (formerly called PCMCIA card; the 32-bit standard is called CardBus).

PCI See peripheral component interconnect.

PCMCIA See Personal Computer Memory Card International Association.

peer processes The entities comprising the corresponding layers of a network architecture such as OSI or TCP/IP on different machines; these appear to communicate directly with each other.

peer-to-peer file sharing Sharing files over the Internet without a central server.

peer-to-peer LAN A LAN in which none of the computers has control over the LAN and they act as client or server computers as necessary.

performance management An ISO network management functional area.

peripheral component interconnect A PC expansion bus standard.

permanent virtual circuit A virtual circuit set up by an administrator for repeated use between the same two devices.

permutation One of the steps involved in secret-key encryption, in which the data is rearranged.

personal area network A network that permits communication between devices that belong to a single owner over very short distances.

Personal Computer Memory Card International Association The organisation responsible for the PC card standard.

phase modulation A technique for encoding digital information by manipulating the phase of an analogue carrier signal.

phishing attack The attacker tries to trick the victim into giving up private information by sending out fake e-mails and/or making a fake Web site.

photodiode A detector that generates an electrical pulse when light falls upon it.

physical layer The OSI layer concerned with the transmission of bit patterns over a communications channel.

physical topology The physical configuration of a network.

piconet See personal area network.

ping of death An attack in which the attacker tries to overwhelm a server computer by flooding it with ping packets.

ping A utility program used to check for reachability of a host.

PKI See public-key infrastructure.

plaintext The message used as input to an encryption algorithm.

platform as a service Computing infrastructure (including an operating system) is made available to paying customers over a network, normally the Internet.

PM See phase modulation.

PN sequence See pseudo-noise sequence.

POe See power over Ethernet.

point-to-point link A link from one place to one other place.

polymorphic virus A virus that can change its form automatically, which makes it more difficult to detect.

POP See post office protocol.

POP3 POP version 3.

port mapping table A table used by a NAT router to tell it which device on the internal network is sending or receiving data via the external address at any one time.

port scanning A method that an attacker can use to find out what TCP or UDP ports are open in a network device or a network.

port A number that TCP and UDP use to map incoming data to an application running on a computer.

port A physical interface.

positive acknowledgement A signal that informs a transmitting device that the receiver has successfully received data.

post office protocol A protocol for retrieving e-mail from a server.

power over Ethernet A system which carries an electricity supply along CAT 3 or CAT 5 cables at the same time as Ethernet signals.

preamble The first field in an Ethernet frame; warns stations on the network that a frame is coming.

presentation layer The OSI layer that deals with data formatting, data compression and data encryption.

PRI See primary rate interface.

primary rate interface A form of ISDN that offers thirty 64-kbps B channels (23 in North America) and a 64-kbps D channel.

private (or internal or corporate) cloud Offers services to a restricted population of users, hidden behind a firewall.

private IP address An address that can be used only within a private network.

private-key encryption See secret-key encryption.

probe An RMON agent that reports the information that it collects from a network segment.

profile Gives a Microsoft® Windows® user a personal desktop environment.

proprietary standard A standard devised by a vendor for use with the company's products.

protocol analyser Special software or hardware that is able to capture and interpret network frames and packets.

protocol field A field in the IPv4 header that indicates the higher-layer protocol (usually TCP or UDP) that is being carried in the IP datagram.

protocol stack A set of protocols that work together.

protocol A set of rules for communication.

proxy agent Translates between SNMP and proprietary software.

proxy server An intermediary system involved in VoIP call set-up when the SIP protocol is in use. (More generally, a server that lets clients make indirect network connections to other network servers.)

pseudo-noise sequence A signal used in CDMA mobile phone systems.

PSTN See public switched telephone network.

public cloud Services are made available to the general public over the Internet.

public switched telephone network The ordinary, fixed-line telephone network that has been in use for a century or so.

public-key encryption An encryption system in which different keys are used for encryption and decryption—a public key that everybody knows and a private key that only the recipient of the message knows.

public-key infrastructure The legal, organisational and technical framework used to support public-key cryptography.

PVC See permanent virtual circuit.

QoS See quality of service.

quality of service The capability of a network to provide a guaranteed throughput level.

radio frequency identification A form of automatic identification technology.

radio A microwave transmitter/receiver that allows a device (computer, phone, etc.) to access a wireless network.

RAID See redundant array of independent disks.

RARP See reverse address resolution protocol.

real-time streaming protocol A protocol that is often used to control the delivery of streamed data over a network.

real-time transport protocol A protocol for transmitting real-time data such as audio and video over the Internet.

reassembly The process of putting back together a fragmented IP datagram.

redundant array of independent disks A system that uses two or more hard drives in combination to give fault tolerance and/or better performance.

Reed–Solomon code An error-correcting code.

registered jack-45 An eight-wire connector for twisted-pair cable, often used to connect computers to a LAN.

remote control A method of remote access to a LAN in which the user's PC on the LAN does the processing but is under the control of the remote PC.

remote monitor An extension to the SNMP MIB that allows the monitoring of remote sites from a central point.

remote node A method of remote access to a LAN in which the remote computer acts as a node or workstation on the LAN.

remote wipe The removal of all data from a mobile device, carried out from a distance as a security measure.

remote-access VPN A VPN that allows home workers to gain secure access to their company's network.

repeater A hardware device that regenerates a digital signal.

request for comments A document that contains technical and organisational notes about the Internet, possibly including definitions of Internet standards such as protocols.

request–response protocol The type of protocol used in a client server system, in which a client requests services and the server provides services in response to the client's requests.

reverse address resolution protocol A mechanism for IP address assignment.

RFC See request for comments.

RFID tag A very small microchip that can be interrogated by radio and can transmit its ID number.

RFID transponder See RFID tag.

RFID See radio frequency identification.

ring A network topology.

RIP See routing information protocol.

RJ-45 See registered jack-45.

RMON alarm group Will set off an alarm if preset parameters are exceeded.

RMON event group Allows a network administrator to define events for a probe, enabling it to log these events or send an SNMP trap.

RMON filter group Can be used to configure a probe to select individual packets for observation.

RMON history group Can be used to take snapshots of the network.

RMON host group Gathers information about certain hosts.

RMON HostTopN Lists the top network hosts rated according to a base statistic specified by the network management system.

RMON matrix group Keeps tables of statistics about the number of packets, bytes and errors sent between two addresses.

RMON packet capture group Used to copy packets from the filter group into buffer memory.

RMON statistics group Details Ethernet statistics, such as collisions and multicasts.

RMON See remote monitor.

roaming The ability of a WLAN device to move from one WLAN AP coverage area to another with no interruption to the service.

rootkit A special form of remote-access Trojan horse that can give an intruder complete control of a remote computer.

route summarisation The ability to represent a block of addresses by just one summary address using CIDR.

router configuration file A file containing rules and instructions to control the way in which data packets flow through a router.

router discovery request A procedure that a host that has not been configured with a default gateway uses to find out available routers.

router solicitation request An ICMP message that is the first step in the router discovery procedure.

router A computer that can make decisions about where an incoming network packet should be sent next, using information contained in its routing table.

routing information protocol A distance-vector routing protocol.

routing protocol A protocol that allows routers to inform each other about networks that they know about, without human intervention.

routing table A table that contains a router's knowledge about open paths through networks.

RS232-C The former name of EIA/TIA-232.

RTCP See RTP control protocol.

RTP control protocol A control protocol that works together with RTP.

RTP See real-time transport protocol.

RTSP See real-time streaming protocol.

runt An illegally short Ethernet frame.

SaaS See software as a service.

SAN See storage area network.

SATA See serial advanced technology attachment.

screened twisted-pair cable A form of twisted-pair cable in which there is an outer braided or foil shield.

SCSI See small computer system interface.

ScTP See screened twisted-pair cable.

SDH See synchronous digital hierarchy.

SDSL See symmetric DSL.

Search for Extraterrestrial Intelligence A grid computing initiative employing the unused processor cycles of thousands of computers to search for signals from intelligent beings in outer space.

second-generation mobile phone network A digital mobile phone network that uses TDMA (or rarely CDMA); GSM is the most widely used kind.

secret-key encryption A form of encryption that uses the same mathematical key for encryption and decryption.

secure real-time transport protocol Secure form of the real-time transport protocol.

secure shell A protocol and program that includes all the functionality of telnet, but is secure.

secure single sign-on A system that requires users to log into a network once only and thus get access to all the resources that they are allowed to use.

secure sockets layer/transport layer security Two very similar protocols that provide secure communications on the Internet.

security as a service See cloud-based security services.

security management An ISO network management functional area.

security policy specification language A special language for writing security policies, devised by the IETF.

security policy A document that gives rules for access, states how policies are enforced and explains the basic architecture of a security environment.

segment A portion of a larger network.

segment The TCP protocol data unit.

segmentation In TCP, the process in which data is divided into segments.

selective retransmission An ARQ retransmission system in which only the blocks that have errors are retransmitted.

sequence number A number given to a frame or segment of data when it is transmitted.

serial advanced technology attachment interface A serial hard disk drive interface.

serial ATA See serial advanced technology attachment.

serial data transfer A method of data transfer where only one wire carries the data and only 1 bit is transmitted at a time.

serial interface A port on a computer for serial transfer.

serial interface A port on a router used to connect to a WAN.

server A server-class computer, more powerful than mere workstations.

server Software that provides services in response to a client's requests.

service set identifier A unique name, 32 characters long and attached to all packets on a wireless network, to identify the packets as belonging to that network.

session hijacking A way of taking over somebody else's Web session by getting hold of the session ID.

session ID (session identifier) A cookie that identifies a session that is taking place over the Web.

session initiation protocol A TCP/IP application-layer protocol that can establish, modify and end multimedia sessions, including VoIP calls.

session layer An OSI layer that deals with the establishment, maintenance and termination of a session (a communication path) between two users.

SETI See Search for Extraterrestrial Intelligence.

shielded twisted pair A twisted-pair cable with shielding added to give more protection from interference both from inside and outside the cable.

shielding Metal mesh or aluminium foil that helps to prevent electromagnetic interference.

short message service Facility for text messaging on phones.

shortest path first A link-state routing algorithm.

signature A distinctive bit pattern that betrays the presence of a virus.

simple mail transfer protocol The standard protocol for sending electronic mail over the Internet.

simple network management protocol A TCP/IP application-layer protocol that makes it easy for management information to be exchanged between network devices.

simplex transmission Transmission that takes place only ever in one direction.

single point of failure Any component of a system which if it fails will cause the whole system to stop working.

single-mode fibre A fibre the diameter of whose core is just sufficient for one wavelength of light.

SIP location server A SIP proxy server with which users are able to register their location.

SIP request A SIP message used during call set-up and release.

SIP See session initiation protocol.

site identity button Used with extended validation SSL to indicate that SSL encryption is in use and that the business behind the site is authenticated.

site-to-site VPN A type of VPN that connects remote offices over the Internet.

SLAAC See StateLess address auto-configuration.

sliding window A flow-control mechanism.

small computer system interface An interface standard and command set for attaching peripheral devices to computers and transferring data.

SMON See switch monitoring.

SMS See short message service.

SMTP See simple mail transfer protocol.

smurf attack A DOS attack in which a network connected to the Internet is swamped with replies to pings that it did not send.

SNMP agent Software that runs on a managed network device; it stores management data and responds to requests from the SNMP manager.

SNMP community string A field in the SNMP versions 1 and 2 packet that acted as a password, transmitted in clear text.

SNMP get An SNMP message type that lets the SNMP manager retrieve MIB object values from the SNMP agent.

SNMP manager Software running on a network management station that can query SNMP agents, get responses from these and make changes to variables by means of SNMP commands.

SNMP MIB A database of objects (variables) that can be accessed by agents and can have changes made to them using SNMP.

SNMP set An SNMP message type that allows the SNMP manager to set MIB object values at the agent.

SNMP trap An SNMP message type that lets the agent tell the SNMP manager about significant occurrences.

SNMP See simple network management protocol.

social engineering Tricking people into compromising security by getting them either to do something or to give up confidential information.

software as a service Applications are hosted by a vendor or service provider and made available to customers over a network, typically the Internet.

SONET See synchronous optical NETwork.

source address Identifies the sending computer.

source A sending computer.

spam filter Software that applies rules to e-mail and tries to classify it as legitimate or illegitimate.

spam Unsolicited e-mail.

spammer A person who produces spam e-mail.

spear phishing Phishing attacks targeted at particular individuals

SPF See shortest path first.

splitter In ADSL, separates the DSL signal from the analogue telephone service.

spread spectrum A microwave wireless transmission technique.

SPSL See security policy specification language.

spyware Software, installed without the user's knowledge, which gathers data about the way in which a computer is used.

SQL injection attack The attacker adds SQL commands to a database query so as to be able to misuse the database.

SQLi attack See SQL injection attack.

SRTP See secure real-time transport protocol.

SSH See secure shell.

SSID See service set identifier.

SSL alert protocol SSL TCP/IP application-layer protocol.

SSL change cipher spec protocol SSL TCP/IP application-layer protocol.

SSL handshake protocol SSL TCP/IP application-layer protocol.

SSL record protocol Provides security services for TCP/IP application-layer protocols.

SSL/TLS See secure sockets layer/transport layer security.

standards body A body that issues formal standards (standards relevant to computer networking and telecommunications in this instance).

standby UPS UPS whose batteries are used only when there is a power failure.

star topology A network configuration in which the computers are connected to a central hub or switch.

start bit In asynchronous transmission, a bit that alerts the receiving device to the fact that a character is about to be transmitted.

start frame delimiter In 10-Mbps IEEE 802.3 Ethernet, a byte that indicates the end of the timing bits.

start–stop transmission See asynchronous transmission.

stateful address auto-configuration IPv6 address auto-configuration performed using DHCPv6.

stateful inspection firewall A firewall that can keep track of the connections traversing it.

StateLess address auto-configuration A mechanism for giving IPv6 hosts addresses automatically.

static address assignment A form of IP address assignment in which a person has to enter the host's IP address manually.

static route A route that a network administrator configures manually.

status update A microblogging element of social networking websites such as Facebook.

stop bit In asynchronous transmission, a bit that tells the receiver that no more bits will be sent for a while.

stop-and-wait RQ See idle RQ.

storage area network A special network that is dedicated to storage.

store and forward In a packet-switching network, packets are briefly stored at every switch in the communication path before being passed on to the next switch.

store-and-forward mode A mode of operation of a layer-2 switch.

STP See shielded twisted pair.

straight-through cable The standard twisted-pair copper cable used for connecting a computer to a hub or switch.

streaming audio A client–server technology that permits an audio file to begin playing before the entire file has been transmitted.

subnet mask A mask that allows an IPv4 network to be subdivided.

subnet On a TCP/IP network, a subnet (subnetwork) consists of all devices whose IP addresses have the same prefix.

subnetting A technique that is used to make the most efficient use of IPv4 addresses by dividing them into subnets.

substitution One of the steps involved in secret-key encryption, in which one piece of the data is replaced by another.

supernetting An alternative term for route summarisation.

supervisory frame An HDLC frame that deals with flow control and error control.

supplicant In the 802.1X LAN security standard, a device that requires authentication.

SVC See switched virtual circuit.

switch monitoring MIB Facilitates the management of network switches.

switch A networking device that can make a temporary connection between other devices.

switched virtual circuit A virtual circuit that is set up temporarily when needed.

symmetric DSL A form of DSL where the upstream and downstream data rates are the same.

symmetrical encryption See secret-key encryption.

SYN flooding attack An attack in which an attacking source host repeatedly sends forged TCP SYN packets to the victim host.

SYN A packet used in TCP to synchronise the initial sequence numbers on two computers that are initiating a new connection.

synchronous digital hierarchy The ITU standard equivalent of SONET.

synchronous modem A modem suitable for use on an analogue leased line.

synchronous optical network A physical layer standard for fibre-optic transmission systems.

synchronous transmission A transmission technique in which data is sent as a continuous stream and at a constant rate.

T3 A T-carrier digital leased line that offers a data rate of 44.736 Mbps.

tag In 802.1q, a 4-byte label inserted into an Ethernet frame to indicate to which VLAN the frame belongs.

tag In HTML, a label used to mark up the text.

tag In RFID, a transponder.

tape library A storage device which consists of at least one tape drive and a mechanism for loading tapes automatically.

T-carrier A digital leased line service available in North America and Japan.

TCP See transmission control protocol.

TCP/IP suite The protocol stack used in the Internet.

TDD See time division duplex.

TD-LTE See time division LTE.

TDM See time division multiplexing.

TDMA See time division multiple access.

TDR See time-domain reflectometry.

tear down To get rid of a connection between network devices.

Telecommunications Industry Association A standards body.

telnet A client–server terminal emulation protocol and program for TCP/IP networks.

terminal adaptor A device used to connect a computer to the ISDN network.

TFTP See trivial file transfer protocol.

third-generation mobile phone network A digital mobile phone system able to support faster data transfer speeds than second-generation networks; generally uses some form of CDMA.

three-way handshake A procedure used to open a TCP connection and to synchronise both ends of the connection.

throughput The amount of data successfully transferred from one place to another in a given time (unlikely to be such a high figure as the notional data rate).

TIA See Telecommunications Industry Association.

TIA/EIA-232 A physical-layer standard for serial data communications.

ticket In Kerberos, authenticates a Kerberos client as an authorised user.

time division duplex A mode of LTE where there is one carrier, shared by the uplink and downlink.

Time division LTE A variant of LTE (long-term evolution) that uses a different part of the wireless spectrum but is very similar to LTE.

time division multiple access A mobile phone technology in which different users are given different time slots on a channel.

time division multiplexing A type of multiplexing in which bits (or bytes) from several sources are interleaved.

time to live A value in the IP datagram header that limits the number of routers that a datagram is allowed to pass through before it is discarded.

time-domain reflectometry A technique used for cable testing.

timeout The length of time that a sender will wait for an acknowledgement from the receiver before giving up.

time-synchronous authentication system An authentication system in which an intelligent token must be synchronised with the authentication server.

TLS See secure sockets layer/transport layer security.

token ring A type of LAN that uses a token to grant access.

token A pattern of bits which constantly circulates around a Token Ring and is used to give permission to transmit.

token In computer security, a piece of software or hardware that generates a one-time password.

token In data compression, a short bit pattern that is used to replace a longer bit pattern.

top-level domain The last part of an Internet domain name.

topology The configuration (physical or logical) of a network.

TOS field See type of service field.

total internal reflection A phenomenon that keeps a light beam within the core of an optical fibre.

traceroute A utility program that allows one to trace the complete route from one host to another.

traffic class field A field in the IPv6 base header that is used to specify priority.

trailer See frame trailer.

transceiver Transmitter/receiver device, either optical or electrical.

transmission control protocol One of the most important protocols in TCP/IP networks; allows two hosts to establish a connection and exchange data.

transmission medium The medium along which data is transmitted (often, but not always, a cable).

transponder A radio transceiver that automatically transmits an identifying signal when it receives a signal from elsewhere, for example, an RFID tag.

transponder A receiver and transmitter in a communications satellite that relays the signals it receives back to the ground.

transport layer The OSI layer responsible for end-to-end connections between hosts. There is a similar layer in TCP/IP.

tree A network topology (alternative name: hierarchical topology).

trivial file transfer protocol A simpler file transfer protocol than FTP.

Trojan horse A form of malware that hides itself within an apparently legitimate program.

TTL See time to live.

tunnelling A networking technology in which packets belonging to a private network are encapsulated and sent over a public network.

two-factor authentication An authentication protocol that demands two independent ways of verifying identity.

type field In Ethernet II, a field containing a value that indicates which higher-layer protocol is being carried in an incoming frame.

type of service field A field in the IPv4 header that is used to specify priority.

UA See user agent.

UBR See unspecified bit rate.

UC See unified communications.

UDP See user datagram protocol.

ultra-wideband A wireless transmission technique in which streams of very short pulses of energy spread over many frequencies are transmitted.

UMTS See universal mobile telecommunications system.

unicast Packet delivery in which packets are delivered to only one address.

unified communications The integration of several different forms of communication, letting users send and receive all kinds of messages from a single interface.

unified threat management system Integrates multiple security functions in one box.

uniform resource locator A World Wide Web address.

uninterruptible power supply A device that contains a battery which will provide power for some time in the event of a power cut.

universal mobile telecommunications system A technology used for 3G mobile phone systems.

unnumbered frame An HDLC frame that carries line setup information.

unshielded twisted pair Twisted-pair cable consisting of four pairs of copper wires with no shielding.

unspecified address The address that an IPv6 host uses when it does not know its own address.

unspecified bit rate An ATM class of service that gives no guarantees as to if or when transmitted data will arrive at the destination.

uploading The process of moving files from the local client to a remote server.

UPS See uninterruptible power supply.

URL See uniform resource locator.

user agent An e-mail client.

user datagram protocol A connectionless alternative to TCP in the TCP/IP protocol stack.

utilisation A measure of how much of a network's bandwidth is being used at a certain time.

UTM See unified threat management system.

UTP See unshielded twisted pair.

UWB See ultra-wideband.

VANET See vehicular ad hoc network.

variable bit rate An ATM class of service for LAN-type traffic.

variable-length subnet mask Allows an organisation to use more than one subnet mask inside the same network address space.

VBR See variable bit rate.

VDSL2 See very high-speed digital subscriber line 2.

vehicular ad hoc network A kind of MANET in which vehicles are networked together.

version field The field in the IP header that indicates which version of IP is being used.

vertical cabling The network cabling that runs between floors of a building.

very high-speed digital subscriber line 2 A high-speed version of DSL.

video on demand A system that allows users to choose and watch video over a network.

videoconferencing Holding a meeting between participants located at two or more sites, via simultaneous, two-way video and audio transmissions.

virtual circuit number A number that identifies a virtual circuit.

virtual circuit A connection between two devices that appears to be a physical path, though the actual physical path along which successive packets travel may vary.

virtual communication The apparently direct communication that seems to take place between two peer processes in the higher layers of a network architecture.

virtual LAN A LAN that does not exist physically, but consists of a logical group of devices or users, selected from the devices or users on an actual, physical LAN.

virtual private LAN service A service that securely connects two or more Ethernet LANs over an MPLS network.

virtual private network A service that provides the equivalent of a private network but runs over a public network.

virtual server A software implementation of a physical server computer, which behaves just as if it were a physical computer.

virus Self-replicating code that is attached to another file.

VLAN See virtual LAN.

VLSM See variable-length subnet mask.

voice over IP Hardware and software that allows people to use IP networks to carry telephone calls.

VoIP See voice over IP.

VPLS See virtual private LAN service.

VPN See virtual private network.

W3C See World Wide Web Consortium.

wake on LAN A facility on an NIC that allows the host computer to be switched on by sending it a special packet over the network.

WAN See wide area network.

wavelength division multiplexing A technique that allows data from different channels to be carried at very high rates over a single strand of optical fibre.

WCDMA See wideband CDMA.

WDM See wavelength division multiplexing.

Web browser A piece of software that presents data from the World Wide Web.

Web page A document on the World Wide Web, usually formatted in HTML or XTML.

well-known port number A port number (below 1024) that is used for a standard TCP/IP application.

WEP See wired equivalent privacy.

whaling Spear phishing that is targeted at very important individuals.

whitelist A list of legitimate sources of e-mail.

wide area network A network that connects computers over long distances.

wideband CDMA A variant of CDMA that can support multimedia communications at high speeds.

Wi-Fi hotspot A place where one can access the Internet via Wi-Fi.

Wi-Fi protected access A security protocol for WLANs.

Wi-Fi See Wireless Fidelity.

wildcard mask A mask whose bits define the scope of a router's access control list address filter.

WiMAX See worldwide interoperability for microwave access.

window advertisement An indication of how many bytes of buffer space a TCP receiver has available.

window size The number of outstanding, unacknowledged bytes in a sliding window system.

windowing system A flow-control mechanism.

wired equivalent privacy The first security protocol that was used with WLANs.

wired LAN A LAN that uses cables as its transmission medium.

wireless bridge A device that can be used to extend a WLAN between buildings or to connect LANs over a distance of up to several miles.

wireless communication Communication without cables.

Wireless Fidelity An alternative term for 802.11x WLANs.

wireless LAN A LAN that does not use cables as its transmission medium.

wireless local loop The use of a wireless technology to replace the copper local loop.

wireless router Combines a router, an access point, a network switch and often a firewall in one box.

wireless USB A wireless replacement for wired USB, based on UWB technology.

wiring closet A walk-in cupboard that contains racks of network hardware.

WLAN See wireless LAN.

World Wide Web Consortium A standards body that develops specifications and software for the World Wide Web.

World Wide Web An easily accessible information service offered over the Internet.

worldwide interoperability for microwave access A microwave radio-based wireless technology which has fixed and mobile versions.

worm Malware that can spread itself through networks automatically, copying itself from computer to computer.

WPA See Wi-Fi protected access.

WPA2 The second version of WPA.

WUSB See wireless USB.

X window A client–server system that offers a windowing environment on UNIX and Linux computers.

X.25 A standard protocol suite for packet-switching WANs.

xDSL A generic term for all forms of DSL.

XHTML See extensible HyperText markup language.

XML See extensible markup language.

zero-day attack Tries to take advantage of weaknesses in software for which there is as yet no cure.

ZigBee A short-range wireless communication standard with low power demands that is based on the IEEE802.15.4 standard.

zombie A computer that is under the control of an attacker, who can make use of it in a DDOS attack.

Index

J. Cowley, *Communications and Networking: An Introduction*, Undergraduate Topics
in Computer Science, DOI 10.1007/978-1-4471-4357-4,
© Springer-Verlag London 2012

Made in the USA
Lexington, KY
26 July 2014